CW01023611

DUCATI MOTORCYCLES

Alan Cathcart

DUCATI
MOTORCYCLES

OSPREY

Published in 1983 by Osprey Publishing Limited
12–14 Long Acre, London WC2E 9LP
Member company of the George Philip Group

© Copyright Alan Cathcart 1983

This book is copyrighted under the Berne Convention. All
rights reserved. Apart from any fair dealing for the purpose of
private study, research, criticism or review, as permitted under
the Copyright Act, 1956, no part of this publication may be
reproduced, stored in a retrieval system, or transmitted in any
form or by any means, electronic, electrical, chemical,
mechanical, optical, photocopying, recording, or otherwise,
without prior written permission. All enquiries should be
addressed to the publisher.

British Library Cataloguing in Publication Data
Cathcart, Alan
    Ducati motorcycles.
    1. Ducati motorcycles
    I. Title
    629.2 275   TL448.D8
ISBN 0-85045-510-3

Editor Tim Parker
Design Roger Daniels

Filmset by Tameside Filmsetting Ltd
Ashton-under-Lyne, Lancs
Printed & bound by Butler & Tanner Ltd
Frome, Somerset

Contents

Foreword by Ing. Fabio Taglioni

It is a pleasure at Mr. Cathcart's request to write a brief introduction
to this book, which sets out the history of Ducati Meccanica and so partly
of myself too, in as much as I was responsible for almost all the products
which this company has presented in the marketplace. To the reader who does
not know me personally it will perhaps appear curious that a single person
was able to create such a remarkable number of products. I'd therefore like
to explain to you how it was possible for this to come about.

My working philosophy has always been founded on the co-operation of all
my colleagues, without regard to position or title: each of them has always
given their all with pride, sacrifice and passionate commitment with the
result that all my ideas, once discussed, were developed with maximum speed and
precision.

What has been the fundamental principal of all my designs?
The answer is contained in a single word: simplicity, carried to its ultimate
extreme. My father, who was my mentor right up until his death, once said to
me: 'Remember that, when you copy something that someone else has done, you're
always going to be behind in your thinking. Also, any component that forms part of
a mechanical design can break, so try to eliminate whatever is not essential
to the efficient function of the engine.'

These fundamental concepts have thus inspired my entire working life, and
experimentation with the new and unproved a constant feature of it. Thus
the desmodromic head, which some people might claim to be an imitation of
an existing system, came about as a result of a process of rationalisation:
it was actually the result of a union between a twin-camshaft design that
opened the valves, and a single camshaft that closed them. It was speedily
simplified into the current even more straightforward system which is
still just as efficient.

Even the V4 came about as the consequence of emphasis on engineering
economy: the aim was to produce an engine that was narrower, lighter and
vibrated less than its rivals. The various parallel twins of *my* design (that is,
the 125, 250 and 350) in fact gave birth to the V4 within the constraints of
the original design, amended somewhat in the case of the two front cylinders
for obvious reasons.

Fabio Taglioni
Bologna
July 1983

ƆUCATI MECCANICA S.p.A. - BOLOGNA

Ho il piacere di scrivere, su richiesta del Sig.Cathcart, una breve introduzione a questo libro che espone la storia della Ducati Meccanica ed anche parte della mia, in quanto diretto responsabile della quasi totalità dei prodotti che questa azienda ha immesso sul mercato. Al lettore che non mi conosce personalmente forse parrà strano che una persona sola abbia realizzato un così notevole numero di prodotti. Ebbene sono qui per spiegarVi come ciò è potuto accadere.

La mia filosofia di lavoro si è sempre basata sulla cooperazione di tutti i miei collaboratori senza distinzione di grado e di capacità: ognuno di loro ha sempre dato tutto quanto era possibile con orgoglio, abnegazione e passione e, di conseguenza, tutti i miei pensieri, una volta discussi, venivano sviluppati con la massima velocità e precisione.

Quale é stato il principio fondamentale di tutte le mie realizzazioni?

Si spiega con una sola parola : - Semplicità - portata all'estremo possibile. Mio padre, che mi é stato maestro fino alla morte, mi disse un giorno : "Ricorda che, copiando quello che hanno fatto gli altri, arrivi sempre in ritardo. Qualunque pezzo che compone un complessivo meccanico può rompersi, quindi cerca di eliminare tutto quanto non é essenziale al suo corretto funzionamento".

Questi concetti fondamentali hanno quindi ispirato ogni mia costruzione ed il segno del nuovo e dell'inedito vi può essere riscontrato. Anche il desmodromico, che alcuni possono ritenere una imitazione di sistemi già noti, é nato invece come conseguenza di un ragionamento applicativo: infatti era composto all'inizio dall'unione di un bialbero che apriva le valvole e da un monoalbero che le chiudeva. In seguito é stato semplificato nell'attuale meno macchinoso, ma pur sempre efficiente.

Anche il 4V é nato come conseguenza di un ragionamento economico: fare un motore più stretto, più leggero e che non vibri. Tutti i motori a cilindri paralleli di mia costruzione (125 - 250 - 350) nacquero infatti 4 cilindri a V sulla stesura del primitivo progetto, mutilati poi dei due cilindri anteriori per ragioni ovvie.

DM - MOD. 4

7

Preface

I suppose you might say I've always had a thing about Ducatis. Back in the 1960s when the idea of a desmodromic road bike seemed as likely as the thought that the Japanese might produce a bike any larger than 450 cc, I learnt to ride on one of the early 250 singles. The fact that I also discovered the joys of sitting out a thunderstorm with drowned electrics, or groping my way through Warwickshire lanes at night to the dim accompaniment of the frail 6V headlamp somehow only served to deepen the special mystique that enveloped that little Bologna ohc thumper. Everyone's first bike has a special place in their hearts, but it seems that once you're bitten by the Ducati bug, you stay hooked – and that's what happened to me.

Years later, when I pucked up enough courage to try my hand at road racing for the first time long after most people have settled for a more sedentary life in front of the fireplace of watching the dahlias grow, once again it was a little Ducati 250 single that provided the entree into this most demanding of sports. It was (and still remains) a near ideal mount for the beginner: safe, sure handling allied to a sometimes startling degree of performance allows the learner racer to concentrate on finding out about the complexities of road racing without getting in over his head.

In time, I progressed up the capacity and performance ladder to a brace of the 750 SS production racers, those lean, legendary desmo-headed Imola replicas which in their time were the fastest road-legal bike in the world. Any chance I might ever have had of evading the spell of Dr. T's wand disappeared the first moment I sat on one of these wonderful machines, which 10 years and more after it first appeared on the streets of the world still sets the standard by which the handling and feel of a bike must be judged.

As I became more heavily involved with latter-day racing, both as a rider and in my new-found profession as a racing journalist, I still looked fondly back towards the past, and was able to discover two of the most jewel-like historic Ducati racers ever made – a 125 dohc Grand Prix and the even rarer desmo 125 twin once raced by Mike Hailwood. Owning and restoring these machines, then later riding them in Classic events only deepened my regard for the man whom all Ducati enthusiasts the world rightly hold in awesome respect: Ing. Fabio Taglioni. A man of proliferate genius – by the time of his retirement from Ducati in 1982 he had designed over 1000 different engines of various kinds from a single-cylinder diesel to a 1260 cc V4 – Dr. T has never compromised his engineering beliefs and principles even if it meant flying in the face of accepted fashion. Take his decision not to tread the turbocharging or four-valve cylinder routes now so popular elsewhere, for example: careful experimentation in parallel with his desmodromic two-valve designs proved the greater efficacy of the latter, hence his decision to stick to his guns – but for all the right engineering reasons rather than a simple refusal to consider alternative designs just because they didn't fit in with his own beliefs.

It's without disrespect to riders of other marques when I say that as a rule it's conceded that Ducati owners are not only generally the most enthusiastic, but also the most technically aware group of motorcyclists in their respective countries. For this reason, and the fact that the Ducati owner's brand loyalty is almost certainly second to none, as a committed *ducatisti* and motorcycle literature freak I've found it curious beyond comprehension that no book attempting to tell the story of the Bologna marque and its products has ever been published until now. When Tim Parker of Osprey Publishing suggested I should write such a book, I soon discovered why: there are practically no factory records before the late 1960s, and though Ing.

Taglioni offered willing and gracious assistance, many of his notebooks and drawings have been lost down the years in various fires and office moves, so records of the early history of the company and especially of the more exotic prototypes are extremely scant. Moreover, the history of Ducati down the years has been surprisingly poorly documented: magazine writers have preferred to concentrate on road tests of the production models, perhaps indicating inadvertently that the main attraction of Ducati machines is in actually riding them!

So when I first began this project two years ago, I had no idea of the difficulties that awaited me in terms of digging out the real story of the Bologna factory and its products. Fortunately, the world-wide clan of fellow Ducati fans rapidly came to my aid with encouragement and assistance, and to all of them whom it has not been possible to thank by name in the acknowledgements section, I offer my sincere gratitude. Needless to say, much of the information I received was conflicting: as an example, there are four different quoted power figures for the 250 Diana Mark 3 model, all for the same year! Wherever possible I've tried to dig to the bottom of the story to get at the truth, but even then I may not have been entirely successful in every case. If any reader has corroborated information which contradicts anything I have stated in this book, I hope he or she will get in touch with me so we may update the facts hopefully in any future editions,

and will at the same time accept that I have done my best to sort out the true facts.

As I was finishing the book off, I got advance word of the tie-up between Ducati and Cagiva which is dealt with in a separate epilogue to the volume. Whether the marriage between the two companies will indeed be consummated remains to be seen, but while the band of *Ducatisti* around the world are as fervent as present in their support for the desmodromic V-twin concept, there seems little doubt that one way or another we'll all be able to buy a Ducati in the future: it just may have a different name on the fuel tank.

For in the end the one thing that the products of Borgo Panigale down the years have possessed above all else is that mystical element known as 'soul'. In these days of plastic these and disposable thats, when the Japanese manufacturers flood the motorcycle market of the world with an ever-widening range of new models, designs and technology, one European firm above all others has become known for its adherence to the traditional values of motorcycling, whether on the road or track: lithe, lissom and lean, economical, efficient and fast, its products today stand for everything that motorcycle riding should be all about. That company is Ducati, and this is its story.

Alan Cathcart
London
June 1983

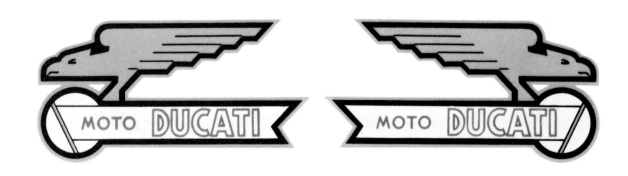

I

The start of it all

Bologna lies at the foot of the Apennine mountains, Italy's backbone, in a commanding position governing the vast and wealthy Emilia-Romagna region of which it is the capital. Seat of the oldest university in Europe, and according to many the gastronomic centre of Italy, it's an ancient city with its roots deep in the Middle Ages and the time of the independent city-states, whose rulers created the artistic miracle of the Renaissance.

But Bologna is no airy-fairy living museum, as so many of its neighbours, such as Florence to the south, have become in the wake of the world-wide growth of tourism. Few of the massive air-conditioned buses which ply the golden triangle between Venice, Florence and Rome stop for more than a couple of hours in this, one of Italy's most historic cities. Instead they breeze past on the multi-lane ringway, heading for the Autostrada del Sole and one more stop on the grand tour: if it's Tuesday, it must be Florence.

For Bologna is a working city, albeit one with a proud heritage and almost unaltered medieval core whose rabbit-warren maze of streets and alleyways would transport the visitor back in time if it wasn't for the ever-present mass of motor-cars. Though the one-way system has evidently been designed to prove so frustrating that visitors are intimidated from driving in the city centre, there's little chance of these historic streets being banned to motor vehicles. For more than any other city in this nation of automotive enthusiasts, Bologna is irrevocably wedded to the motor-car and, above all, the motorcycle.

Located at the crossroads of Italy's transportation system, Bologna has permanent importance in the 20th century as a road and rail centre: most traffic between southern and central Italy and the north, must pass through it. The Bolognese and their near neighbours in Modena to the north-west consequently embrace the heart and soul of the

transportation industry: such famous names on four and two wheels as Ferrari, Maserati, Lamborghini, De Tomaso, Morini, Minarelli, Malanca, Villa, and so on originated and are produced in the Bologna region. However, the most famous in the world of motorcycling, is Ducati.

Bologna's industries are many and varied, not only concentrating on the engineering and automotive component side but also embracing electronics, optics, agricultural machinery and so forth. One of its most famous sons was Guglielmo Marconi, the inventor of the wireless, and in the 1920s Bologna was one of the European centres of the radiophonic industry. In 1926, two brothers named Adriano and Marcello Ducati founded a company to specialize in the production of valves, condensors and other radiophonic components, in time leading to the manufacture of their own wireless sets and other electrical goods. The firm, entitled the Società Scientifica Radiobrevetti Ducati, expanded greatly in the wake of the radio boom in the 1930s, the more so since under Mussolini's rule Italy was gradually being transformed from an agricultural and rural society with its roots deep in the Middle Ages, to an increasingly urban and industrial one. Moreover, the Fascist Party's emphasis on spreading its fanatical message through the speeches of its leader meant that a high priority was assigned to getting a radio into every Italian household, however poor and even primitive, so that the strident tones of *Il Duce's* haranguing could reach even those places which the 20th century had otherwise barely touched. Under such circumstances, it was scarcely surprising that, by 1939, the Ducati company employed the massive total of 7000 workers.

Benito Mussolini had swept to power in October 1922 on the crest of a wave of popular support for his Fascist Party. He was committed to modernizing the country and to completing the process of unification still left unfinished after Garibaldi's soldiers had created the modern Italian state through the *Risorgimento* of 1870. Though Mussolini undoubtedly achieved much of lasting benefit to the Italian nation, it was only at the expense of a ruthless suppression of the opposition, which saw the right to strike abolished in 1926, and the elimination of his personal opponents, principally the Socialist leader Giacomo Matteotti, whom he had murdered. Forced to leave the League of Nations in the face of world-wide opposition to his invasion of Abyssinia in 1935, Mussolini joined into formal alliance with his friend and idol Adolf Hitler, creating the Axis in 1936 with Nazi Germany.

The ever-closer modelling of the Italian state and its industrial strategy on that of Germany inevitably led to a greater emphasis on manufacture of war material. Thus by 1940 the Ducati company's primary interests lay in the manufacture of military equipment, principally field radios, gun sights and other artillery optical components. This made the factory, located on the western side of Bologna in a suburb named Borgo Panigale, a prime target for enemy action in later years.

When the Second World War broke out in 1939, Italy officially remained a 'non-belligerent' – though still tied to Germany by treaty. It was not until the following year, after the rout of the Allied Expeditionary Force at Dunkirk and the fall of France, that Mussolini formally committed his country to war with the Allies, confident by then that he would be joining the winning side. He could scarcely have been more wrong.

Whatever little enthusiasm the Italian nation as a whole may have had for supporting their leader's dreams of glory swiftly evaporated after Pearl Harbor and the entry of the USA into the war on the Allied side in 1941. Many Italian families had relatives in the States, part of that great flood of immigrants who had poured through the Ellis Island immigration terminal around the turn of the century, mostly to be entered in the census register as 'WOP' – 'Without Passport'. After the Allied invasion of Sicily in July 1943, Fascism's days were numbered, as many Italians realized that their sympathies lay more with the American forces than with their supposed Nazi allies, who had in any case had to bail the unenthusiastic Italian army out of deep trouble on more than a few occasions in Greece and North Africa.

On 25 July, 1943, Benito Mussolini was forced to resign as Prime Minister – his nominal title – and was imprisoned in Rome, while a new government led by Marshall Badoglio negotiated an armistice with the Allied forces led by General Eisenhower. After protracted haggling over terms, a cease-fire was announced on 8 September, 1943, stranding millions of Italian soldiers abroad. They were promptly disarmed by their former German allies, and interned.

At this stage Italy was still a divided country, with the Allied advance progressing only very slowly from the south. When Mussolini escaped from prison with German help, he was able to flee to the north and there set up a puppet Fascist republic, notable primarily for its brutality.

Bologna lay in the heart of the new Fascist state, and was still a part of it when winter came at the end of 1944, with the Allied advance ground to a halt along the line of the Apennines, north of Florence. So close to the front line, though, Bologna was within easy range of the Allied bombardment, and its industrial importance meant that the city came under heavy attack from enemy bombing. The Ducati factory at Borgo Panigale was badly hit on a number of occasions, but still maintained production: the only difference now was that the occupying German forces were the recipients of its products, rather than the new disbanded Italian army.

Conditions for the civilian population on both sides of the front line were by then as bad as they have been in any European country since the Great War: even postwar Germany, its cities mere piles of rubble after ceaseless RAF and USAF bombing, did not suffer so greatly by comparison. For the war literally covered the whole of Italy, as the Germans fought bitterly across the entire breadth of the country to stave off the Allied advance. Even the tiniest village and remotest monastery became a military objective. Rejected by the Germans as turncoats and untrustworthy former allies, and by the US and British forces as former belligerents who, in spite of renouncing the struggle, were never accepted as fully fledged allies, the Italian nation on both sides of the slowly moving border simply starved. Deprived of even the most essential of life's necessities, the country lapsed again into even more abject a poverty than that from which Mussolini had partially rescued it.

Conditions were not quite so bad in Turin, the capital of the Piedmont region, some 200 miles north-west of Bologna. Home of the massive Fiat industrial complex, producing everything from fighter aircraft to light tanks, Turin was of sufficient strategic importance for the Germans to keep it well supplied and defended. Nevertheless, the Torinese,

The factory entrance at Via A.C. Ducati, 3, in the eastern suburb of Bologna, Borgo Panigale

Farinelli was one of the first people to realize that postwar Italy would be desperately starved of means of personal transportation. That was already the case, as blanket petrol rationing imposed by occupying forces on both sides of the front line meant that private vehicles, even motorcycles, simply could not be used due to a lack of worthwhile fuel in available quantity. There were some ingenious but makeshift solutions to this: some home-grown engineers converted their little Fiats to run on an exotic brew of home-produced alcohol, and there were many cases of vehicles, including motorcycles, running on distilled wine. But for the most part people either had to rely on what little public transport there was to get about, walk or better still to use bicycles, which were in plentiful supply.

Farinelli and his colleagues at Siata realized that a small-capacity internal combustion engine with a low enough compression ratio to run on practically any kind of available fuel, which could be attached to a pushbike in order to give it some means of motive power other than the rider's own efforts, would fulfil a vital need for mobility in postwar Italy. A semi-destroyed nation, almost completely deprived of its own means of transportation, would create the perfect opportunity for such a lightweight engine, which he termed a *micromotor* and, once the fashion spread to Britain five years later, was called a 'clip-on'. Accordingly, soon after the Armistice in 1943, he began to draw the design of such an engine, working in secret and with great courage, since such action was directly contrary to the dictates of Mussolini's Republican government and the occupying German forces.

Gathering together sufficient raw materials to construct a prototype was even more difficult and risky, since it involved diverting war-related commodities for his own use. But by dint of performing some amazing feats of juggling, and with the help of some forged requisition orders, Farinelli managed to build his first prototype and have it running on the streets of Turin by the autumn of 1944. Not only because its short stub exhaust produced a high-pitched, yapping note, but also because he had an understandable affection for a project with which he was closely entwined emotionally, he dubbed the little 48 cc engine the *Cucciolo* – his little puppy dog.

Developing just a single brake horsepower at 4500 rpm from its little four-stroke engine, the Cucciolo could be fitted to almost any design of bicycle, retaining the original chain and pedal crank, which provided not only the means of

like the vast majority of their fellow-countrymen, were already praying for peace, and had been counting the days since the Armistice, when the whole of Italy, including their region, would no longer be at war.

Some, indeed, were even sufficiently far-sighted to begin making plans for the period after the coming Liberation. One such person was a remarkable man named Avv. Aldo Farinelli, a qualified lawyer, engineer and writer who was then associated with a small but successful Torinese firm entitled Siata – the Società Italiana per Applicazione Tecniche Auto-Aviatorie. That mouthful meant that the company's war work consisted of high-technology engineering work carried out under the supervision of the occupying German forces. But before the war Siata had made a considerable name for themselves as manufacturers of tuning kits and parts for souping up Fiat saloons and sports cars, while in the years to come they'd receive considerable recognition for sports cars of their own manufacture, including a 1500 cc V8-engined device that bristled with technical interest.

starting but also offered the possibility of 'light pedal assistance' up anything over a slight incline. A delightful postwar advertizing photo shows a trio of *cucciolisti* breezing up a hill with the snow-topped Alps in the background, passing a group of labouring cyclists, whose envious glances conveyed the message: buy one, and you too can coast up hills. Reality may not have been quite so sublime, but the little engine, weighing a mere 7.8 kg, added little to the overall weight of the bike, and moreover was exceptionally economical: it was almost certainly the first-ever motorcycle engine to attain the remarkable fuel consumption figure of 100 km per litre – around 280 miles per Imperial gallon.

Farinelli had thus achieved his target; all that was required now was an end to the war so that Siata could put it into production. Turin was heavily bombarded during the winter of 1944–45, and the Fascist regime grew ever more tyrannical; there was no chance of starting to manufacture the Cucciolo before the cease-fire, but at least plans could be laid. Other Italians were helping to bring about an end to the war in Italy: the partisan guerrillas operating in the countryside mounted ever more daring raids. Several were caught and shot by their Fascist fellow-countrymen and their Nazi allies, but many more continued the struggle.

In the early spring of 1945, the Allied forces broke through in a new offensive, and the Fascist Republic fell. At the same time as his supposed friend and hero Hitler was holed-up in his Berlin bunker with Russian troops inching ever closer, Mussolini tried to flee from Italy, but was captured by a group of partisans and executed on a lonely road near Lake Como on 28 April, 1945. Italy was liberated from the cruel force which had gripped it for over 22 years.

Siata wasted no time; on 26 July, barely one month after the official liberation of the country and the formation of a new government responsible for the whole state, they announced plans to construct the Cucciolo for sale to the public: it was the first new automotive design to appear in postwar Europe. Commercial production and distribution were slow to get started, however, as not only were raw materials very scarce but the ravaged state of the country in the aftermath of its three years as the bloody battleground of southern Europe made any kind of commercial enterprise difficult.

Early production examples were eagerly snapped up by local Torinese customers, however; the Cucciolo's low compression ratio meant that it would run on petrol as low as 65 octane, while still giving good economy and evident reliability. The message spread, encouraging Siata to open a sales office at Via Leonardo da Vinci 23 in Turin to deal with the flood of enquiries. By the start of 1946 this had become so great that the production facilities offered by what was essentially a small specialist engineering workshop proved inadequate: the solution was to look for another company to take over the task of manufacture.

Bologna had been even worse hit by Allied bombing than Turin, and the Ducati factory at Borgo Panigale had been all but destroyed. Worse still, the company's wartime production line was clearly inapposite to peacetime, and the patterns for its prewar radio designs had been destroyed in the blitz. Its only assets were the remnants of its workforce, by now reduced to a state of poverty and looking eagerly to their employers for some means of earning a living, their experience in high-precision light engineering and the Italian capacity – contrary to the belief of many Anglo-Saxons – for hard work. But first the Ducati family had to find something to make.

It's not clear at this distance in time how Siata in Turin and Ducati in Bologna ever came into contact with each other. The two firms were in different fields, though perhaps may have had some dealings in the course of their repective war work. Moreover, the 200 miles distance between the two cities was a yawning chasm in postwar Italy, with communications and travel facilities crippled by the war. The key seems likely to have been an organization entitled the Instituto per la Reconstruzione Industriale (IRI); founded by Mussolini, and inherited by the postwar Christian Democrat-controlled elected government, IRI was a state holding company through which the government controlled its substantial investments in private industry, principally in the engineering, insurance, banking and transportation sectors. These were never less than 50 per cent, but not usually much more (though there were exceptions); the remaining shares were often held by wealthy private institutions, or most commonly by Opus Dei, the investment arm of the Roman Catholic Church, or, in other words, the Vatican. Since Mussolini's time, up to the present day, central government in Italy has always been prepared to step in to acquire a controlling stock interest in parts of the economy, wherever private enterprise showed itself unable or unwilling to exercise sufficiently dynamic initiative. Private industry came to realize that failure to respond to the challenge of changing markets, for example, would threaten it with seizure by the government – even a Centre-Right Christian

The Ducati Meccanica factory in the mid-60s, before it was redeveloped in the next decade

Democrat one. Such a fate, for example, befell the Alfa Romeo car giant – while its Fiat rival, under the helm of the ebullient Agnelli family, stayed in private hands.

In the immediate postwar period IRI's principal purpose was to use state funds – such as they were – to get war-damaged industries restarted in order to re-establish the economy. But money, like almost every other commodity in the war-torn country, was desperately short, not helped by the fact that after the surrender in 1943 the Germans had seized the entire Italian gold reserve stocks as they retreated north. Though it was recovered intact, only a proportion of it was returned by the Allies, who demanded and received substantial war damages from its previous enemy: this was an important result of Italy's not being accepted as a full ally after 1943. The consequence was that the country was starved of capital, even government funds; only a massive influx of US dollars from friends and relatives in the USA saved the country

from bankruptcy and allowed it to pay off the crippling war debts.

Enter the Vatican. The Pope and Mussolini had been sworn enemies until a partial reconciliation had been effected in the interests of the war effort; the Vatican, however, remained neutral throughout the conflict, and the Vatican City a non-belligerent zone. This meant that the Church's vast wealth was largely untouched by the war, and part of it was put at the disposal of a stricken postwar Italy.

Working with the Vatican as a partner, IRI identified certain key businesses which had before the war provided employment on a substantial scale but which needed capital for reconstruction purposes after the conflict. With 7000 workers in 1940 (rising to 9000 by 1943) Ducati were precisely the sort of company IRI wanted to help – but at a price.

That price was a government takeover, which left the Ducati family with minimal compensation but provided the company with capital to rebuild the factory, repair their machine tools and purchase new equipment as time went by. Additionally, IRI funded a research department, which soon after the war came up with a revolutionary pocket camera that predated any of Kodak's products by some years. Unfortunately, it was in many ways too advanced, and though it sold in reasonably large numbers, the postwar consumer society took longer to establish in Italy than elsewhere in Western Europe, and the *Microcamera Ducati* eventually died a death in the late 1940s. Many examples are still in use today.

Instead of microcameras, it was micromotors that provided the Ducati company with its postwar salvation. IRI was probably on the lookout for successful new products for which there was a ready market but insufficient production capacity. The Cucciolo engine was exactly the type of product they would have had in mind, and suited Ducati's engineering capability and experience. A deal was concluded with Siata, originally to manufacture the engines for the Turin company to market, then later to take over the complete operation, paying Siata and Aldo Farinelli a royalty on each engine sold. By 1946, Ducati were in the motorcycle business.

Four decades later, when the roads of the world are inundated with 50 cc mopeds providing basic transportation for millions of people, it's difficult to realize just how revolutionary a concept the Cucciolo and the dozens of imitators it spawned in postwar Europe represented. For sure, there had been other previous attempts to produce powered bicycles, such as the Wall Autowheel in Britain in the immediate post-Great War period, but they either lacked sound engineering or a suitably receptive market, or both. The Cucciolo was the first successful moped/micromotor (or *bicimotore* as it was also called) in the history of motorcycling, born out of the critical shortage of other means of getting about in a country that would take many years to recover fully from the effects of a war that few of its inhabitants had ever really wanted. The Cucciolo swiftly conquered Italy; originally offered only in engine form, not as a complete bike, by 1946 over 15,000 were in use, rising to 25,000 in 1947, with several thousand being exported to other countries equally in need of such mobility. By early 1949, over 60,000 Cucciolos were in use on the roads of Italy, being used for every conceivable purpose, including racing. Naturally, competitors were not slow to seize the opportunity of a share of this eager market, and a host of other *micromotori* manufacturers flooded the showrooms with their products, almost all cheap, easily produced two-strokes, some of which faded back into obscurity almost as soon as they appeared. Others, such as the popular Mosquito, made by the old-established Garelli factory, or the smaller Alpino and Minimotor models survived, but by 1949 the total of all the other manufacturers' products on the streets of Italy only equalled the number of Cucciolos – another 60,000 vehicles. Ducati had 50 per cent of the market, and to celebrate their taking over the whole operation under licence from Siata opened their own showroom in 1947 at Largo Augusto 7, in Milan. A network of dealers was established, many of whom still represent the company today.

There were a number of reasons for the Cucciolo's success, not least the fact that it never hurt to be first in the field if you can do so with a product that is superior and longer-lasting than its subsequent competition. Siata had not been seduced by the attractions of the less complicated two-stroke engine. Instead, they designed a very simple four-stroke engine which had a longer life, used less fuel, did not require the nuisance of adding oil to petrol in precise premix quantities, and needed a decoke only every 7000–8000 km. Moreover, the better torque offered by its four-stroke engine made it a favourite in mountainous districts: Ducati were quick to capitalize in advertisements on the feat of a group of nine members of the Cucciolo Club Torino, who, on 20 February, 1949, rode their little machines from Turin to the Italian customs post at Molaretto at the top of the Moncenisio Pass, 8000 feet up in the nearby Alps. It was deep mid-winter, with the roads covered with snow and impassable to four-wheel traffic. The inevitable photo of the group of cold but cheerful *cucciolisti* beside the market stone at the top of the pass made good press, besides which it also brought home to the unconverted the fact that owners of the little bikes thought sufficiently highly of them to form local owner's clubs for joint outings and the like. 'Why be an outsider? Join the happy band!' enticed the adverts. Thousands did.

Delightful period shot of an early Cucciolo clip-on. Note the rear skirt guard and the bicycle dynamo lighting set

2

Cucciolo – **little pup**

The Cucciolo engine was unusual in four-stroke terms in having pullrod rather than pushrod valve gear. The original design was known as the T1 (Type 1), and formed the basis for later developments beginning in 1949. The ribbed crankcase was cast in unit with the finned cylinder, inclined forward by 20 degrees, using silumin alloy, which was the secret of the light weight of the unit as a whole. A cast-iron sleeve was shrunk into the barrel, with an alloy piston running on a forged steel conrod; there were two compression piston rings, and one scraper ring.

The crankcase split vertically to reveal the engine's internals: the sturdy crankshaft ran in two ball bearings, one sunk into the wall of the right-hand case, the other running in a housing bolted to the inside of the wet, multi-plate metallic clutch. This was supported by another bearing in the wall of the left-outside flywheel. This contained a four-pole magneto – made by Ducati themselves, the forerunner of the Ducati Elettrotecnica company's activities today – which provided not only a 15W/6V output for the lighting system, but also the ignition for the single 14 mm plug fitted in an inclined position in the front of the head; for many years Maserati plugs were standard original equipment, till the high-performance car firm's offshoot in nearby Modena discontinued manufacture.

The two-speed gearbox was driven by a large primary gear directly off the clutch, and in turn incorporated on its layshaft the single camshaft lobe, which drove the valve gear. Final drive was by means of the bicycle's original toothed crank, which could be clamped complete with pedals to the unit. An ingenious selector system meant that the position of the pedal crank dictated the choice of gear. If the clutch lever was pulled in and the pedals rotated so that the left one pointed forward, first gear was automatically selected. If the left pedal

pointed backwards, you were in second, while neutral – naturally enough – was found between the two, with the pedal pointing towards the ground. Later models were offered with a choice of either this simple but effective system, or with a vintage-type hand change, or else with a modern-style twistgrip control.

The single cam drove the twin 12 mm valves by means of long pullrods up the back of the cylinder, either side of the inlet tract. Running in their own channels incorporated in the casting of the one-piece head and barrel, these were bolted to short rockers which in turn pivoted on two upright beams incorporated in the head casting: the plug sat between these. Valve lift was 3.5 mm, and symmetrical valve timing of 8/32 and 32/8 on the earlier models were the hallmarks of a workhorse rather than a competition engine. The engine ran so cool that a very soft plug could be used – plug fouling was almost unheard of, another important advantage over the more temperamental 2-strokes – and with an ignition advance of 24 degrees and a 6.25:1 compression ratio, the little, nearly 'square' 39 × 40 mm engine would run on very low-octane fuel.

There was no kick-starter, the engine being fired up by the usual moped trick of pedalling it in gear, and of course pedal assistance could be rendered whether the gearbox was engaged or not. The 9 mm Weber carburettor – specially made for the Cucciolo in later years with an adjacent float chamber and ultra-long induction tract – gave the exceptional economy which was the engine's hallmark under almost any conditions: climbing hills or running flat-out at the top speed of just over 30 mph seemed to have little effect on consumption figures.

There was no oil pump as such; instead, the 0.4 litre of lubricant, inserted through a filler behind the flywheel, was thrown up from the wet-sump by the clutch primary gear into a small chamber above the crank, where it was drip-fed by gravity. This ingenious and simple system was in keeping with the entire concept of the unit-construction engine: designed to be used by people who had probably never touched a car or motorcycle engine in their lives before, maintenance was reduced to a minimum, and though it was recommended that the oil level should be checked every 250 km, the Cucciolo would continue to run without adverse effects even if the quantity of oil in the crankcase got very low, so effective was the lubrication system. Engine life appears to have been exceptional, with many owners reporting 25,000 km and more from their little *micromotori*.

Performance naturally depended on the weight of the cycle parts into which the engine was fitted, as well as of the rider, and was adequate rather than exceptional. From the single bhp at 4500 rpm of the prototype, the T1 was gradually improved to 1.25 bhp at the same revs by 1949, then to 1.35 bhp at 5150 rpm in 1952, and finally 1.5 bhp by the end of its production run in 1959. The engine was safe up to 5500 rpm or thereabouts, at the expense of a

certain amount of vibration, but it was pointless wringing the little pup's neck since performance was unaffected even in the lower gear. The engine was happiest running at around 4000 rpm, and would pull from practically zero. It was an ideal design for a new generation of postwar converts to motorcycling.

At the end of 1948, production facilities at the Borgo Panigale factory were increased to allow 245 Cucciolo engines to be produced each eight-hour working day. A new Cucciolo every two minutes, and still demand showed no sign of abating. A photograph of the production line at the time nevertheless shows that this substantial enterprise, producing over 60,000 units a year, was run more along radiophonic industry lines than a motorcycle factory. Rows of workers seated on wooden chairs working on embryo engines which they passed to one another along steel-topped tables constituted the assembly line, but it was a far cry from Farinelli's primitive working conditions.

To mark the increase in their production capacity, Ducati's directors also decided to extend the model line. The opportunity was also taken to redesign the engine slightly in light of experience: the crankcase was no longer split along the axis of the conrod, but instead became a single casting with a screwed-on cover behind the flywheel on the left side. The cylinder became detachable, bolted on via a four-stud flange under the barrel, which was however still cast in unit with the head. Previously, it had been necessary to disassemble the engine completely to carry out any work more complicated than adjusting valve clearances. Now the crankcase cover could be simply unscrewed to permit easy access to the whole engine. The oil filler was moved to the front of the engine, and the following year the valve gear, still using coil springs, was enclosed.

To combat the inroads some of the cheaper two-strokes had been making on their market, Ducati introduced the T-'zero' (T0), which had a slightly lower compression ratio, single-speed clutchless transmission and reduced performance. The redesigned T1 became the T2, while a large-capacity model was introduced, dubbed the T3.

This new model marked the first step on the trial of increased engine capacities which would eventually lead to the 860 cc V-twins over 25 years later. The essential layout of the T3 was the same as the T2, but with the cylinder bored out to 43.8 mm for the extra capacity to make a 60 cc engine. A three-speed gearbox with foot change was featured, separate from the bicycle-type pedal cranks which were still employed for starting and for the more

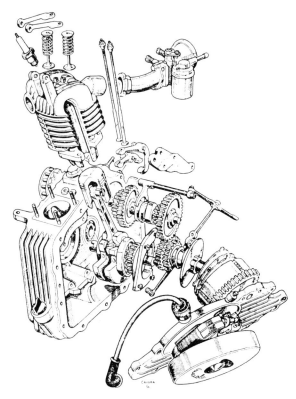

A Cucciolo engine drawing first published in February 1949 in Motociclismo. *Delightfully simple and yet robust*

Co-riders Zitelli (left) and Tamarozzi (right – with glasses, but without his famous cigar) are congratulated by Giovanni Fiorio after their record-breaking stint at Monza on 16 May, 1951. Note the rudimentary streamlining and copius padding

daunting hills. Other details were the same as for the smaller-capacity models, though a top speed of just on 40 mph was now possible.

The Italian passion for competition led many Cucciolo owners to strip their machines down and enter them in the popular *Micromotore* class for up to 50 cc racing bikes. The T3 was also race-prepared, but was not competitive in the 65 cc class against Moto Guzzi's two-stroke Guzzino. In the smaller-capacity category though, Cucciolo riders had great success, though competition from the more easily tuned two-strokes, especially the Alpino, was very fierce. The factory encouraged this by producing a Sport version of the T2 in 1948, which was available to special order. An oversize piston was fitted to bring the capacity up to a full 50 cc, the compression ration raised to 8.9:1 (necessitating use of a 70/30 petrol-benzole mixture), ignition advance increased to 32 degrees, and the power output to 2 bhp at the maximum safe 5700 rpm. This was the first racing Ducati engine, and it enabled Cucciolo riders to win races all over Italy at speeds as high as 60 km/h average. Star rider

was Amilcare Bonfanti, who scored five wins in 1948 against the two-stroke opposition, but success was not confined to male riders and short-distance events. A lady member of the Turin Cucciolo Club, Sga. Bianca Germonio, won the 50 cc class in the Milano–San Remo long-distance race the same year, over an inter-city course of 160 miles. Cucciolos were even victorious in scrambles, Giulio Drei winning two events at Ravenna and Lugo at the season's end.

But it was in hillclimbs, where four-stroke torque told over the still relatively unsophisticated two-strokes, that Cucciolos really shone. An enterprising Roman tuning shop, Lario, produced a series of kits that enabled owners to improve their engines to the same level of tune as the factory's T2 Sport, and provided a similar service to riders of the 60 cc T3. The result was a series of successes for Cucciolo riders: at the prestigious Monte Mario climb near Rome in 1949, for example, Cucciolos not only placed 1-2-3 in the 50 cc class, with winner Giuseppe Flemini averaging 51.85 km/h uphill, but Romano Levantini also scooped the 100 cc category on his little 60 cc Cucciolo, averaging 59.26 km/h against machines up to 40 per cent greater in engine capacity. Compare this to the new course record set the same day by Bruno Francisci on the works 500 Guzzi of 90.58 km/h, and the performance of the little Ducatis becomes apparent.

Cucciolos were also sold abroad in large quantities, and were even manufactured under licence in France by Ets. Rochet of Paris. In Britain, the engine was later imported by Britax Concessionaires, an offshoot of the motorcycle accessory company, who offered it for sale from 1953 onwards either as a clip-on or as a complete machine, originally using a Royal Enfield bicycle as the frame. In due course Britax designed their own set of cycle parts, featuring a rigid rear end and blade girder forks with rubber band front suspension. A fully enclosed version was marketed as the Britax Scooterette, and sold for just under £100, albeit not in any quantity. Equally unsuccessful was a racing version complete with hand-beaten alloy streamling and dropped handlebars; the Britax Hurricane thus achieved the distinction not only of being the first British 50 cc racing machine but also the first production racer to be offered for sale anywhere in the world with a streamlined fairing as standard equipment. Unfortunately, the British public was not yet ready for tiddler racing, and in any case the extra weight of the quite advanced dustbin-type fairing meant that the Hurricane's performance did not live up to its name.

Cucciolo engine unit in the metal. Neat, with racy inlet stub

Only a few were sold, though a couple do still exist in private hands.

In the early years of its production the Cucciolo was only offered for sale as an engine unit, which prompted some Italian entrepreneurs to purchase a quantity supply from Ducati, build their own frames, and market a complete mini-motorcycle, much as is the case with Minarelli engines today. Chief amongst these was the Motoclipper, whose grandiose badge depicting a *Cutty Sark*-like China clipper sailing ship first appeared in early 1948. Its constructors, the equally grandly named Società Generale Prodotti Industriale, opted for a bicycle-type frame with leading link front forks and torsion bar rear suspension. All three engine types were available, but the 60 cc T3 had some tuning work carried out on its 43.8 × 40 mm engine to produce

1.8 bhp at only 4500 rpm, with the aid of a 15 mm Weber carburettor. The 24 in wheels were fitted with 2.25 section tyres, and a single 110 mm diameter brake was fitted to the rear wheel. A hefty 5.5-litre fuel tank sat on the top frame tube, giving a pleasant line to the little bike, which weighed 45 kg and offered a claimed 60 km/h top speed. More to the point, though, in a country still suffering from fuel shortages, was its still exceptional fuel consumption of 225 mpg.

By the time the Motoclipper appeared at the Milan Show in October 1948, the rear suspension had been changed from the torsion bars to a cleverly simple design featuring a coil spring wrapped round the swinging arm spindle and bearing on the fork at each end. In spite of an intensive advertising campaign, however, the Motoclipper was not a huge success, although it did sell in reasonable numbers, especially since the T3 version could also be had with a pillion as an optional extra: for a nation as sociable as the Italians, this was an undoubted attraction!

Not much better fortune befell the Necchi, a rival Cucciolo-engined marque introduced in 1949, which looked even more of a real motorcycle, with saddle tank, two-wheel brakes and plunger rear

A 1955 Britax Hurricane 50 cc production racer, powered by the Cucciolo pullrod engine. It weighed 90 lb and originally featured rubber-band front suspension, though this was later dropped in favour of telescopic forks. The alloy streamlining made the Hurricane the first British bike to be so equipped as standard, but factory rider Arnold Jones reaped little success on the bike

suspension; its potential market in a country still struggling to recover from the war was too small, for the boy racer set of later years did not yet have the discretionary spending to buy such a bike, and their elders were not yet disposed to pay a substantial additional sum for the benefits offered by a sophisticated version of what was only supposed to be basic transportation: if they wanted more, they bought a scooter.

That 1948 Milan Show did however see Ducati themselves take the first step towards manufacture of their own complete machine when they introduced the Girino, a three-wheel transporter powered by the T3 Cucciolo engine (the T2 could be had as an option at lesser cost). The engine was mounted over the single rear wheel in a Vespa-like compartment; the driver sat just in front of the rear wheel with the fuel tank behind him. Flat handlebars steered twin front wheels via hub-centre steering, with the flatbed to carry the maximum payload of 120 kg stretching in front of the driver and ending just in front of the twin front wheels. The Girino (meaning helmsman) was not a commercial success, though, for the simple reason that a light but bulky load would obscure the driver's forward vision, a fact wittily pointed out by Aldo Farinelli, the Cucciolo's designer, when he visited the Show. There he saw a display featuring a trio of Motoclippers mounted on the Girino's flatbed. 'I never thought my little puppy would be able to tug along a fleet of clippers,' he is reported to have said, 'even with a helmsman aboard. The trouble is, though, I think he'll need radar to navigate with!' Many a true word spoken in jest.

By 1950 almost 200,000 Cucciolo engines had been manufactured, and Ducati decided to extend their range further by marketing a complete motorcycle based on the little pullrod engine. To begin with, though, they had no frame-making expertise or facilities, so instead turned to an outside contractor to make the cycle parts for them. The firm selected was another company which had been heavily dependent on military contracts during the war and was no searching for new fields to work in: Aero Caproni of Trento, in the far north-western German-speaking corner of Italy, in the foothills of the Dolomites. Caproni had been Italy's principal manufacturer of fighter-bomber aircraft before and during the Second World War, and like their fighter and seaplane counterparts a few hundred miles to the west, Aer Macchi, decided to diversify into the motorcycle growth industry in the late 1940s.

In fact, Caproni had a loose connection with motorcycles from before the war, since in 1935 they

had acquired the aircraft interests and designs of the Roman CNA company, which had also produced a supercharged, 500 cc four-cylinder racing bike known as the Rondine. Caproni then had no interest in motorcycles, so passed the Rondine and its development engineer and rider, Piero Taruffi, along to the Gilera motorcycle company, who were then on the lookout for a means of instant success in competition. Thanks to Taruffi and works rider Dorino Serafini they achieved it: Serafini won the 1939 European Championship, beating the blown BMWs in the process, while Taruffi captured a host of world speed records, including the outright (for motorcycles) mark, before war broke out.

Caproni had scarcely more experience than Ducati in building motorcycle frames, but here again the hand of IRI may be detected in putting the two companies together. The result was a well-designed little machine built around 22 in. wheels, with s/s Caproni brakes fitted to both. A telescopic front fork with coil springing was featured, while at the rear a very modern-looking cantilever design was employed, with the spring tube running up under the seat and damping provided by means of twin friction units mounted on either side of the swinging arm. Fitted with the 60 cc engine, tuned to produce 2.25 bhp at 5000 rpm, the first Ducati motorcycle weighed 44.5 kg, had a top speed of 40 mph, and returned just under 200 mpg with the aid of a 15 mm Weber and even longer induction tract than before.

The arrangement with Caproni lasted less than a year, for in May 1950 the aircraft firm announced their own 50 cc flyweight, with advanced pressed-steel frame, the Capriolo. This too had an ohv four-stroke engine, though with pushrod valve gear rather than the Cucciolo's pullrods. At the same time though, Ducati had also taken the first step forward from the basic design on which the company had depended since its initiation into the motorcycle field by introducing its own 65 cc pushrod engine in March 1950, dealt with in the next chapter.

The Capriolo's arrival on the scene put Ducati under some commercial pressure, since they no longer offered the only four-stroke micromotor on the market. Even though they took over production of their complete motorcycle from Caproni, the spate of flyweight designs now on the market caused profit margins to be cut to the minimum, as manufacturers slashed prices in an effort to be competitive. Ducati were no exception, cutting the price of the clip-on T2 engine from 55,000 to 44,000 lire in early 1950, and the complete T3 machine

Last of the 'little pups'. Real suspension, comfort and some performance

from 143,000 to 123,000 lire. Further inroads into their market were being made by the scooter craze, led by the massive Piaggio and Innocenti industrial giants with their Vespa and Lambretta models respectively. Even worse, a law was passed in 1950 restricting *bicimotore* such as the Cucciolo to a maximum speed of 35 km/h on Italian roads, rendering them even less attractive to a speed-conscious nation. And further proposed legislation requiring the little machines to be registered and driving licences to be compulsory for the riders was only narrowly averted, after an intensive lobby.

Ducati's efforts to maintain the Cucciolo's popularity led the company into the competition field for the first time. Italians have always been interested in and conscious of world speed records, and Ducati decided to cash in on this by assisting one of the most ardent *cucciolisti*, Ugo Tamarozzi, to launch an attack on the medium- and long-distance 50 cc records, which, even better from a publicity standpoint, were then held by a German Victoria machine. The opportunity for much nationalistic flag-waving and associated publicity thereby presented itself, which could do no harm into the bargain.

Ugo Tamarozzi was a remarkable man; a jovial, bespectacled enthusiast, he was over 50 years old when the war ended, which made his later achievements all the more notable. An ardent Cucciolo fan, he used his little bike for every conceivable purpose with some success, not only racing it to victories over much younger men but also using it for scrambles in the winter and reliability trials and hillclimbs all year round. In 1951 he entered the International Six Days Trial,

held in Italy that year, on his 50 cc Cucciolo, winning a bronze medal after scoring clean sheets on five out of the six days. His trademark was a fat cigar which he chewed incessantly, even while racing; it's doubtful if the top speed of his little machine was great enough to extinguish it!

Tamarozzi prepared his own machine with works assistance before launching an attack on the Victoria records on 5 March, 1951 at Monza. Using a petrol/benzole 50/50 mixture and a 12 mm Dell'Orto carburettor mounted directly on to the cylinder, compression ratio raised to 9.5:1 and a stripped-down frame with the rear wheel spokes covered by a light-alloy disc as a token concession to streamlining – no other fairing was fitted – Tamarozzi set 12 new 50 cc world records from 10 km (at 62.717 km/h) to six hours (at 65.548 km/h). Fastest mark was the 100 miles at 66.092 km/h, and the little bike ran perfectly throughout, with the aid of a scrupulously observed 3500 rpm rev limit.

Ducati were overjoyed, and mounted a formidable advertizing campaign to capitalize on Tamarozzi's success. But more was to come: realizing that an even greater haul of records could have been acquired with a higher rev limit and, even more important, a second rider – a continuous six-hour stint in the highly uncomfortable saddle of such a tiny machine was a considerable feat of endurance for anyone, let alone a man no longer in the prime of life – Tamarozzi returned to Monza on 16 May for another crack. This time the bike was prepared by Ducati in the factory, under the guidance of chief engineer Giovanni Fiorio, who also attended the record attempt. Fiorio raised the compression ratio to 10:1, raised the benzole content of the fuel, and installed a different cam. The result was an engine that ran for 12 hours at the remarkable speed of 6800 rpm, yet differed very little in the important areas from the standard road product. Tamarozzi, assisted by co-rider Glauco Zitelli, achieved no less than 20 new world records, breaking all his own marks handsomely – the 10 km mark went up by over 15 per cent for example to 72.756 km/h. Longest distance covered was the 12-hour record, which was captured at 67.156 km/h, and once again the little bike ran without the slightest trouble throughout the attempt.

Ducati were particularly glad to achieve their targets in order to counteract the rather embarrassing results of their inaugural effort in the famous Milano–Taranto long-distance race a couple of weeks later. This marathon single-stage event, 1400 km long and run the length of Italy, was highly regarded by the motorcycle-buying public, who placed great emphasis on success in it as well as in the Giro d'Italia multi-stage event for sports machines up to 175 cc. The introduction of a 50 cc class caused Ducati to offer assistance to several private owners on their Cucciolos, but the result was total disaster, with all half-dozen bikes retiring before the half-distance mark at Rome. One had, however, briefly appeared in the top 10 class runners, when one of Ducati's own employees, Alberto Farne, reached 10th place at Bologna before retiring 20 miles later on the climb up the Apennine pass to Florence. Farne's son Franco would later become a key figure for over 25 years in the fortunes of the Borgo Panigale factory in competition.

So while Alpino, Capriolo and the rest of their competitors were able to advertize their success in the Milano–Taranto, Ducati leant heavily on Tamarozzi and Zitelli's world records to show the speed and dependability of the little Cucciolo. Just to rub the message in, in what was to become a recurrent tactic of the factory's just before the important Milan Show, Ducati sent Tamarozzi back to Monza a third time on 13 November, 1951, only a month after his sterling efforts in the ISDT. With a team of five other riders, amongst them Alberto Farne, the cigar-chewing veteran scooped a total of 27 world records, beating all the previous marks (the 10 km speed was now up to 76.400 km/h) and gaining new ones up to 48 hours at 63.200 km/h. Once again, the little 50 cc pullrod ran faultlessly, the only difficulty the team encountered being one of coping with a typically foggy Milanese night with only a frail 6V lighting system to pierce the murk.

That left just two 50 cc records still held by Victoria, the short-distance marks of the standing start and flying kilometre. Though the Cucciolo was anything but a sprinter, the fact irked Tamarozzi enough to have a crack at these records in a final visit to Monza on 16 January, 1952. With the machine stripped of every ounce of surplus weight and tuned for maximum power rather than for endurance, he succeeded in completing a clean sweep of the capacity speed records by setting two new world marks of 63.268 km/h for the standing start, and 77.753 km/h for the flying kilo, both on a still unfaired machine.

The Ducati 50 cc world records stood for nearly five years, and were only partially beaten in the end by the fully streamined Guazzoni two-stroke. As a feat of endurance and reliability on the part of both man and machine, the little Cucciolo's successes were all the more remarkable for the fact that the machine was effectively unfaired, and differed only very little from a standard road model: the cycle

The Ducati team for the 1951 ISDT, held that year in Italy. Ugo Tamarozzi is second from the left, and obtained a silver medal in the event on his Cucciolo

parts in fact were those of an ordinary customer machine, lightened where possible. In the future, only specialist record-breaking designs would be able to break the Ducati Cucciolo's marks.

This success established the Cucciolo afresh in the eyes of the public, and ensured its continued success for some years to come. Progressively updated over the years to 65 cc, in which guise it would attain a speed of 70 km/h – nearly 45 mph – the model also gained a more modern and less bicycle-like set of cycle parts, with 18 in. rims, pressed-steel frame and conventional telescopic rear suspension being introduced in the course of the 1950s. Though the Cucciolo name was in time officially dropped in favour of supposedly more snappy model denominations such as the '55 M' or '65 TL', the little bike would always be known to a generation of Italians who owed their postwar mobility to it as the 'little puppy': to many, it was at least as well loved as the real thing.

25

3

Finding the way

The increasing affluence of postwar Italy caused manufacturers of every kind of consumer merchandise to take a fresh look at their customers' needs and desires as the 1950s began. Motorcycles were no exception, and two trends became apparent.

Though the country as a whole was still a long way from its goal of postwar prosperity, there was a great deal more money around than had been the case four years before. Customers who had previously relied on a *bicimotore* to get around on were now looking for something more sophisticated, while at the same time some of those for whom even a Cucciolo clip-on engine had been out of reach financially in the immediate aftermath were now able to afford such a basic transport.

The latter market was catered for by an increasing proliferation of micromotor manufacturers engaged in every more intensive competition to wrest a bigger slice of the cake for themselves. Ducati's entire collection of eggs was in this basket, and though the Cucciolo was sufficiently well established to retain market leadership, its production was increasingly less profitable in the wake of the price war. Diversification was a necessity that the IRI bosses would have pointed out.

However, the only way that the Ducati model range could go was up. Here a bitter struggle was already being waged between the makers of two contrasting types of two-wheeler: the scooter and the lightweight motorcycle. In some cases the latter were scaled-up flyweights, in other scaled-down large-capacity machines, but conventional bikes were having a hard time of it at the hands of the Vespa and Lambretta, whose fully enclosed design and simple operation proved attractive to customers who felt daunted by the much more 'mechanical' appearance of the motorbikes. Scooters seemed cleaner and more practical: you just sat on them as you would in a chair, and didn't have to worry about flapping clothes getting caught

in the works, or such like. They sounded quieter too, and offered some weather protection.

Faced with this two-edged competition, Ducati decided to hedge their bets by producing one of each type of design. The motorcycle appeared first, in March 1950, when the Ducati 60 Sport was introduced. This had a conventional pushrod ohv engine which in fact measured 65 cc and produced 2.5 bhp at 5500 rpm, fitted into a pressed-steel frame, also designed and initially produced by Caproni, and very similar to the Cucciolo's. However, twin hydraulic rear units were employed from the outset, and the basic model featured leg guards as standard in an obvious counter to one of the scooter's benefits. Dry weight was 48 kg, with the claimed top speed around 70 km/h, and the light alloy crankcase contained an enclosed flywheel and three-speed gearbox operated by a typical Italian rocking-pedal arrangement that would be a feature of Ducati's machines up to the advent of the V-twins. The cast-iron cylinder was inclined forward by 25 degrees, and the valves set at an included angle of 100 degrees, compared to the Cucciolo's parallel valve layout, on the longest side of a pent-roof combustion chamber. Designer Giovanni Fiorio had also included a vane-type oil pump, with an external steel pipe feeding the valve gear up the right side of the cylinder, and 17 in. rims.

The 60 Sport was an immediate success, and in due course was renamed the 65 TS, in which guise it continued to be available well into the 1960s. In later times, from 1955 onwards, it was available with a sporty-looking handlebar fairing, the leg guards having become an optional extra from 1952 on: the day of the boy racer had arrived!

RIGHT *The unsuccessful Cruiser, which though technically interesting was too powerful and heavy to combat the Lambretta and Vespa competition. It used a 175 cc ohv engine fitted horizontally under the Ghia-designed bodywork*

★ POSITIONED BETWEEN FRONT AND REAR
WHEELS FOR MAXIMUM STABILITY

★ PROVIDING DIRECT CHAIN DRIVE
FOR POSITIVE TRACTION

★ OFFERING A 48c.c. FOUR-STROKE O.H.V ENGINE WITH TWO-
SPEED FOOT CHANGE PRE-SELECTOR GEARBOX ALSO
SUPPLIED WITH HAND CHANGE GEARS at slight extra charge

★ SMOOTH, EASY MOTOR CYCLING FOR ALL AT THE RATE
OF OVER 250 M.P.G. CRUISING AT 25-30 M.P.H.
BUILT-IN 6 VOLT DYNAMO LIGHTING

★ A MIRACLE OF COMPACT PRECISION
ENGINEERING, weighing only 17½ lb

DEMONSTRABLY SUPERIOR !

1,265 MILES IN 32 HOURS (AVERAGE
SPEED 39.8 M.P.H.) AT THRUXTON.
9-10 OCTOBER, 1953.

AT MONZA (ITALY), 1951 :—

		Standing Start
1 Km. in 59.6 secs.		39.5 m.p.h.
47.6 miles in 1 hour		47.6 m.p.h.
229.6 miles in 5 hours		45.9 m.p.h.
520 miles in 12 hours		43.3 m.p.h.
990 miles in 24 hours		41.3 m.p.h.
1,885.5 miles in 48 hours		39.3 m.p.h.

THRUXTON ENDURANCE TEST, 1953
(Photo by W. Lee)

'CUCCIOLO'

LITTLE PUP *Introduced by* **Britax** **£40** H.P. TERMS AVAILABLE

The greatest, speediest, and most flexible small engine ever produced!

The 'Cucciolo' (little pup) Cycle Auxiliary Motor is making cycling news in all parts of the world because it incorporates absolutely new and sensational features never before embodied in so small a motor unit.

Manufactured by the Italian DUCATI concern, famed for fine engineering, the 'Cucciolo' consists of a 48c.c. four-stroke—O.H.V. assembly with a two-speed pre-selector gearbox. Advanced as this is, it offers the additional advantages of a direct chain drive, like all the best types of motor cycles, together with a lighting current supplied by a separate L.T. coil. Moreover, its cunning positioning between front and rear wheels

makes for perfect balance and stability.

The engine develops 1.25 b.h.p. at 5,250 r.p.m. and pedalling can be assumed as in normal cycling..

No oil has to be mixed with the fuel—another big feature ! Lubrication is independent and fully automatic and the multiple metal plate clutch works in the oil bath.

Altogether the 'Cucciolo' is an outstanding example of precision engineering — smooth running, flexible and reliable, providing effortless motor cycling for all at the rate of over 250 m.p.g. cruising at 25-30 m.p.h. Make a point of looking at this sensational little motor when it next passes you !

FIRST CLASS AWARDS :
A.C.U. Trial 1952
A.C.U. Trial 1953
Completed London to Cardiff run
under severe winter conditions.
Completed London to Paris run in
9 hours, February, 1953.
Completed Witney Club Trial, 1953.
Completed Exeter Trial, January, 1954.
The only machine under 50c.c. to race
at HARRINGAY, WIMBLEDON and
RAYLEIGH SPEEDWAYS.
all with **NO MECHANICAL FAILURES !**

EXETER TRIAL, 1954 (Photo by Len Thorpe)

BRITAX (London) LTD. 115.129 CARLTON VALE, LONDON, N.W.6 · · · Telephone : MAIDA VALE 9351 (7 lines)

ABOVE *The Britax brochure from 1954 lauding the exploits and the abilities of the Cucciolo engine*

The Milan Show at the start of 1952 saw an uprated version of the pushrod ohv design introduced, the 98, available in three versions depending on the state of tune, but all employing the same Ducati-designed pressed steel open frame which appears in retrospect to be a small-scale version of the NSU Max. The single-seater 98N and dual seat 98T were the basic models, fitted with a three-speed gearbox just as the 65, but the 98 Sport already pointed the direction in which Ducati would follow in future years. The 48 × 52 mm engine initially produced 5.8 bhp at 7500 rpm, with a compression ratio of 8:1, rising to 6.9 bhp in later years. This was good for a top speed of 87 km/h for the little 98 cc bike, which in due course became 95 km/h with the later version and could be dramatically increased further with the aid of special tuning parts available from a variety of specialists. Fuel consumption was around 110 mpg, and weight held down to 89 kg with the aid of such features as 17 in. alloy rims as standard. Quite large diameter sls brakes were fitted, the front one employing an air scoop for cooling. The front of the crankcase was also finned to provide what the factory incorrectly claimed was a 'cooling radiator': all that meant was that the cheaper versions didn't have this feature. Performance was quite brisk with the aid of a four-speed gearbox in unit with the engine, and with – as on all Ducatis ever made – a geared primary drive. Ignition was by flywheel magneto, and a delightful period touch was the provision of a hand tyre-pump, carried on the top of the chainguard.

That same Milan Show in January 1952 also saw the launch of the other string to Ducati's bow, and a surprising one it was too. Their 175 cc ohv Cruiser was the first four-stroke scooter to be produced anywhere in the world and it incorporated many innovative features. Ducati were surprisingly coy at the time as to the identity of the machine's *progettista*, admitting only that it was 'a well-known car design and engineering company'. In due course the identity of this firm was revealed as being the famous Ghia design house, both then and since better known for their luxury car designs than for any two-wheeled expertise, and now as part of Ford after a period under the control of Alessandro de Tomaso.

Giovanni Fiorio had, however, designed the mechanical package, which consisted of a transversely located horizontal single-cylinder ohv engine lying under the rider's seat, bolted to an automatic hydraulic torque-converter gearbox via a casting which also incorporated the rear suspension

swinging arm pivot. The gearbox ran longitudinally under the dual seat, driving the rear wheel via a crown wheel and pinion with short stub axle. The substantial alloy gearbox casting, in fact, constituted the suspension arm, damped by a single unit fitted on the opposite side from the rear wheel. Front suspension was by telescopic forks, and the whole machine clothed in a stylish but unremarkable Ghia-designed bodywork which bore more than a passing resemblance to the popular Lambretta. An electric starter was fitted as standard.

With 7.5 bhp available from the 175 cc engine, the Ducati Cruiser had to be detuned to meet the 80 km/h speed limit imposed by the government on scooter-type machines. Fuel consumption though was comparable with the two-stroke competition at 95 mpg, and as a technical innovation the design was hailed as the most interesting new machine at the Show. Unfortunately, it was much less successful commercially, for a variety of reasons which seem so obvious in retrospect that it's amazing the Ducati directors did not realize them at the time.

For the Cruiser, while breaking new ground in the scooter world, violated a number of the principles that made scooters attractive in the first place to those who bought them. Ducati after all could not have hoped to attract customers for the Cruiser from the ranks of motorcyclists, but from amongst the thousands and thousands of Vespa and Lambretta owners. Yet their scooter design was a motorcyclist's idea of what a scooter ought to be like, but wasn't: the four-stroke engine required more maintenance, such as messy oil changes, attention to the valves and so forth, and was also noisier. The automatic gearbox, while a praiseworthy effort at making things easier for the rider, was complicated and gave rise to many warranty claims. The machine was heavier, and required more ability on the part of the owner to ride, as well as being more difficult to lift on to its stand – in fact the engine was more powerful and bigger than necessary.

For these and the reason that Ducati simply did not have the reputation enjoyed by Vespa and Lambretta for making scooters, the Cruiser was not a success. Relatively few *cucciolisti* transferred to it from their little *bicimotore*, preferring the proven

OPPOSITE ABOVE *The sporty pushrod 98 Touring Lusso at the 1954 Milan Show. Behind on the left is a light truck version of the Cruiser; on the right is an early 98 Sport*
OPPOSITE BELOW *A 1956 version of the pushrod 98 Sport, complete with boy racer handlebar fairing. Probably the first proper Ducati motorcycle to have been imported into Britain*

simplicity of the established two-strokes: it was a market reaction other motorcycle manufacturers, particularly Triumph in Britain over a decade later, would have done well to have noted. Scooters and motorcycles are two different concepts: it has never paid to mix them, but even Ducati didn't learn that lesson, as we shall see later.

Only a couple of thousand Cruisers were made in the two years before the model was withdrawn from production. Fortunately, their bow's other string, in the form of the pushrod ohv motorcycle, was much more successful, remaining in production until the mid-1960s, by which time over 100,000 examples had been produced. More importantly, it provided the company with both an entrée into the world of proper motorcycles and a reasonably sound financial base from which to plan future diversification of the model line.

Meantime the electrical side of the Ducati company had been developing successfully as well, to the point that in 1953 the decision was made to split the operation into two distinct enterprises, each independent of the other though occupying adjoining factories in a street now renamed Via Adriano Ducati in honour of the eldest brother, the firm's principal founder. The present-day motorcycle manufacturer was thus created: Ducati Meccanica SpA, while Ducati Elettronica SpA as it was then known, went its own way under separate direction.

Head of the new bike company was Dr. Giuseppe Montano, a convivial and dynamic man whose far-sightedness was largely responsible for the success the company enjoyed in later years. Under Montano, the final stages of the modernization and reconstruction of the Borgo Panigale factory were completed with the aid of government capital. By 1954, production capacity of 120 bikes a day was being consistently met, and photographs of the era show the spacious new factory to be very modern and well lit.

Montano was – fortunately for Ducati – a thorough-going motorcycle enthusiast in spite of being a government-appointed director, and was moreover a keen fan of racing. Under him, Ducati's competition activities grew from the occasional lending hand to a worthwhile customer, to a fully fledged racing team participating in everything from the Italian Novice (cadetti) Championship to Grands Prix. Montano was the first person of authority at Ducati to recognize that the sport-mad Italian public buys in the shops what wins on the tracks. Before an official works Ducati racer ever turned a wheel in public, Montano was on record as

saying that he believed Ducati had to go racing successfully in order to acquire the sporting image and heritage that other longer-established companies such as Guzzi and Gilera, let alone the more recent MV and Mondial firms, already possessed through their competition victories.

Before, Ducati's commercial rivals were the dozens of other micromotor/moped manufacturers amongst whom they stood out simply by virtue of the Cucciolo's massive sales and overwhelming public acceptance. In moving up to the world of proper motorcycles, even small-capacity ones, they were taking on companies who had been in business much longer than they, and who had gained public recognition through literally dozens of victories on racing tracks all over the world. Ducati needed such an image themselves, but rather than build a fleet of exotic factory racers bearing little or no resemblance to the products they sold to the public, it was Montano's policy decision that Ducati's competition bikes should be based on their road range. It was a policy that was not only successfully implemented by the team that he gathered round him but has continued to stand the company in good stead by its continued observance up to and including the present day.

Montano was realistic enough to accept that the ohv pushrod range could never be competitive in road racing, but did offer possibilities in off-road competition. Scrambles and enduro versions of the 98 Sport were prepared and used with some success, culminating in two silver medals for Alberto Farne and Giovanni Malaguti (later to build his own brand of lightweight motorcycles) in the 1954 International Six Days, held that year in Wales. As the smallest machines entered in that year's ISDT, the little Ducatis caused much favourable comment by their performance, and the event marked the first notable overseas success for the Bologna marque in competition. There would be many more to follow in future years.

Montano realized, however, that victory in road racing was what sold bikes in Italy, and especially success in the Milano-Taranto and Giro d'Italia marathons which then dominated the Italian competition calendar. Realizing that the engineering team he'd acquired weren't up to the task of designing suitable machinery, he decided to hire his own men. It was thus that in 1954 the man who more than any other has been responsible for the plethora of innovative, exciting and successful motorcycle designs to pour out of the Borgo Panigale factory in the last 30 years, joined the firm of Ducati Meccanica SpA: Ing. Fabio Taglioni.

4

Overnight success

When Taglioni left Mondial and joined Ducati in 1954, his brief from Montano was straightforward. As technical director and chief designer, he was to be responsible for producing a new range of sporting machines which would not only bring Ducati success on the track but would also form the basis of a line of road bikes of various capacities.

Taglioni has always adhered to the principal of scaling up: 'a good little 'un makes a better big 'un' than vice versa. His basic design would therefore be a 100 cc machine which could be transformed into a 125 or 175 cc version simply by changing the cylinder bore. It's a remarkable fact that the same bottom-end design was employed on all Taglioni Ducati singles from 100 up to 203 cc, whether road or race, with the same basic format when beefed-up providing the essential ingredients of the later road singles, both desmo and valve spring, up to 436 cc. If you get it right first time, and the design will accept the additional stresses of increased cubic capacity and power output, why change? Such was Taglioni's reasoning, and it means that all Ducati singles produced over the next 20 years were clearly descended from that first little 100 cc machine: the Gran Sport.

Nicknamed the *Marianna* by its thousands of affectionate owners, the 100 Gran Sport was announced to the public in March 1955. Taglioni had worked very fast to produce the bike, for the Giro d'Italia took place in April and Montano and he were reluctant to let another year pass by without the chance of Ducati success in the event. The first track tests were held at the Mondena *aeroauto-dromo* circuit in February, and startled onlookers, including representatives from rival factories. In the cauldron of Italian racing, even the efforts of a previously unsung company such as Ducati were closely followed. The fact that the Marianna not only looked right but went well on its first semi-public appearance worried rival factories.

When the model was officially launched on 5 March, 1955, it was seen that Taglioni had introduced a new degree of sophistication to the 100 cc class, hitherto dominated by the spritely pushrod ohv Laverdas, by opting for an ohc engine design. In view of the fact that the Marianna's technical specification provided the basis for all future single-cylinder Ducatis, it's worth examining its features in some detail. Aspects which would be adhered to in the future included a 10 degree forward inclination of the light alloy cylinder; a cast iron sleeve; vertically split crankcases with forward finning and a small integral sump; unit-construction gearbox; oil bath clutch with gear-driven primary; camshaft drive by vertical shaft and bevel gears up the right side of the engine, employing the hunting tooth principle; battery and coil ignition, with the points located on the front right side of the engine and driven off the bottom bevel by a spur gear; 80 degree included valve angle; forged three-ring piston with deep valve inserts and profiled at the bottom to clear the flywheels; three-piece built-up crankshaft with full-disc flywheels forged integrally with their shafts, drilled axially for lightness and running on two ball thrust bearings with the end loading obtained by a star washer on the drive-side shaft; forged steel conrod with double T-section stiffening, running on caged roller bearing; and force-fed lubrication of the big end and camshaft(s), with horizontal oil filter and fling feed oiling to the constant-mesh transmission and cylinder. Given the speed with which he was forced to work to produce the first expression of this basic design concept, it's a remarkable testament to Taglioni's talent that so little of it would change over the next two decades and more.

The 98 cc engine of the Gran Sport measured 49.4 × 52 mm, and produced 9 bhp at 9000 rpm on a compression ratio of 8.5:1. This was a crankshaft figure, translating to 8 bhp at the rear wheel;

Taglioni has always bèen at great pains to emphasize the difference between the two. By 1956, the cr was up to 9.7:1 with the availability of 100 octane pump fuel on Italian roads, with peak power than up to 9.4 bhp and produced at 9800 rpm. The engine was however safe to 11,500 rpm, providing a useful margin of safety in the vent of a missed gear or neck-and-neck struggle to the line. One of the reasons Taglioni has always been lionized by the riders who've performed for him over the years is that he realizes that to err is human: no Joe Craig or Domenico Agusta, who flew into tyrannical rages if they felt that some poor rider – an unfortunate necessity at best in any case – was misusing one of their beloved machines, Taglioni has always adopted a philosophical approach to the in-evitabilities of human frailty, which in turn has led him to build a safety margin into his designs wherever possible. Such an attitude would be one of the reasons behind his later adoption of positive valve control.

For the time being though, the Marianna employed conventional twin hairpin valve springs, left exposed, and a 20 mm Dell'Orto carburettor with a long venturi, which, thanks to the forward inclination of the cylinder and 15 degrees of downdraught employed, required a section to be cut out of the fuel tank for clearance. Unlike on later Ducati singles, the cambox was separate from the head, both cast in light alloy, with the camshaft operating the two valves via short rockers. A four-speed gearbox was fitted, but thanks to the wide spread of power this was not initially a problem, especially with the straight exhaust pipe originally fitted. Later models with more extreme valve timing and small reverse cone megaphone were a little more temperamental.

Finally, since a headlamp and horn were fitted as standard, not only to comply with Italian sports machine regulations but also because of the night section on the Milano–Taranto, a generator was fitted on the left-hand side of the crankshaft, charging the 6V battery located under the seat.

The cycle parts also acted as the prototype for later Ducati singles, consisting of an open-cradle, single downtube design with the engine acting as a semi-stressed member. Small separate engine plates were originally employed at the front of the crankcase, but in later years these would come to be incorporated into the construction of the frame. The long seat could be used for a pillion if necessary, but in view of its kicked-up rear end was more likely to be employed for lying prone on the tank to cheat the wind of every ounce of speed. Seventeen-inch rims helped to present a low profile, and an optional extra for racing events was an alloy bikini fairing which enclosed the clip-on handlebars completely, small slots being cut in the side for the rider's knuckles to clear. A 50.5 in. wheelbase helped to provide quick and positive steering, while telescopic suspension front and rear was by then the norm. A

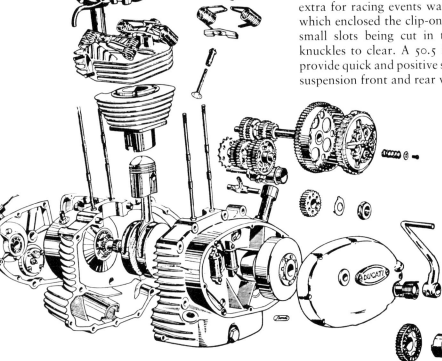

An exploded drawing of the 98 cc Gran Sport engine which, in the bike known affectionately as the Marianna, formed the basis of future Ducati units. This was Ing. Taglioni's first design for the company

Mariannas on test at Modena Aeroautodrome in April 1956, a week before the Giro d'Italia in which the model made such a dramatic debut (Zagari)

compressed air bottle was fitted as standard to the left rear frame tube, in place of the usual hand pump, thus further emphasizing the machine's sporting purpose. The 18-litre steel fuel tank gave a 420-mile range at just over 100 mpg at racing speeds, an important factor in the long-distance races at which the bike was aimed, since it thus enabled refuelling stops to be cut to a minimum. Dry weight was exactly 80 kg.

At a time when almost all other factories in Italy – or indeed anywhere else – were restricted to employing pushrod valve gear on their lightweight production machines, the significance of Taglioni's decision to use the classic bevel gear solution on the Marianna should not be underestimated. While undoubtedly the best solution to the problem in engineering terms, bevel drive ohc required careful choice of material and high manufacturing tolerances, as well as skilful assembly. It's a tribute to the quality of manufacture at the Ducati factory that this increasingly expensive method of opening and closing the valves could be employed with complete success for nigh on 30 years – far longer commercially than with any other marque. The fact that it could have been introduced at all in the first place in 1955 was only due to the new high-precision machine tools installed at the Borgo Panigale factory under Montano's supervision. His far-

sightedness would pay considerable dividends in future years.

With a top speed of 130 km/h, the 100 Gran Sport seemed to be a likely contender for honours at the beginning of the 1955 racing season. Even Ducati, though, cannot have been prepared for the amazing success which the Marianna achieved so soon after its launch, especially since the team of riders which they had recruited to ride the bike contained none of the established stars of the lightweight racing world.

Instead, Ducati's line-up of what journalist Vic Willoughby charmingly termed at the time their 'star midgets' – men whose riding prowess was matched by their diminutive stature, making them ideally suited to get the best out of the little bikes – was composed of up-and-coming local riders from the Bologna area who were for the most part in only their second or for some third year of competition. Clad in identical team helmets painted the distinctive Ducati striped colours of dark red and white, with a single initial 'D' on the front, Leopoldo Tartarini and Franco Villa (later to become bike manufacturers in their own right under the Italjet and Villa names respectively) were joined on works 98 cc Mariannas by Gianni Degli Antoni,

33

Italo Fantuzzi and Giuliano Maoggi. Additionally, Taglioni had somehow found time to breathe on the more humble pushrod 98 Sport, with the result that no less than 37 Ducati-mounted riders lined up for the start of the Giro d'Italia, a bare six weeks after the announcement of the Gran Sport model. Many of those mounted on the pushrod models received factory assistance in preparing their machines for the race. In consequence, so many Ducati-entered riders were to take part in Italian events that it was found necessary to adopt different colour stripes on the riders' helmets for ease of identification. Another motif was the figure of a prancing horse on the side of the fairing. This was the same emblem as used by the Scuderia Ferrari car team, and owes its origins to the most famous son of Lugo, Taglioni's home town. He was Italy's most celebrated World War I fighter pilot ace, Barracca, whom Taglioni much admired, hence the emblem.

The result of the Marianna's competition debut in the Giro d'Italia must have exceeded even Taglioni's wildest dreams. Whereas in 1954 the pushrod Ducatis had been totally swamped by the ohv Laverdas in the 100 cc class, in 1955 the tables were turned completely. Each of the nine inter-city stages, run off on successive days over distances of up to 500 km each, were won by Ducati riders, with Villa taking the flag in the first stage from the team's base in Bologna to Trieste. Degli Antoni had finished a lowly 27th place in that stage while he ran in a new engine, but in the second stage from Trieste to Padua he ran away from the field to win at an average of over 100 km/h. On the seventh leg over the long, straight roads of the southern Mezzogiorno, he won again at an average speed for the 400 km from Taranto to Cosenza of 112.03 km/h – an amazing figure for a 100 cc machine at any time.

When the race returned to Bologna for the finish, the factory employees turned out *en masse* to greet a Ducati grand slam. Out of 37 Ducati-mounted starters no less than 28 machines finished the 3400 km event. Gianni Degli Antoni not only won the 100 cc class handsomely at an average speed throughout the event of 98.90 km/h but also finished fifth overall against all the larger-capacity machines, and together with Villa in 2nd place, Fantuzzi 3rd and youngster Bruno Spaggiari in 4th spot on a pushrod 98 Sport, beat all the 125 cc finishers, including class winner Paolo Campanelli's factory-entered Benelli. The previous Laverda class record was smashed by the incredible figure of 12.47 km/h for the whole event, and to make matters worse for the Breganze firm, not a single one of their bikes finished the course, so hot had been the pace set by the Ducati

squad: every finisher in the 100 cc class was Ducati-mounted. Almost the only disappointment was that one of the Mariannas failed to finish: Tartarini, at one time a likely winner, had fallen off so often in trying to stave off Degli Antoni's charge from behind that he ended up destroying the motorcycle. Had Degli Antoni not been forced to take things easily on that first stage, he would almost certainly have been third overall.

Ducati had practically stopped any form of advertizing for the past two years – they had

RIGHT *The start of the 1955 Milano–Taranto in dead of night. Two bikes on left are works Gran Sports*
BELOW *A line-up of Ducatisti at Modena in April 1957, with the machines they would ride in the last Giro d'Italia later that month. The machines are a mixed bag of 100 and 125 Gran Sports (Zagari)*

relatively little to boast about – but now in the wake of this overwhelming victory they responded by launching an intensive campaign based on what was unabashedly termed *il miraculo del motogiro 1955*. Great emphasis was rightly laid on the fact that the little Gran Sport had comprehensively beaten all the 125s – why buy bigger when you can get a faster, more economical smaller bike – and additionally an interesting and prophetic angle was introduced by an advert which showed a penny-farthing bicycle and a Fiat 600 car stationed on either side of a yawning chasm. The gap was spanned by a triumphal arch composed of the various models of Ducati lightweight motorcycles, which were hailed in full-size print as 'The Bridge Between the Bicycle and the Automobile'. In view of later events, the message could hardly have been more apt.

Not surprisingly, Marianna sales took off like a rocket after the Giro d'Italia success, with waiting lists up to two months long becoming commonplace in spite of the factory's every effort to meet demand. The pushrod 98, which had also covered itself with glory in the event, also became very popular, and the whole exercise proved the validity of Montano's decision to become involved in racing.

Just 10 days after completing the rigorous Motogiro, Degli Antoni – by now recognized as team leader – and the rest of the Marianna-mounted squad were in action in a quite different type of event at a venue which would come to hold great significance to Ducati enthusiasts: Imola. An hour's drive from the Bologna factory, together with the once-a-year Modena event, Imola was to become Ducati's home track, and it was prophetic that the first appearance of the factory team in a short circuit race should be there. The result was just as successful as the Giro d'Italia, with Degli Antoni leading the field home in the 100 cc race, with Villa in 2nd place. In some ways even more significant though was the name of the 3rd place man, also Marianna-mounted: Franco Farne, then a Ducati apprentice enjoying his first factory ride on one of the ohc machines. He was to become Taglioni's right-hand man for the next three decades.

Mariannas were now being delivered to private owners, and one of these, Marcello Dama, used his little 98 cc machine, then barely tun in, to record an interesting victory at the end of May in the prestigious *Corsa del Mare* sprint. This 'Race to the Sea' took place between Rome and its neighbouring seaside resort Ostia, along the dead straight autostrada, which thus enabled interesting top speed comparisons to be made. In winning the 100 cc class, Dama averaged 122.449 km/h from a

ABOVE *Two of the most famous and enduring names at Modena in April 1956: Bruno Spaggiari (left) and Franco Farne, the latter seated on a 98 cc Gran Sport (Zagari)*
RIGHT *Franco Farne, (Modena 1956) with fellow-rider Casadei and mechanic Pietro Regazzi on the right (Zagari)*

standing start, indicating that the performance of the Mariannas sold to customers was on a par with that of the works bikes.

The next big event however was the Milano–Taranto classic, the major long-distance event of the season eagerly contested by all the Italian factories. Aware of their previously disappointing performances in this race, Ducati redoubled their efforts in preparing for the 1955 version, and were rewarded by another crushing victory in the 100 cc class. Degli Antoni led the way home again at an average speed for the 1400 km single-stage event of 103.172 km/h, placing 16th overall against the other machines of up to 500 cc capacity, some of which were fully fledged Grand Prix machines, such as Bruno Francisci's winning four-cylinder Gilera. By completing the course in just over $13\frac{1}{2}$ hours, Degli Antoni also led home the winner of the 125 class – none other than his team-mate Giuliano Maoggi, making the unheralded debut of the 125 cc version of the Gran Sport Ducati. His factory machine beat the works MV Agusta by over two minutes, thus winning for the Bologna team the first round in what would prove to be a

recurrent battle for the best part of the next decade. Ducatis placed 1-2-3-4 in the 100 cc category, Villa leading home privateer Ettore Scamondi and Spaggiari for the minor placings.

Taglioni had stated when the Marianna was announced that he planned to produce 125 and 175 cc versions, but the first hint that one of these would appear so soon only came when the entry list for the Milano–Taranto was published just before the event. Ducati had realized with the results of the Motogiro just how competitive their 100 cc machine was against the 125s, so working with the speed which now appeared to be second nature to him, Taglioni bored out the Marianna to produce the 125 Gran Sport, with engine dimensions of 55.3 × 52 mm. In doing so, he had produced the first 'oversquare' ohc Ducati engine, in which the bore

size is greater than the stroke. While this would become a trademark of future Ducatis, and indeed would become a commonly accepted engineering practice in the motorcycle world, it was very far from being so in 1955, when current wisdom held that a longer stroke was preferable in the interests of increased torque and reduced piston speed. By careful attention to producing a sound bottom-end design, thus permitting increased revs, as well as to proper breathing, Taglioni was able to achieve the increased engine efficiency and greater specific power in terms of the brake mean effective pressure (bmep) of an oversquare engine. The 125 Gran Sport was his first such unit.

The sohc 125 produced 12 bhp at 9800 rpm, using a 22 mm carb and running on a slightly lower compression ratio than the 98 cc version, but otherwise identical to it mechanically. Safe maximum engine revs were 11,400 rpm – again practically the same. The complete bike, employing the same frame as the Marianna, weighed 85 kg, the difference resulting from the use of 18 in. rims and a larger front brake.

After the successes enjoyed in long-distance racing Ducati now turned their attention to the short circuits and *circuiti cittadine* road races round the streets of Italian cities such as Perugia, Riccione, Vigevano, Faenza, Cattolica, Pesaro and the like. These dangerous but exciting courses, often lined with houses, trees, walls and serried ranks of spectators, were an integral part of the Italian racing scene, and were moreover important from the publicity standpoint for the manufacturers, since it offered potential buyers the opportunity to see for themselves at first hand how rival machines performed over roads they themselves rode on every day.

Mario Carini and Sandro Ciceri with their Nardi-streamlined 100 Gran Sport at Monza on 30 November, 1956. They scooped a total of 44 world class records, covering the 100, 125, 175 and 250 cc classes

Several of the races counted for the Italian Junior Championship, the 100 cc crown in which was won for 1955 by Ducati's Franco Villa in his first full season of racing. This gave the firm a complete sweep of the 100 cc category in Italian events that season, and a nice handle on which to hang their participation in the Milan Show at the end of the year. This saw the appearance of a Taglioni-inspired 125 cc version of the pushrod engine, in later years to rejoice in the rather ill-thought-out name of the Bronco! Its engine too measured 55.3 × 52 mm, producing 6.5 bhp at 6500 rpm, enough for a top speed of 97 km/h from the 100 kg machine. An attractive-looking duplex cradle frame turned out to be a forerunner of the later Grand Prix machines, since it's worth noting that not only did all small-capacity ohc Ducatis have the same bottom-end design, they also had the same frame pick-up points as the pushrod singles, rendering the engines interchangeable.

Though the 125 and 100 Gran Sport models were now catalogued as 'for competition only', they were true dual-purpose machines and were used by many owners as regular daily transport during the week,

before being raced in local or even more distant events at the weekend. They could even be ridden to the track before having the road equipment removed for racing, and in this way were in every way the Latin equivalent of the contemporary BSA Gold Star. Unfortunately, they also had the same effect as the Goldie on their respective category of racing, for by 1958 Ducati domination of the 100 cc class was such that it was scrapped altogether, and the 125 category reorganized in favour of a series of formula classes. Success has its penalties, too.

In due course a 175 cc version of the Gran Sport was produced, measuring 62 × 57.8 mm by means of both boring *and* stroking the 98 cc engine. This produced 16 bhp at 9000 rpm, good for a top speed of 155 km/h, but only appeared in a couple of races at the end of 1956 before being replaced for the 1957 season by the unsuccessful valve spring twin and the 175 Sport, which was the precursor of the 1960s model range.

Meantime, during the course of 1956, the Marianna was developed further to produce 12 bhp at 10,500 rpm, raising the top speed slightly to 135 km/h but better still making for brisker acceleration, still with a four-speed gearbox. The 125 Gran Sport was taken up to 10,000 rpm, at which point it produced 14 bhp and did 150 km/h – all speeds quoted were with only a handlebar fairing at best. This increased performance was sufficient to keep Ducati ahead of the opposition in both the 100 and 125 classes in sports machine competition. Giuliano Maoggi won the Giro d'Italia outright on his 125, defeating the entire 175 cc class, backed up by team-mate Maranghi in second place on a similar bike. Ducati won all nine stages, and once again swamped the 100 cc class.

It was the same story in the last-ever Milano–Taranto; neither this race nor the Moto-giro were held again after 1957 in the wake of the Mille Miglia car race tragedy that year, after which open roads, inter-city racing was banned in Italy. A new name, Alberto Gandossi, won the 100 cc class at 99.744 km/h, while Degli Antoni secured victory in the 125 category at 103.176 km/h to register an amazing 6th place overall: he beat all the 175 cc class runners, and all but two 500s and three 250s in a superlative ride that again yielded Ducati much useful publicity.

The burgeoning sales of the Gran Sports prompted Ducati to offer an interesting service to private owners who wished to race their bikes. They could if they wished send their mechanic or tuner to the factory for an instruction course in how to prepare and maintain the bikes for racing – or even

attend themselves if, as was often the case, they looked after their own bike. Furthermore, a spares kit could be obtained from the racing department at Borgo Panigale which consisted of a large wooden chest containing all the tools necessary to work on the bike plus tuning parts and the most commonly used spares, including a full set of sprockets. It was an imaginative move which was eagerly responded to by dozens of competitors, and was yet another reason for the popularity of the Marianna and its larger-capacity sister.

Ducati once again won a plethora of sports-machine events throughout Italy, and even abroad in other parts of Europe, where the marque's name was beginning to be made. At the end of 1956, the Marianna's reputation as the dominant machine in its class was firmly cemented when two private owners, Mario Carini and Sandro Ciceri, took the latter's 100 Gran Sport to a grand total of 44 world records at Monza on 30 November, just in time for

Ducati made the most of their sweeping success in the 1955 Giro d'Italia

IIIº Giro d'Italia Motociclistico

la moto

DUCATI

ha **TRIONFALMENTE CONCLUSO**

la lunga corsa dominando la classifica generale (classe 100 cc.) con:

1º GIANNI DEGLI ANTONI
in ore 34.44'35", alla media di km. 98,907, precedendo tutte le 125 cmc. (quinto assoluto)

2º FRANCESCO VILLA
in ore 35.32'59", precedendo tutte le 125 (undicesimo assoluto)

3º ITALO FANTUZZI
in ore 35.44'55", precedendo tutte le 125 (quindicesimo assoluto)

4º BRUNO SPAGGIARI
in ore 35.57'51", precedendo tutte le 125 (diciassettesimo assoluto)

5º GIULIANO MAOGGI
in ore 35.58'36" (ventesimo assoluto)

6º ETTORE SCAMANDRI
in ore 35.59'16"

. . . .

arrivando al traguardo finale con 28 delle 37 macchine partite

Catene Regina Extra   Candele "Marelli"

DUCATI MECCANICA S. p. A. - BOLOGNA
(BORGO PANIGALE) CASELLA POSTALE 313
TEL. 53-851 (quattro linee) TELEGRAMMI "DUCATIMEC„ BOLOGNA

il ponte

dalla bicicletta   **all' automobile**

'The bridge between the bicycle and the car' was Ducati's advertising thrust in the mid-50s. They certainly had identified their competition accurately: the car represented is a Fiat 600

the feat to be splashed at the important Milan Show.

Though the actual machine was privately owned, Ducati had lent factory assistance by preparing the engine and commissioning a specially designed all-enveloping alloy streamlining for the standard cycle parts from the Milan firm of Nardi e Danese, who already had considerable renown in the car world for their success in the field, especially when applied to small-capacity Fiat specials, one of which was actually a Siata: the wheel had come full circle!

Nardi's design, achieved with the help of a wind tunnel, featured an open cockpit and small Plexiglas screen rather than the fully enclosed teardrop type of streamlining then in vogue for record attempts. That it worked well was proved by the speeds which the distinctively striped machine was able to attain: with the only modification to the engine consisting of a 25 mm Dell'Orto instead of the 20 mm standard carburettor, and correspondingly opened-up inlet tract, the Marianna was timed at 171.910 km/h in a

straight line. Records gained were for distances from 50 km at 164.443 km/h up to 1000 km completed in just under six and a half hours at 154.556 km/h. These records were valid in four classes (11 in each): the 100 cc, previously held by Demm and Guazzoni; 125 and 175 cc (Lambretta); and the 250 cc (Moto Guzzi). And all that with a 98 cc production motorcycle!

The sohc Gran Sport gradually slipped into the background after this record-breaking success, as it was replaced on the competition front by the dohc Grand Prix and desmo models, and as a customer racer by the 125 Super Sport, announced at the Bari Show in September 1957. The killing-off of the 100 cc class by the Italian Federation as a result of the Marianna's total dominance of the category had much to do with this, though several owners converted their bikes to 125 cc and continued racing them with great success. But the long-distance races such as the Motogiro and Milano–Taranto – the 'terrible twins' as the Italian motorcycle press had christened them – were the Marianna's happy hunting ground, and when these were stopped the time for a more specialized racing model, incorporating the lessons of the factory's first handful of years on the sporting scene, had come.

But the Gran Sport had a couple of final successes which stamp it as one of the finest motorcycle designs ever produced: most important was its success in the 1957 Barcelona 24 hour race, covered in a later chapter, which set the scene for Ducati's consistent supremacy in this prestigious event.

Likewise, an important piece of flag-waving lay behind the last appearance of the Gran Sport in major competition, this time in the USA. At the request of the Berliner Corporation, who had begun to import Ducatis into the States in 1957, Bologna sent Franco Villa across to America in the early 1960s to contest some key events there with a 250 cc version of the Gran Sport, measuring 74 × 57.8 mm and producing 25 bhp at 9000 rpm. His visit was successful, and though at the time Ducati did not have a fully fledged 250 with which to compete in American lightweight events, which were predominantly for that category, the large-capacity version of the Marianna design acquitted itself with honour, and provided the basis of the ohc 250 road range.

Back in 1956, though, Ducati and Taglioni were already planning bigger and better things, with an eye on the Grand Prix scene. A single ohc design based on a modified road machine would not be sufficient for success on this front, however; a more sophisticated and powerful engine would be needed.

5

Desmodromics debut

In deciding to move up to fully fledged Grand Prix racing in 1956, Ducati could not have chosen a more difficult or more competitive time at which to do so.

Having thus far concentrated their efforts on small-capacity machines, the 125 cc GP class was their obvious target. Yet in what was in retrospect one of the golden ages of Grand Prix motorcycle racing, a host of factories were engaged in a bitter struggle for supremacy that saw the level of technological achievement necessary to reap success raised ever higher with each successive race, not only in the 125 class but in all categories.

Though the German NSU team had retired undefeated from the 125 and 250 classes, the Teutonic cudgel was being taken up by their neighbours on the other side of the Iron Curtain, the East German MZs under the ingenious hand of the father of the modern racing two-stroke, Walter Kaaden. Against them were ranged a mass of sparring Italian factories: MV Agusta had taken over the mantle of champions after NSU's withdrawl, thanks largely to the brilliant riding of the greatest lightweight rider of the era, Carlo Ubbiali. But after a period in the doldrums, the formerly all-conquering Mondial team, the original 125 cc World Champions, were making a determined comeback with conventional but well-developed dohc singles, while Ducati's Bolognese neighbours Morini were trying hard to keep up. However, potentially the greatest threat to MV's supremacy came from Italy's then greatest and most successful racing team in the large-capacity classes: Gilera. Their 125 dohc twin was the first multi-cylinder design to appear in the class, and in the brave Romolo Ferri they had a potential race-winner to ride the machine in its debut season of 1956.

Though by now one of the largest motorcycle manufacturers in Italy, with over 700 employees generating an output of around 20,000 machines a year, Ducati's resources in terms of GP experience in taking on these established teams were very slender. What they did have, however, was unbridled enthusiasm, some courageous and ambitious riders then coming into their prime, and in 35-year-old Fabio Taglioni a designer and development engineer full of invention and persistence, who had proved by the success of the Marianna and its derivatives in 1955 his capacity to get things right first time. It was a sound basis on which to build a team to take on the world's best.

Taglioni's first shot in this new battle was a dohc version of the 125 Gran Sport, which had been rumoured to exist for some time before its eventual announcement on 25 February, 1956. Identical in every way to its predecessor from the base of the cambox down, the *Bialbero* Gran Sport was intended to be the factory's representative in the Modified Sports machines category for the coming Italian season, while the sohc version would continue to compete in the MSDS (*macchine sport derivate dalla serie*) class for production sports machines. For the 1957 season this convoluted terminology would be cleaned up, with the classes henceforward known as Formula 2 (effectively outright racers derived from production machines, rather like today's TT Formula category, but with substantial engine modifications permitted, such as the fitting of twin-cam heads) and Formula 3 (production sports racers fitted with full lighting sets and other road-going paraphernalia). Formula 1 would be for outright racing bikes available to private owners in minimum quantities, and in time Ducati would shine in all three categories.

But for now the Bialbero 125 Gran Sport was Taglioni's first move in the direction of Grand Prix participation; recognizing that his first priority was to chase the increased power that he knew lay higher up the rev scale, and could only be attained with the help of better breathing, extended valve

timings with greater overlap and reduced reciprocating weight, a twin-cam head was a logical
first move. This single modification yielded an
immediate and substantial increase in power of 30
per cent over the output of the sohc engine at that
time, producing 15.5 bhp at 10,500 rpm without any
adverse effect on engine life, thanks to the inherent
safety margin that Taglioni had designed into the
Marianna's engine.

Testing that winter was seriously disrupted for
Ducati (as well as for their Italian rivals) by one of
the hardest winters since the end of the war. Monza
lay under a continuous cloak of snow, and though
the Ducati team's local test track at Modena was
kept more or less clear, thanks to its principal use as
airfield for the local flying club, any serious tests of
the new machine were badly hampered by the
adverse weather which persisted into the early
spring.

Working, however, with the aid of the factory's
excellent brake-testing facilities, Taglioni increased
the Bialbero's output to 16 bhp by the simple
expedient of raising the engine revs to their
maximum safe ceiling of 11,500 rpm. This step,
though, brought several attendant problems, not
least the fact that the power figure was insufficient
to be competitive with the opposition. Provini had
won the Italian Senior title the year before with a
dohc Mondial single that was known to be
producing 17 bhp reliably and presumably would
churn out even more in 1956, but this paled before
the 19–20 bhp of the works MV singles which
would, at least, be matched by the new Gilera twin.
More power was badly needed before it was worth
racing the bike at that level.

Nevertheless, even at that uncompetitive pitch
the dohc Ducati's performance brought the
question of mechanical unreliability into play. At
sustained peak revs the power figure would dip
occasionally as the separate cast-alloy cambox and
the cylinder head parted company briefly from the
cylinder. Taglioni cured this by casting the head and
cambox as one, the result being a beautiful,
complicated casting with every ounce of excess
weight removed that remains today a masterpiece of
the metallurgist's art.

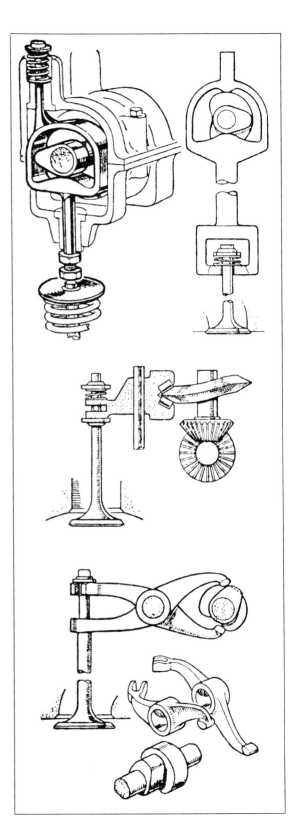

*How desmodramic valve gear developed; top left, 1912
Peugeot; top right, 1914 Delage; centre, the Bignan Sport
system; bottom, Mercedes-Benz GP car of the 50s*

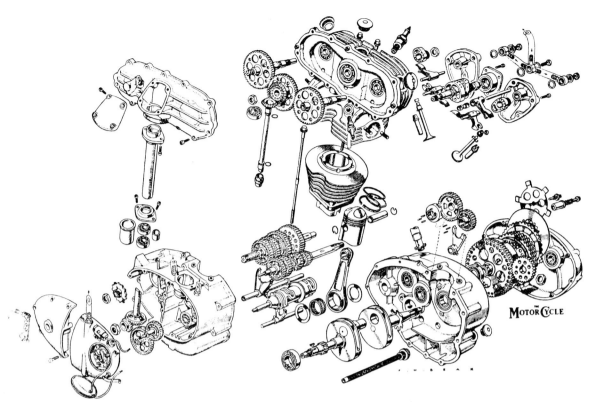

Exploded drawing of the 125 desmo Ducati GP engine of 1958. From the cylinder head joint downwards, the unit is identical to its dohc valve-spring predecessor

More serious though was the fact that he had used up every ounce of his safety margin, so that a moment's inattention in the heat of battle and a missed gear would result in the piston instantly hitting a valve and bending it. Running on a 9.5:1 compression ratio, the valve-to-piston clearance was so small that no margin of error was possible at such high revs, with that design.

The reason for this problem, which seems self-evident to most motorcyclists since it's an inherent drawback of most internal combustion engines employing poppet valves, lies in the use of the springs to control the opening and closing action of the valves themselves. The greater the engine speed, the fiercer the rates of acceleration and deceleration of the valve gear, and when on a racing engine high revs are accompanied by extended valve openings to enable the engine to breathe more freely, this problem is compounded. Sooner or later, the engine speed in rpm terms becomes so great that the valve springs can no longer cope, even if two or even three are fitted to the same valve. At this point the inertia forces in the valve gear take over and the valve springs, which on most engines are responsible for carrying out the job of closing the valves, can no longer keep the cam followers in contact with the closing profile of the camshaft. This means that the valve(s) in question, instead of closing as the piston rises in the cylinder, 'float' in the open or semi-open position; inevitably, the piston clouts the valve, bending it with at the least a resultant loss of compression and at the worst breaking the valve head off and destroying the engine.

The problem of valve float is one which has plagued internal combustion engine designers since the very earliest days of competition, well before the First World War. The most common solution, dating back to the Fiat S.61 of 1908, and the GP Peugeot car of 1912 designed by Ernest Henry and his 500 cc dohc twin-cylinder motorcycle of the same era, as well as the Indian board racers of pre-1914 America, is to reduce the size of the valves and thus lower their reciprocating weight, while at the same time maintaining or even increasing valve area by resorting to the use of paired valves, in other words the four-valve head. Lighter (because smaller) valves meant that higher engine speeds could be attained with the same valve springs before valve float set in.

The four-valve head was not universally adopted,

although the 1921 Triumph Ricardo and TT winning Rudges were notable exceptions, and even eventually fell into disfavour, since bottom-end design was not at that time sufficiently advanced – mostly due to inadequacy of materials – to permit the increased speed potential made possible. It was only in the early 1960s that Honda reintroduced the concept to the motorcycle world, at the same time proving the additional benefits of four-valve design such as more complete combustion thanks to a centrally located plug and increased gas flow with commensurately greater mixture turbulence.

So in the 1950s the problem remained: how to prevent valve float at high engine speeds, and thereby not only increase power out put but at the same time do so reliably? The answer, Taglioni believed, lay in positive valve control, or desmodromic valve gear. Taken from the Greek words *desmos* and *dromos*, desmodromic literally translates as 'controlled run', and was by no means a new concept, although, like four-valve heads, it had been tried without much success in the past.

Though some case has been made by Norton enthusiasts claiming that James 'Pa' Norton was the first designer to apply the desmodromic principle to valve gear, based on some drawings he supposedly prepared in 1909, it is generally accepted that the first person to experiment with valve gear which both opened and closed the valves by positive means was the British engineer F. H. Arnott in 1910. Ernest Henry used a valve-operating system in his 1912 GP Peugeot which appeared to give positive valve closing using a stirrup-shaped follower, but it was not desmodromic because the valve stem was not attached to the follower. There was no question of using the opposing forces of two springs although there was a light return spring on the stirrup. The forerunner of what was to come was the valve gear of the French Delage GP car engine of 1914, which featured two cams per valve, one to open it and one to close it, using a stirrup-shaped follower vaguely like that of the peugeot. It was extremely effective, but development time was too short and there were problems in machining the closing cams to match the opening cams.

Various experiments were conducted in several countries between the wars on the principles of desmodromic design. Some occasionally, such as the French Bignan Sport car engine of the mid-1920s, actually reached fruition, without advancing the concept very far. In the case of the Bignan, which actually appeared at the 1926 Paris Salon, the problem was compounded by the curious cam design, which featured a vertical shaft driven by

ABOVE AND RIGHT *Two views of the clutch side of 125 Grand Prix dohc valve-spring engines of succeeding years. That on the left is a 1957 model, with the Marianna-type single*

bevel gears off the crank, to which was attached a disc cam, a swash-plate, whose periphery engaged with a grooved boss on the valve stem. The valve was thus raised and lowered as the disc cam turned. The problem was of course the high rate of cam wear, compounded by the difficulty of machining it accurately. The desmodromic Bignan was not a success.

In July 1954, the motor racing world was shocked to the soles of its feet by one of the most dramatic racing debuts ever seen in four-wheel sport, when the Mercedes-Benz team made a triumphal return to Grand Prix racing after peace was declared in 1945, scoring a 1-2-3 victory in the French GP run on the ultra-fast Reims-Thillois track. In doing so they humbled the might of the Italian Maserati and Ferrari teams, whose formerly all-conquering red machines were made to look passé by the sophisticated, streamlined silver cars from Germany. Mercedes team leader Juan Manuel Fangio went on to win the 1954 World Championship

downtube frame with bifurcated cradle; on the right is a 1958 model with proper twin-loop cradle. Note subtle changes to the engine castings between the years (Zagari)

easily from his veteran team-mate Karl Kling, repeating the feat the following year, this time with a less vulnerable open-wheeled version of the same car, and followed home in the points table by a more youthful colleague, Britain's Stirling Moss. With the 2½-litre straight-8 GP engine punched out to a full three litres and fitted with advanced sports car bodywork similar to the GP streamliners, the 300SLR Mercedes also scooped the World Sports Car Championship in 1955. The highlight was Moss's win in the Mille Miglia, accompanied by former World Champion sidecar passenger and noted journalist Denis Jenkinson. At the other end of the scale, it was in a similar SLR Mercedes that Frenchman Pierre Levegh plunged at high speed into the pit straight grandstand during the Le Mans 24 Hour race that year, reaping a terrible toll of dead and injured spectators in the worst motor racing tragedy of modern times.

At the end of the 1955 season Mercedes retired from racing as suddenly as they had re-entered it,

having – like their NSU motorcycle compatriots the year before – achieved everything they could have hoped to do. The significance of their racing involvement in motorcycle terms lies in the design of the engine, for the Mercedes-Benz GP engine and its sports car derivative saw the first successful exploitation of the desmodromic valve-gear principle.

The 2500 cc Mercedes GP engine produced just on 260 bhp at 10,000 rpm from its 16-valve sohc in-line 8-cylinders. For the mid-1950s this was a remarkable engine speed for 300 cc-plus individual cylinders to run at, and the fact that the cars achieved an unsurpassable reputation for both speed and reliability – 1-2 finishes were the order of the day in the 300-mile GPs of the time – only served to strengthen the attraction of the desmodromic principle. In Italy, the lesson was well learnt, though not, surprisingly, at the Ferrari or Maserati factories, whose cars never succeeded in rivalling Mercedes during the two years they were in competition. Instead, it was left to two of the six Maserati brothers, who had created the Osca factory after having sold off the company bearing their own name to the Orsi family many years earlier, to produce the country's first successful desmo engine, a 1500 cc four-cylinder fitted into a sports car chassis. The car's major claim to fame was one of its patrons – flamboyant, Italo-Argentinian Alessandro de Tomaso and his American heiress girlfriend Elizabeth Haskell (now Isabel de Tomaso). It was an interesting engine and car, but not often a major race winner.

The honour of producing the first Italian des-modromic engine might instead have gone elsewhere if the Boselli family who controlled the Mondial motorcycle company had given the young Fabio Taglioni his head when he worked for them for just one year in 1953–54, before leaving to join Ducati. Taglioni had been a longtime devotee of positive valve control since his days at Bologna University just after the war, but Mondial's engineering policy was too inherently conservative and Count Boselli, the head of the firm, would not permit Taglioni to build such an engine. Ironically, after the initial success of the Ducati desmo, Boselli did allow his engineers to produce a 125 cc prototype with four-cam desmodromic valve gear; tested at Monza in 1957, it produced a claimed 20 bhp at 13,000 rpm, but was never raced as the factory retired from competition at the end of that season after winning both 125 and 250 world titles with the conventional dohc singles.

Initial testing with the Ducati Bialbero 125, once

ABOVE *A 1957 125 dohc GP, devoid of its dustbin for which the large scoops on the Amadoro brakes pointed downwards to combat brake fade from overheating. The 'anatomical' tank permitted the rider to get under the screen, with cutout for the steeply angled carburettor (Zagari)*

LEFT *1958 Grand Prix. The revised frame featured upward sloping top rails which rendered the tank cutout unnecessary, an updated crankcase made for a more rigid chassis mounting (Zagari)*

the weather had improved in the spring of 1956, convinced Taglioni that it was not the answer to the company's hopes for success at the highest level, and this impression was confirmed when the twin-cam failed to shine on its first few outings in the hands of Degli Antoni and others. Though top speed was well up on the sohc Gran Sport at 170 km/h, thanks partly to a handlebar fairing and streamlined seat unit, the machine was not fast enough to pose a threat to the MV singles, which had been timed at over 180 km/h during the course of the Italian GP at Monza the previous September, let alone the new Gilera twin. It would, however, serve as a useful basis for a production racer for

private owners, which moreover would be eligible for the modified production class (soon to become Formula 2) in Italian events, provided the machine was run without a fairing and with the road bike's 22 mm carburettor fitted. For open class events, a 27 mm or even 29 mm Dell'Orto could be substituted for increased top-end power, while all-enveloping dustbin fairings were available from a variety of sources from backstreet panel-beaters to aerodynamic specialists such as Nardi. Thus in due course, in time for the 1957 season, the Ducati 125 Grand Prix production racer was to be made available in limited quantity to selected clients.

During the couple of years of the Grand Prix model's production it was developed alongside the factory desmo machines, to which it was indeed identical from the cylinder head joint downwards. The cycle parts initially resembled the Marianna's, with the 1957 addition of a twin-loop subframe under the engine to strengthen the single-tube frame; later this was changed for 1958 to a full twin-loop duplex design with a single top frame tube under the tank bifurcating into twin rear top tubes on which the seat was fitted. The double-cradle frame was well braced around the steering head, and the tiny 48 in. wheelbase meant that smaller riders were at a premium to get the best out of the machine. For the 1957 season the use of dustbin fairings meant that the twin Amadoro magnesium alloy brakes, a 180 mm sls unit in front and 170 mm sls rear, had long, curved air scoops reaching forward into the airstream underneath the axles to grab every last scrap of cooling air: brake fade due to overheated linings was a major problem with full streamlining during this period. After the FIM banned this type of fairing after 1957, largely at the behest of Count Agusta, whose MVs were never as stable as their opponents with dustbin fairings fitted, Ducatis, like most other bikes, simply dispensed with the air scoop extensions and reversed their brake plates to place the scoops above the axle. Thirty millimetre telescopic forks were fitted to the Grand Prix models, whose unfaired weight was just under 90 kg. Eighteen-inch rims were fitted front and rear, with 2.50 section front and 2.75 rear tyres.

The dohc valve-spring engine could eventually be taken to 12,000 rpm, producing 17 bhp by the end of 1958. At this engine speed though, valve clearances were very critical, and most owners preferred to run their engines at least 1000 rpm slower in the interests of reliability. The principal sacrifice lay in reduced acceleration, as the top speed was not much less than 175 km/h in the end. The addition of a fifth gear, squeezed into the space outside the crankcase wall behind the clutch, in the primary drive compartment, was incorporated into the very first 1956 prototype and became a standard fitting. There was even room to fit a sixth set of gears, but this was only done on the desmos, whose valve timing was much more radical than the valve spring bikes, resulting in a narrower powerband. The Grand Prix would pull from around 8000 rpm with the 27 mm carburettor fitted and, like the desmos, had twin-plug ignition as standard, with two 3V coils fixed to the front frame down-tubes and fed by the 6V battery under the seat. The second plug was a 10 mm one, squeezed into a gap behind the top bevel, between it and the inlet tract. The Gran Sport's generator was discarded, in favour of total-loss ignition. Bore and stroke were identical to all ohc 125 Ducati singles, at 55.25 (usually rounded up to 55.3) × 52 mm.

Around 50 dohc Grand Prix Ducatis were made by the factory up to the end of 1959, and found their way all over the world, where they achieved great success. In 1958 alone, for example, Ducati GP-mounted privateers won races in Great Britain, Germany, Holland, France, USA, Ireland, Chile, Venezuela, Argentina, Uruguay, Sweden, Algeria, Australia, Belgium and, of course, their native Italy. Highlight of the year for the customers of the Bologna factory must surely have been German Hans Spellner's victory in the Jugoslavia GP at Opatija, defeating the highly-fancied Czech CZ team led by Malina in front of a crowd of 60,000. For many years 125 Grand Prix Ducatis would still be racing competitively in many countries, sometimes taken out to 200 or even 220 cc for the 250 class, and providing a dependable ride even at the highest level for riders on their way up the road racing tree. Perhaps the best-known example was Rhodesian Jim Redman, who made his Isle of Man 125 debut on a dohc Ducati in the 1960 TT, finishing 13th: at the very next Grand Prix, in Holland, he joined the Honda works team, and the rest is history!

Long after the factory retired from racing the Grand Prix Ducati would still be winning, defeating much younger and more technically advanced machines which had not, however, had the benefit of its painstaking development alongside one of the most advanced and successful factory racing bikes of its era: the 125 Ducati Desmo. Taglioni had begun work on a design for a demodromic head soon after joining Ducati in 1954; during the following year he produced the first prototype, having had his faith in the concept strengthened by the success of the Mercedes-Benz and Osca car designs. When the Bialbero's various problems of reliability and uncompetitive power output became apparent, he swiftly switched development to the desmodromic head.

The Mercedes desmodromic system relied on a single overhead camshaft on which were mounted 16 pairs of cams for the two valves per each of the eight cylinders. Each pair of cams controlled the valve action via a set of scissor rockers, clamped to the valve by means of collars: it was a system that in time would become familiar to exponents of the Ducati marque as well, but not yet.

Instead, Taglioni modified the principle by using a triple-camshaft arrangement, with the opening cams mounted on the two outer shafts, and the two closing cams fitted to the single central shaft, operating the valves by means of forked rockers bearing on flanged collars located by split wire rings sprung into annular grooves in the stems. The

The author's 125 GP Ducati, a dohc valvespring model dating from 1958 which Ing. Taglioni, however, believes perhaps to be one of the works desmos which was fitted with a twin cam head and sold to the public. In this case, it may well be the ex-Fron Purslow bike

degree of accuracy necessary to achieve the required tolerances was considerable, and not only the design but also the machining and grinding represented quite a technical feat for even a well-equipped (though small by automotive standards) factory such as Ducati in those days before computer-operated machine tools and electronic equipment.

An indication of the extreme camshaft form made possible by the adoption of desmodromic valve gear came from the amount of lift on each valve: the inlet rose 8.1 mm (as compared to 7.5 mm on the dohc valve-spring Grand Prix) and the exhaust moved 7.4 mm (against 7.0 mm), both with the same opening and closing points as on the GP engine, with which it shared other basic design features. The valves ran in bronze guides, and seated on alloy-bronze rings shrunk into the head, while all cams were a taper fit on their shafts and were extensively drilled along the side of the lobes for lightness. Valve clearance adjustment was effected by changing the valve collars and caps, which were made in different thicknesses – again a very high-precision task. The entire valve gear was contained in another beautifully made alloy casting incorporating the cylinder head, with the engine again identical from the head joint down to the Gran Sport, apart from the addition of a 5th and

sometimes 6th gear, the removal of the generator and the adoption of twin-plug total-loss ignition by battery and coils. Proof of the Desmo's humble origins was apparent in the blanked-off kickstart boss on the left crankcase.

Though the principal advantage of the desmo head was the fact that it dispensed with the use of valve springs, causing valve float to become a thing of the past, light rocker-return springs were originally fitted to close the valves mechanically the last 0.012 in. and thus ensure full engine compression at low rpm, for consequent ease of starting; allowance for heat expansion without excessive rubbing loads meant the valves could not be seated completely when cold. Taglioni's decision to incorporate these small springs into the original desmo design was surprising, since it was already common knowledge that Mercedes had originally done the same thing, then later dispensed with the springs altogether, relying on valve momentum and gas pressure in the cylinder to close the valves completely. Perhaps he wanted to eliminate a possible problem in the early stages of the design, but at any rate the springs were indeed dispensed with completely by the time the engine was used in competition. Their absence accounted for the fact that, when a 125 Desmo Ducati's engine was turned slowly by hand, it seemed to have very poor compression; only when it was spun quickly, as was the case when it was bump-started, would the valves seat firmly and full compression be achieved.

Running with a compression ratio of 10:1, the desmo 125 single featured a 31 mm inlet valve and 27mm exhaust, and normally used a 27 mm Dell'-Orto carburettor just like the dohc Grand Prix, though for fast, open circuits a 29 mm unit was fitted. Initial power output was not much greater than the valve spring engine's, yielding 17 bhp at 12,500 rpm, but the difference was in the fantastic safety margin which the desmodromic valve gear gave. Riders were able to take advantage of this, particularly under braking, since with the safe engine speed now increased to 14,000 rpm – a remarkable figure for a single-cylinder four-stroke even by today's standards – they could afford to buzz the engine on the overrun with impunity. Ducati riders suddenly became the last of the late brakers, for as well as using their double-sided front stoppers to outbrake their opponents, they could also run the engine on occasions to an incredible 15,000 rpm for added effect. Not surprisingly, bottom-end life was drastically shortened by such

treatment, which in turn meant new crankshaft bearings after every race. But this was a small price to pay for the advantages afforded by desmodromic valve gear, which immediately catapulted Ducati into Grand Prix contention once preliminary tests were concluded.

By the summer of 1956 Taglioni was ready to put his desmodromic concept to the test. Both he and his colleagues at the factory, including, by now, Dr. Cosimo Calcagnile – for over 25 years the firm's sales director – were particularly eager to do well at the prestigious Italian GP at Monza in September, the results of which had an important bearing on retail bike sales in Italy. Taglioni, however, wanted to debut the bike well away from the pressures of Italian racing and especially away from the prying gaze of the local press, in case any problems showed up in the heat of competition which might then be put right before the Monza race.

It was thus that the debut of the Taglioni-designed Ducati Desmo 125 took place without any advance announcement at the distant Swedish GP at Hedemora, on 15 July, 1956. The Swedish race was not at that time a classic event, counting for the World Championship, but it was well supported by

Amadoro brakes as fitted to the 125 Desmos and GP models. Left is a 1958 unit, of smaller diameter and with top-mounted airscoops, as fitted to naked machines or those fitted with *new-style dolphin fairings in which the front wheel was exposed. Right is a 1957 rear brake, from the days of fully-enclosed dustbin (Zagari)*

the leading privateers as well as, on this occasion, by the works Norton team. Entailing a round trip journey of nearly 5000 km and no less than four ferry crossings, it was also certainly remote enough from Bologna to suit Taglioni's purpose. Gianni Degli Antoni, who had not only showed himself to be the fastest of the works riders but had also assisted Taglioni greatly in the development of all his Ducati designs thus far, was entered to ride a single 125 Desmo, supported by local ace Olle Nygren – later to become more famous as a topline speedway rider – on the sohc Gran Sport with which he had won the 1955 Swedish title.

The result was a devastating victory for the lone Desmo Ducati, and another first-time win in its debut event for one of Taglioni's designs. Fitted with Nardi-designed dustbin streamlining, painted the distinctive factory striped colours, Degli Antoni's little machine took the lead from Nygren on the first lap to open up an enormous lead in the extremely hot conditions; the track was in fact in a dangerous condition, with melting tar being combated by the organizers with sand and cement dust. But Degli Antoni made no mistakes and romped home to a convincing victory, lapping every other finisher in the process, including Nygren, whose engine went sick in the effort to keep up with the flying Desmo; he later had some consolation by

A 1957 works desmo 125 with distinctively-painted red and white stripes. The prancing horse has the same significance as the Ferrari badge: it was the emblem of the Italian WW1 fighter pilot ace Baracca. He came from Ing. Taglioni's home town of Lugo, near Ravenna, and was a distant relative

finishing 5th in the 500 event on his G45 Matchless behind the works Norton team led by Geoff Duke.

The Desmo's first win had been achieved against a field of private MVs and Mondials, but in averaging 136 km/h for the race, with a fastest lap of over 141 km/h, Degli Antoni had shown that the bike was ready to be tested against the best that the other factory teams could put forward. Unfortunately, he was never to have the chance of doing so himself, for after making the long return journey from Sweden with the bike he was tragically killed on his very next ride during a test session at Monza on 7 August. Putting the Desmo through its paces in readiness for the Italian GP a month later and both his and the factory's World Championship debut, he fell off at the Lesmo Curve and died instantly.

Gianni Degli Antoni's death at the age of 26 was a severe emotional blow to the Ducati team, and set back their efforts to make the Desmo into a race-winner. A former mechanic for the Stanguellini racing car team, Antoni had ridden previously for the MV Agusta Junior squad before joining Ducati as team leader and Taglioni's chief development rider. With his mechanical knowledge and racing experience he was a key man in the Borgo Panigale racing department, and was moreover at that time the only person with experience of racing a desmodromic model in competition.

Not surprisingly, the Monza race was a *débâcle* for the Ducati team, still under the cloud cast by the death of their leading rider. Artusi held 5th place on a Desmo going into the last lap, but stopped during the course of it to join the rest of his team-mates in

retirement. After the elation of the Swedish win, and the ensuing high hopes for success at Monza, it was a cruel disappointment. With the Italian GP then the last major race of the season, there was nothing for it but to hope for better things next year.

Continuing work on the desmodromic engine over the winter, Taglioni managed to raise the power output slightly, to just on 18 bhp, still at 12,500 rpm with that all-important safety margin. He also produced a 98 cc version for the last year of the 100 cc Formula 2 class, to be ridden by Franco Farne; this 49.4 × 52 mm Marianna-based engine ran on an 11:1 compression ratio and yielded 12 bhp at 13,000 rpm, enough for a top speed without fairing (not permitted under F2 rules) of 140 km/h. A massive 14-rider team was engaged to contest everything from the Grands Prix to the Italian novice title, and the Borgo Panigale factory echoed to the roar of one racing engine after another being run up on the testbed. After the highs and lows of 1956, great hopes were in store for success in 1957.

ABOVE *Gianni Degli Antoni at Faenza in 1956 on the works Ducati 125 double-knocker. He finished second to world champion Carlo Ubbiali's MV in one of Ducati's first major successes in short circuit racing (Zagari)*
TOP *The field gets away in the 125 race on the Faenza street circuit in 1956. Visible are Ubbiali (MV, 3), Venturi (MV, 5), Degli Antoni (Ducati, 10), Copeta (MV, 4), Nava (Mondial, 14), Artusi (Ducati, 9) and Ferri (Gilera twin, 8) (Zagari)*

6

Great Expectations – 1957 and 1958

The 1957 racing season started off well enough for Ducati, with a crushing victory – as was by now becoming expected – in the last-ever Giro d'Italia, run off at the end of April just a week before the tragic Mille Miglia, which resulted in a new appraisal of all kinds of road racing in Italy.

Though Tartarini on a new 175 cc twin-cylinder Ducati prototype with a dohc valve-spring head retired on the 3rd stage without ever really shining, Ducatis won the first 12 places overall with Graziano's 125 Gran Sport the victor after Spaggiari on a similar bike retired on the first stage. Mandolini was the 100 cc class winner on his Marianna: such was Ducati's dominance of the category that there were no other makes even entered. It was a hollow victory, and when the Milano–Taranto event was cancelled one of Ducati's principal fields of competition, the long-distance road races, had disappeared.

Back in Bologna the decision was made to spend one more year developing the Desmo before contesting the GPs seriously, not only to ensure that the bikes would be completely competitive but also to permit Taglioni, who had been devoting his principal attention to the racing machines, to concentrate on producing some new models for the road. This meant that the large squad of riders would have their activities confined to Italy, though another successful excursion was made to Sweden for the Hedemora event, resulting in a first-to-fifth sweep of the leaderboard by Ducati riders. The only classic GP entered officially was the home event at Monza, in which Gandossi on the factory 125 Desmo distinguished himself by falling off in the lead on the first lap, bringing down two-thirds of the rival Mondial team in the shape of that year's World Champions Tarquinio Provini and Cecil Sandford.

If at international level Ducatis had yet to shine, in Italian events they were well-nigh unbeatable, dominating the Formula 2 and 3 categories. Franco

Farne won the Italian Junior title, and a year of steady development brought the Desmo 125's performance up to a level with that of the opposition. The engine was now producing 19 bhp at 13,000 rpm, and problems encountered with the pistons holding up to that engine speed were solved by using Mahle forged units, still with two compression rings and a single scraper, and with deep valve inserts. Nimonic valves were now used.

Meanwhile the factory's flag had been successfully carried at home and abroad by their customers aboard the dohc Grand Prix models, which would, however, for the 1958 season, be required to dispense with their full streamlining in favour of dolphin-type fairings. The Ducati 125s were thus fitted with an extremely slim alloy fairing – later copied by Fi-Glass in Britain in fibreglass – which seemed to mould itself to the machine and required a slot to be cut in the right leading edge for the curve of the exhaust pipe to sweep through. Very light-alloy 15-litre fuel tanks of a revised shape were also fitted, and the new twin-loop frame was developed during the course of the 1957 Italian season.

Before the start of 1958 the racing world was startled by a simultaneous announcement from Gilera, Motor Guzzi and Mondial that they would be withdrawing from competition immediately. Each had spent handsomely in search of success, and together had won all four 1957 solo world titles. The reason for their decision was not hard to discern: the growing affluence of postwar Italy had seen its population progress from getting about on foot or by public transport, to a clip-on *bicimotore* such as the Cucciolo, and thence to a more powerful scooter or proper motorcycle which could carry a pillion or even have a sidecar attached to bring the

Ducati's spring test sessions at Modena became an integral part of the build-up to each season. Here in April of 1957 Fantuzzi warms up his 125 Desmo Sport Italian F2 machine. Mechanic Ruggero Mazza watches (Zagari)

family along on outings. But in 1955 a significant
event occurred which was to have a profound
bearing on the future of the Italian motorcycle
industry: the first real Italian postwar mini-car, the
Fiat *Nuova* 500, was announced. With its little
500 cc twin-cylinder four-stroke engine, it was
aimed four-square at the motorcyclist, and the
attractions of a (sun)roof over one's head, four seats
(or even more at a pinch) and all the other comforts
of four-wheeled motoring with economy of fuel
consumption and purchase price proved irresistible
to even the most diehard motorcyclist, especially if –
as was frequently the case – he was a family man
too. Soon the roads of Italy were flooded with the
little cars, and the fortunes of the local motorcycle
manufacturers, whether as large as Guzzi or as
small as Mondial, plunged accordingly.

Having achieved a succession of world titles, it
was easier for the big three to withdraw from racing
than for a company like Ducati, which had already
made a substantial investment in terms of time and
effort, not to mention money, in preparing to aim
for Grand Prix success, without having yet had the
chance to reap the dividends. In any case, their bike
sales, riding high on the wave of success generated
by the Marianna and its descendants, were holding
up well, and there were new models in the pipeline
for which it would be important to establish some
background of sporting success. Finally, and most
important of all, racing had now become a way of
life at Ducati: the excitement of the search for
competition success ran in the factory's veins,
imbuing each employee with a collective enthusiasm for victory and the sport.

In any case, competition in the 125 class would
still be as keen as ever. Though the Gilera twin
would disappear without ever really achieving its
true potential, the factory Mondials were in private
hands and the team's former chief mechanic
Giuseppe Pattoni was engaged in producing the first
of his line of jewel-like, hand-made Paton specials,
using for the 125 a Mondial bottom half as a basis.
Then, too, the East German MZ team was
becoming ever more competitive, though one of
their principal riders from the previous season,
Swiss ace Luigi Taveri, would be riding a Ducati
Desmo for the Bologna factory in the 1958 season.

The principal opposition though, as seemed
always to be the case in the classic era of road
racing, would come from MV Agusta, for whom the
brilliant Carlo Ubbiali, already three times a World
Champion in the 125 and 250 categories, would be
joined for the 1958 season by the reigning 125 title
holder, Tarquinio Provini. With Count Agusta

An early 125 desmo prototype engine

*Ducati built and discarded several prototypes with both
desmodromic and valvespring valve gear. This 125 desmo
dates from 1957–58, and has a completely different crankcase
than the later works bikes as well as an interim frame in
which the single downtube is heavily gusseted. The forks
have fabricated yokes, similar to those on the later 125 twin.
This machine eventually found its way to the USA*

A 1958–59 works desmo with sculpted crankcase to save weight and larger fuel tank, requiring a carburettor cutout. Instead of the rear engine plates, the upper part of the crankcase is gripped by two tubes welded to the rear of the cradle frame, with the battery mounted on top. Compare this to the bike in the lower picture on page 46 (Zagari)

eager to avenge his defeat at the hands of the Mondials in both classes the previous year, Ducati's task would be hard indeed.

But Taglioni and Ducati were ready. One hundred-hour bench tests at full throttle had seen the 125 Desmo single come through with flying colours, and Taglioni was already working on a twin-cylinder version in case MV should put on the track their dohc twin, which was already running. In addition to Taveri, the by now experienced pair of *Ducatisti*, Bruno Spaggiari and Alberto Gandossi, would contest the Grands Prix, with support at various times from the former rider of the Gilera twin, Romolo Ferri, and Franco Villa, now returned to the fold after a couple of seasons spent riding Mondials. And for Ducati's first visit to what would 20 years later become one of their happy hunting grounds, the Isle of Man, they engaged the services of a local ace, later to become the greatest trials rider in the history of the sport: Sammy Miller.

Once again, a 14-rider Ducati team was announced to contest the various championships, this time with even greater success. Franco Farne

was nominated as team leader in the assault on the Italian 125 F2 (of Junior) title, and he opened the season in fine style with a win in pouring rain at the seaside race at Riccione in April, run along both sides of the promenade. On his unfaired 125 Desmo, he led home six other Ducatis in the top 10 places, split only by a pair of MVs and Silario's lone Paton prototype. Two weeks later, however, in the second round over the street course at Busto Arsizio, he was surprisingly beaten after a fierce struggle by Silvio Grassetti's Benelli, though still retained his championship lead after two rounds.

In the highly prestigious Italian Senior championship, though, things went even more successfully for the Ducati team. In the first round at Modena on 25 April, Gandossi won convincingly on the track on which Ducati did much of their testing, beating Ubbiali's MV into second place by nine seconds, with Provini 3rd. But Ferri and Spaggiari were 4th and 5th for Ducati in a race which saw the Bologna bikes only fitted with handlebar fairings after the dustbin ban, while the MV team were already sporting their new-style dolphin, full fairings. The defeat was a shock for Count Agusta, who had expected his experienced team to win handsomely; that they did not, in spite of a new lap record set by Ubbiali in his vain pursuit of the flying Desmo, was a portent of things to come.

Ducati's sudden competitiveness, along with MV's worst fears, was confirmed at the next round on 11 May at Marina Ravenna – another promenade race beside the Adriatic. Now fitted with full fairings, Ducatis romped to a 1-2 victory, Spaggiari leading home Ferri to set new lap and race records. MV were humbled, and to rub it in even more, both Ubbiali and Provini suffered the indignity of being lapped by the victorious Desmo in finishing 3rd and 4th respectively.

But the first of a series of unfortunate injuries which would leave its mark on the season had already occurred, when Alberto Gandossi, who had by now taken over the mantle of team leader after Degli Antoni's death, was injured in a collision with a car on his road bike just before the Ravenna race. Though not seriously hurt, he was unable to pass fit to ride at the event, leaving a fortunate Ubbiali sharing the lead of the championship after two rounds with the consistent Ferri.

Meantime Luigi Taveri had had his first ride for Ducati, winning the non-championship Saar GP in Germany of 4 May on his Desmo 125, ahead of Degner and Fugner on works MZs. He thus not only scored the factory's first overseas victory of the 1958 season but also obtained a useful psychological advantage over his former team-mates before the World Championship events kicked off. On the same day Franco Farne took his unfaired machine to the Rome–Ostia *Corsa del Mare*, winning the 125 class at 150.047 km/h: over 90 mph from a standing start on an unstreamlined 125 cc motorcycle! Three weeks later he was in action again in the third round of the Junior title chase at Gallarate, winning easily to open up his lead in the points table. Eight Ducatis packed the top 10 places, with only two MV Agustas in the points scorers in a further setback which was made all the worse by the fact that the street circuit passed by the front gate of the MV factory!

Meantime, Ducati had been preparing for the long journey to the Isle of Man and the first round of the 1958 World Championships over the Clypse course. Gandossi had by now recovered sufficiently to ride, backed up by Taveri and Ferri. Taglioni had, however, studied the Island's special conditions thoroughly and concluded that it would be sensible to engage a couple of local specialists to back the factory riders up. Sammy Miller had been most unfortunate not to win the 250 TT the year before, when he fell off on the very last corner with a seized gearbox and had to push his works Mondial home from Governors Bridge to finish 4th. With Mondial out of racing he was without a ride, and was thus snapped up by Ducati, who also provided a bike for leading privateer and continental circus regular Dave Chadwick.

Ducati had a useful boost when in the pre-TT event at Aintree their British agent, Fron Purslow, scored an important win on his dohc Grand Prix. More significant, though, was the name of the rider he beat into second place on a dohc MV Agusta: 18-year-old teenage sensation Mike Hailwood, then in his second season of racing and already hailed by the British press as a future World Champion.

Hailwood was the son of a wealthy motorcycle dealer who controlled what was then Britain's largest chain of retail outlets, King's of Oxford. Stan Hailwood – himself an ex-racer – had decided early on that his only son was going to race as well, even though Mike originally professed more interest in playing jazz music and did not have much enthusiasm for bike racing. But Stan Hailwood was a man accustomed to having his own way, and when Mike's debut races produced a string of successes against older, more experienced competitors, he swiftly fell in love with the sport.

In his early days Mike suffered in one way from having a millionaire father, in that critics attributed his success to the fact that his father was able to buy

him the best possible equipment and hire the services of one of the finest tuners in the business, Bill Lacey, to look after it. But by 1958 even the most short-sighted of his detractors were forced to admit that Mike had great talent: in later years he would prove it by winning races on machines that nobody else could or would ride so hard.

Later to be successful in all capacity classes, often riding four or even five different bikes to success in the course of a single afternoon, Mike was still, in the summer of 1958, concentrating on the smaller-capacity classes while he gained valuable experience. The previous winter he'd raced in South Africa at his father's behest, with an older, more experienced team-mate to coach him and show him the ropes: Dave Chadwick, now a fully fledged member of the Ducati works team for the TT.

Up till now Hailwood had raced mostly MV Agustas in the 125 class, but the speed of Purslow's valve-spring Ducati had impressed Stan Hailwood mightily. With his customary thoroughness, he set to, to use his many Italian contacts in helping him find out as much as he could about the company, then almost completely unknown in Britain, before approaching them. What he discovered caused him to reassess the brand of machinery which his son was riding in the smallest capacity class.

First though there was the TT to be considered, in which Mike was due to make his Isle of Man debut on a pair of 125 Patons, which his father had obtained from Giuseppe Pattoni primarily for this one event. Pattoni recalls that Stan Hailwood quizzed him thoroughly about the Ducatis, and especially on the desmo versions, which were then being seen in Britain for the first time. He could only, with typical honesty, say they were the best bike in their class in Italy at that time.

In the TT itself Ubbiali's vast experience was more than an match for the speed advantage of the Ducatis, and he won the race from Ferri, with Chadwick 3rd and Miller 4th. Gandossi had not yet recovered from his injuries and non-started, an event which would later influence the destination of the world title. Taveri retired with broken piston rings after passing Ubbiali to lead the race on lap 2, while in a replica-winning 7th place on his TT debut came Mike Hailwood on the little Paton.

After speaking to Pattoni and, of course, to Dave Chadwick, who was overjoyed with the performance of his little bike, Stan Hailwood made his move, approaching Taglioni in the Island with a view to obtaining a Ducati ride for Mike as soon as possible. With the additional prod that King's of Oxford could do much to benefit Ducati com-

A Marianna prepared for racing in 1955 – presumably for the Giro d'Italia, since no headlamp is fitted as would have been necessary for the Milano–Taranto. Note the registration plate

mercially if they were to start pushing sales of the road models in Britain, then still practically virgin territory for the Bologna marque, Montano and Taglioni took little time to agree to supply the Hailwoods' Ecurie Sportive with a brace of *Bialberi* for future events. The first of which was to be the next round of the World Championship, the Dutch TT at Assen on 28 June.

Making his continental GP debut on his first-ever ride on a Ducati, Mike Hailwood confirmed his future promise by coming home 10th on the little valve-spring twin-cam – a bike he had great difficulty initially in wrapping his 5 ft 9 in. frame into, so small was the wheelbase. Meantime his team-mate Taveri and MV's Ubbiali were engaged in a tooth and nail struggle for the lead, with victory eventually going to the Italian veteran by 0.2 sec. – just half a length. Taveri still set up a new lap record at 126.76 km/h, 1.4 sec. faster than the existing mark set up the year before by Provini, who finished 3rd. Ducatis packed the other places, though, with Gandossi 4th, Chadwick 5th, Miller 7th and Ferri 9th, just ahead of Hailwood. Ducati had now arrived on the Grand Prix scene as a force to be reckoned with, and moreover, Taglioni's desmodromic design was proving itself remarkably reliable: all six Desmos finished the gruelling race.

A name missing from the rider line-up though was that of Bruno Spaggiari, who had come a cropper in the second round of the Italian Senior championship at Alessandria on 16 June, when he fell off in the lead but still bravely remounted to defeat the MV duo easily to win in record time. His machine skidded on some sand and mounted a kerb, throwing him over the bars; his bravery left him in the lead of the Italian title hunt, but with a broken collar-bone. No sooner had Gandossi returned after injury than the team's other Italian topliner was hurt. Ferri finished 4th on the day, to place 3rd in the points table behind Ubbiali.

Back to the World Championship, though, and the next round at Spa-Francorchamps in Belgium saw the first-ever Ducati Grand Prix victory, with Gandossi averaging 157.860 km/h – nearly 100 mph – on the ultra-fast circuit, to score a crushing victory for the Bologna marque, with Ferri 2nd on another Ducati ahead of Provini's MV. Chadwick – by now a valuable member of the team – beat Ubbiali for 4th spot, with Taveri 6th. It was a triumphant vindication of Taglioni's belief in the value of positive valve control, with the way the Ducati riders were able to leave their braking incredibly late on the approach to the tight La Source hairpin before the start and finish line, letting their engines run to astronomical revs on the overrun, amazing observers. And if any doubts were still harboured as to the top speed superiority of the little bikes over their MV rivals, their performance on this flat-out track certainly dispelled them.

Ubbiali now led the championship with 18 points to the consistent Ferri's 12 and Gandossi's 11 – the car-racing points scoring system was in use then (8-6-4-3-2-1) rather than the modern one with 15 points to the winner and scoring down to 10th place, implemented from 1969 onwards. More importantly, Ducati were now tying with MV on 20 points in the Manufacturers Championship.

Alas, it was too good to last: the next round at Germany's 14 kilometres of long and tortuous Nürburgring brought disaster for the Ducati team in a race which placed a premium on knowledge of the track. Ubbialli led Provini home to score 1-2 for MV, ahead of Degner's MZ, which had thus far been completely overshadowed by the warring Italian four-strokes. Taveri's Desmo broke its crank, Gandossi's threw a rod and the unfortunate Ferri fell off while trying to keep the MVs in sight and sustained multiple fractures which brought a premature end to his racing career. Ducati were in disarray.

As if to illustrate the seesawing fickleness of Grand Prix fortunes, the pendulum swung completely the other way at the next round on Ducati's happy hunting ground at Hedemora in Sweden, now a championship event. MV withdrew from the 350 and 500 classes, whose championships they were certain to win easily anyhow, in order to concentrate their resources on inflicting a decisive blow in the 125 category, where the speed of the Ducatis had evidently surprised them; in the 250 category, they were under threat too from the MZs. It didn't do them much good, though, for not only did Fugner's MZ win the 250 race ahead of Hailwood on an NSU Sportmax, with both MVs retiring, but in the 125 Gandossi used the Ducati's by now substantial speed advantage to good effect, winning comfortably from team-mate Taveri, with Ubbiali and Provini 3rd and 4th. As an indication of how greatly Taglioni had succeeded in developing the 125 Desmo, compare Gandossi's winning average in 1958 on an unchanged track and in similar conditions to Degli Antoni's speed on the bike's victorious debut two years before: 146 km/h against 136 km/h, with the lap record raised from 141 to 149 km/h. Taglioni had brought the bike a long way in two years, especially when it's realized that Degli Antoni's machine was fitted with full streamlining, which was outlawed by 1958.

This result meant that Ducati were still in with a chance of both titles, as the teams began the long haul to Northern Ireland for the Ulster GP – the penultimate round of the championship. Alberto Gandossi was their only hope, and he responded magnificently on his debut ride at Dundrod, one of the world's most difficult and dangerous tracks for the first-timer, by romping away from Ubbiali at the start in typically misty and damp conditions. But in his efforts to stay in front of the vastly experienced MV team leader, Gandossi came off at Leathemstown while in the lead, remounting bravely to finish 4th. The three points scored weren't good enough to stop Ubbiali winning both the race and the pair of titles for MV Agusta, with Taveri's Ducati 2nd on the day, nearly a minute behind; Chadwick was 3rd.

Some consolation was provided by Farne's victory the following day at Fermo to clinch the Italian Junior title on the F2 Desmo by three points from Grassetti's Benelli. Franco Villa, who had won the previous round down in Messina ahead of Farne and the Benelli rider, wound up 3rd in the points table by riding to team orders at Fermo and finishing 2nd.

More compensation for so narrowly missing out on World Championship success in their first real crack at the Grands Prix came to the Ducati factory's way when the final round of the Italian Senior championship was cancelled, leaving Bruno Spaggiari, by now recovered from his broken clavicle, as the new Italian Champion in the 125 class. Ducati were not slow to follow up the fact in their advertising, but they soon had something even better to shout about.

The effort expended in pursuit of success during 1958 had been considerable, so a much reduced scale of activities on the competition front was planned for the following season. In order to go out in a blaze of glory, also to counter the effects of MV's world title success in the eyes of the home crowd, Ducati planned a convincing display of superiority in the Italian GP at Monza, where the high-speed track would favour the Desmos in this, the final major race of the season. And to give added spice to the event, as well as to display their technical prowess, the prototype 125 Desmo twin would be given its competition debut in the hands of Franco Villa, who would also ride one of the recently announced 175 Sport road bikes in the prestigious Formula 3 production machine race the same day.

The fifth of September 1958, was one of the most memorable days in Ducati history. In front of a massive crowd over 100,000 strong, they dominated

Dawn on the Mountain Mile; Vic Willoughby about to test the works 125 desmo on which Sammy Miller had just finished 4th in the 1958 Ultra-Lightweight TT – Ducati's IoM debut. Ing. Taglioni looks suitably pensive, while next to him is Ducati's first British importer Fron Purslow, who also raced one of the little bikes himself with considerable success, in spite of his size!

the Italian 125 GP, sweeping the first five places. Spaggiari won at 155.827 km/h on his return ride, ahead of Gandossi, Villa on the new twin, Chadwick and Taveri. Ubbiali and Provini both blew up their MVs in a vain attempt to stay the fierce pace imposed by the little Desmos from the start, with only new MV rider Enzo Vezzalini reaching the flag in sixth place, humiliatingly lapped by the first three finishers. Count Domenico Agusta, who had gone to MV's home Monza track expecting to glory in the success of his title-winning team, was instead thrown into a towering rage by the Ducati success, which can hardly have been improved when the tiny Morini factory scored a 1-2 victory in the 250 race, with his bikes nowhere.

For Taglioni and Ducati it was the best possible palliative to the bitter disappointment of losing out so narrowly on the world titles, made even sweeter by Villa's perhaps even more important win in the prestigious F3 event on the lone Ducati Sport, which looked as if it had come straight off the showroom floor. The sohc machine averaged 143.005 km/h in a start-to-finish win ahead of the fancied Morinis and Benellis to score the first major victory for the new road bike design. And when on the very same day Leopoldo Tartarini and Giorgio Monetti returned to Bologna after a 60,000 km trip around the world on two similar machines, even a team which had become as dedicated to success as Ducati in the course of the 1958 season were able to concentrate on the good points of the season and forget the bad.

Ducati had reaped a clean sweep of the 125 class in Italian racing, Spaggiari winning the Senior title, Farne the F2 Junior and Antonio Croce the F3 Novice category on a 125 sohc Sport. The factory had scored a narrow second place in both the World Riders and Manufacturers Championships, won three Grands Prix and achieved a clean sweep at Monza in their home classic. Only the brilliance of Carlo Ubbiali had denied them the final satisfaction of a world title. Nevertheless, a concerted effort had brought them success that could only have been dreamed of at the start of the season, and in doing so had proved beyond any question the viability of the Ducati desmodromic design and the talent of the man who created it, Ing. Fabio Taglioni.

OPPOSITE ABOVE *Dave Chadwick sweeps through Cheg-ny-Baa (the wrong way, because the event was held on the Clypse Circuit) en route to 3rd place in the 1958 125 TT behind Ducati team-mate Romolo Ferri on another works desmo and winner Ubbiali's MV*
OPPOSITE BELOW *The streets of Onchan ring with the sound of Ducati exhausts during practice for the 1959 125 TT. Mike Hailwood on the desmo twin chases Bruno Spaggiari on a desmo single through the Nursery Bends on the Clypse Course (Nicholls)*

ABOVE *Luigi Taveri before the start of the 1958 Swedish Grand Prix with his works 125 Desmo single*

TOP *Mike Hailwood rushes his 125 desmo single round the Dundrod circuit on the way to a convincing victory in the 1959 125 cc Ulster GP. He set up new race and lap records, the latter at 84.75 mph (Nicholls)*

7

Laying more foundations

At the Milan Show in December 1956 a new Ducati road model appeared which was to prove the precursor of the entire range of Taglioni-designed sohc singles, both valve spring and desmo, over the next 20 years: the 175 Sport. Accompanied by large banners announcing the recent scoop of 44 world records, including 11 in the 175 class, by Carini and Ciceri on the 100 cc Marianna streamliner, the launch of the largest-capacity Ducati road bike yet made was rightly deemed an important event by the Italian press. For the new machine brought a distinctly sporting flair to the until-now rather lacklustre range of Borgo Panigale products, in which the limited-availability 100 and 125 Gran Sport machines were the only bright spots.

For while the pushrod Ducatis introduced some years before had been shown by Taglioni's careful tuning to have surprising depths of performance, they did not entice the sporting rider, who instead opted for a larger-capacity 175 or 250 Benelli or Guzzi, with the more expensive MV or Morini as a preference if he could afford it. With the Fiat 500 eating into ride-to-work bike and scooter sales, and a hefty marketing effort on the part of Vespa and Lambretta to counter this, manufacturers like Ducati urgently needed to broaden their range to appeal to the committed motorcyclist, who looked for a bit of spice in his model specification and a successful involvement in racing on the part of the factory to give him something to boast about to his friends. Ducati had already taken care of the latter prerequisite, and during 1956 Taglioni worked hard on the design of a new generation of road bikes to add the former.

Because it was the next capacity class up not already covered by the factory's range, the 175 was the first of the new line to be announced. This did not, however, mean that Taglioni had departed from his policy of scaling up rather than down, for the basis of the engine was once again the identical bottom half as first appeared on the Marianna nearly two years before. Engine castings, however, were diecast rather than sandcast, and though the outline specification of the powerplant resembled that of the Gran Sport, there were several detail differences, particularly in the head design.

The sohc head had its valve gear operated by vertical shaft and bevels as on the GS, but the single hairpin valves were fully enclosed and access to the tappets available via the finned rocker covers which would become so familiar in later years to generations of Ducati owners. The engine indeed looked externally well-nigh identical to the 250/350/450 singles of the early 1970s: the mould had been cast.

Measuring 62 × 57.8 mm, the 175 Ducati departed from the period norm by being 7 per cent oversquare, in time one of Taglioni's trademarks. Producing 14 bhp at 7500 rpm, its specific output of 70 bhp/litre was exceptional for a road bike of the period, and fitted into a cleaned-up version of the Gran Sport's single-loop frame weighed only 104 kg with complete road equipment and a pillion seat. Though only a four-speed gearbox was fitted, performance was excellent compared to the opposition, with a top speed of just on 135 km/h. Seventeen-inch wheels were later dropped in favour of 18 in. rims.

At the same time an uprated version was announced, known as the 175 Super Sport. With its gold frame and knobbly tank with arm recesses and clip-on brackets for a tank pad, this little machine became the envious target of every Italian boy racer and not a few in other countries besides. Aimed fair and square at the MSDS class (later to become Formula 3), this little production racer had a lumpier cam and 9.5:1 compression ratio (compared to 8:1 on the Sport), sufficient for a dramatic increase in speed to 150 km/h. Output became 17 bhp at 9300 rpm.

The Ducati 175 Sport: the first step up the larger-capacity scale, in 1957

With a production capacity of 200 machines a day, Ducati were well equipped to respond to the success of the new bike, though in truth that target was rarely if ever attained.

In the following year, 1957, the 175 gained more than a 25 per cent share of its important capacity market, but even more significantly was the basis of the company's *entrée* into the vital US market under the auspices of their newly appointed distributors, the Berliner Corporation.

At the end of 1956 the Ducati road range thus consisted of the 55 and 65 pullrod Cucciolo-based runabouts, the 98 and 125 pushrod machines, and the new 175s, a detuned version of which, the 175T, soon became available. Working swiftly in between

his efforts to perfect the desmo racers, Taglioni extended the ohc concept down the capacity scale, and in September 1957 two new models were introduced at the Bari Show, the first major motorcycle exhibition to be held in the remote Mezzogiorno region of the south of Italy. Their launch here rather than at the more usual Milan Show was an expert piece of marketing by Calcagnile, since not only were they the only new models from any manufacturer on display, but in presenting them here in one of the poorest and thus far most neglected parts of the country, Ducati

The 100 Sport was a perfect small-scale sporting motorcycle, here shown in 1959 form

reaped considerable local sympathy in a region whose affluence was not yet sufficient for the Fiat 500 to have made many inroads: in other words, it was still a traditional bike market.

The new models were the 100 and 125 Sports, both variations on the 175 theme, and already demonstrating Taglioni's future policy of a multiplicity of models, in varying capacities and states of tune, not to mention levels of trim, on a single basic concept. The models shown were the intermediate Sport versions, producing 10 bhp at 8000 rpm from the familiar 55.3 × 52 mm dimensions of the 125, and 8 bhp at 8700 rpm on the 49.4 × 52 mm 98 cc version. The Formula 3 and 'T' versions followed soon after.

Taking time out from his preparations for the company's forthcoming big effort in the World Championship, Taglioni supervised the design of two new engines in the latter half of 1957 which made their debut in two greatly differing vehicles at the beginning of 1958. The first to appear was the *Muletto*, an aptly-named little mule of a three-wheeled workhorse which represented a much more sensible entry into the Vespa-dominated light truck market than the ill-fated Girino. This time the driver sat in front of his maximum 350 kg payload, powered by a low-compression 62 × 66 mm 200 cc pushrod four-stroke ohv engine producing 6 bhp at

5000 rpm. Good fuel consumption of 70 mpg fully loaded was claimed, but though the Muletto sold in reasonable quantities, it never really dented the established models' hold on this specialist market.

Of more lasting moment was the introduction at the Milan Export Trade Fair in April of the first-ever Ducati two-stroke, a 50 cc unit aimed at the growing moped market in which the mechanical sophistication of even as uncomplicated a four-stroke as the Cucciolo was deemed to be unacceptable. Taglioni, whose dislike of two-strokes is well recorded, had little to do with the engine, whose design was delegated to his assistants. For the first few years production was exclusively for the export market, with Mototrans, whose foundation had been one of the principal reasons for the design's creation in the first place, making it under licence in Barcelona for the avidly two-stroke orientated Spanish market.

Villa's success in the most important Formula 3 race yet run, at the Italian GP on Ducati's day of glory in September 1958, gave added impetus to sales of the 175 and its associated models. These received a further boost with Tartarini and Monetti returning safely from a 12-month-long round-the-

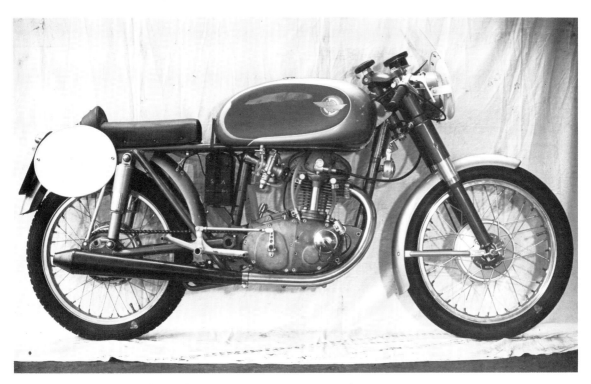

ABOVE *The 1959 125 cc Formula 3 production racer, with sandcast crankcases and full road equipment. As sold in Britain by Kings of Oxford, it was over £50 more expensive than the 500 cc Matchless G50*

BELOW *The 175 Sport with its 'knobbly' tank was a fast and distinctive machine that in 1959 was burdened with the curious twin silencer exhaust styling*

world journey on two 175T Ducatis in completely standard trim. Though the idea of the trip had been Tartarini's, the factory were not slow to realize the commercial implications, and several new markets were successfully opened up to Ducati products as a result of the trip, with Calcagnile and his staff making several follow-up visits to countries which had not thus far figured on the Ducati sales map.

The two riders had left Bologna the year before soon after Tartarini's unsuccessful ride in the Giro d'Italia on the prototype 175 twin. Taking the time-honoured overland route through Yugoslavia, Bulgaria and Turkey to Iran, they crossed uneventfully through Pakistan to the Indian sub-continent. There was already a Ducati dealer in Bombay, where they serviced the bikes, continuing on a flag-waving visit north to Delhi before crossing to Calcutta. In spite of the difficulties of political and natural barriers, they managed to ride through East Pakistan, Assam, Burma and from Rangoon down through the Malay Peninsula to Singapore, where a series of voyages began on ferries and tramp steamers through the East Indies and newly formed republic of Indonesia.

Visiting Sumatra, Java, Borneo and Timor they eventually wound up in New Guinea, braving the cannibalistic tendencies of the local populace to ride along the south-west side of the country before embarking on another ship for the short crossing to Australia: in due course to become one of Ducati's

The 204 cc Elite was Ducati's first step towards the quarter-litre category, in which they were to shine in future years. This is a 1959 model

most important export markets, the country was at that time still virgin territory for the Bologna marque, and again the visit of the two round-the-world travellers and the attendant publicity they received at a time when this type of journey was much less commonplace than it is today, proved invaluable in establishing its name.

Riding south down the Queensland coast to Sydney, they once again stopped for a while to service the two little machines, which had been standing up to the rigours of the trip remarkably well, despite the appalling roads and jungle tracks they had been required to traverse in Asia, heavily loaded. Punctures were the only consistent problem.

From Sydney they rode down through Canberra to Melbourne, the most southerly point on their trip, with Bologna the furthest north. From there they took ship again for the lengthy voyage across the Pacific Ocean, through the Panama Canal, to Venezuela. Disembarking at Caracas, they found themselves embroiled in one of the country's periodic revolutions. Escaping unscathed, they plunged into the dense South American jungle to cross to neighbouring Colombia, a journey made even more fraught by the dangers of meeting the still uncivilized Indian tribes and their poison darts.

ABOVE AND BELOW *The 175 cc category in Italian road racing was an important class in the early 60s. This is a privateer effort to produce a very workmanlike racer out of the basics of a 175 Sport road machine (Zagari)*

Making it safely to Bogota, they then climbed up over the northern tip of the Andes to Ecuador, before following the coastline south through Peru and Chile to Santiago. Here they prepared the bikes for the arduous journey over the Andes to Argentina, through one of the highest road passes in the world: this involved their resetting the ignition timing and carburation to enable the engine to cope with the rarefied atmosphere at an altitude equivalent to the height of the tallest mountains in Europe – over 14,000 feet.

Struggling over the mountain range successfully, the two little machines and their riders arrived in Buenos Aires to a rapturous reception; the large Italian population and well-established Ducati name made them popular heroes. Shrugging off the effects of the liberal hospitality, they took to the road again, only to ferry across the River Plate to Uruguay to find a similar reception awaiting them there. Throughout South America, Ducati-mounted riders had been cleaning up in the 125 racing class that season with dohc Grand Prix models still fitted with dustbin streamlining in spite of the FIM's ban, for it was by now 1958, and

Uruguay was no exception.

Tartarini and Monetti had set themselves the target date of 5 September that year for their return home, telling reporters along the way that they intended getting back in time to see the Ducati team sweep to victory in the Italian GP at Monza that day: they could have had little idea how prophetic their forecast would be! Time was passing quickly though, and they still had another continent to cross, so bearing north again they crossed into Brazil and set sail once again from Rio de Janeiro across the Southern Atlantic to Cape Town.

Crowds of well-wishers greeted their arrival in South Africa, but they could not afford to stay long. Continuing from Johannesburg, they rode north through what was in those days the British-dominated eastern side of Africa, through the soon-to-be independent colonies of Rhodesia and Nyasaland, Tanganyika, Uganda and Kenya. Pausing in Nairobi to refresh the bikes and themselves for the last push home, they avoided Ethiopia, where since 1935 Italians were no longer particularly welcome, and instead crossed the arid wastes of the southern Sudan on what they would later say was the most arduous stretch of the entire journey. From Khartoum they followed the Nile north to Cairo, then struck off east, after a look at the Pyramids, into the desert. Never straying very far from the coastal strip, they rode through Libya to Tunis, from where they took a ferry to Naples. Riding hard over the final stretch, they reached Bologna on 5 September – a day too late to continue on to Monza, but in time to hear the glad tidings from the track over the radio broadcast.

The two intrepid travellers had completed a trip that even today would be a major test of stamina for both man and machine: 60,000 km in little more than a year, over largely unmetalled roads and through some of the most primitive and untamed regions on earth. They had visited over 30 countries along the way, in many of which in those pre-Honda days a motorcycle was a rarity, and though there had been assorted problems *en route*, the two little 175 cc Ducatis had done everything expected of them, especially bearing in mind their standard and unmodified nature. The resultant publicity benefits at both home and abroad were immeasurable, and Ducati were suitably grateful to both men, who had by their feat done so much to establish the name of the Bologna company all over the world.

The one major export area which had been missed out from the itinerary was North America, but here Ducati were already becoming well established thanks to the efforts of their newly appointed concessionaires, Joseph and Michael Berliner. It was largely at their request, in view of the American market's emphasis on larger-capacity machines, that Taglioni produced an overbored version of the 175, announced in November 1958. This was the 204 cc (actually 203.783) Elite, whose 67 × 57.8 cc engine produced 18 bhp at 7500 rpm, on an 8.5:1 compression ratio.

Taglioni had not originally intended to take the 175 engine out this far without redesigning the bottom end, but tests showed the design to be strong enough, and so it proved. The 90 bhp/litre bike had a top speed of 140 km/h, weighed only 106 kg and, fitted with 18 in. wheels as opposed to the original 17 in. of the smaller capacity models, was Ducati's first 'real' middleweight motorcycle. Styling was an important feature, with the blue and gold theme again prominent, later red and gold, and the knobbly/'anatomical' 17-litre tank giving the air of a thoroughbred racer. Less successful was the exhaust pipe styling, with a bifurcated twin-silencer outlet for the single downpipe at one time adopted in a vain attempt to make the bike look more powerful than it really was. With 80 mpg available even with the sports-type SS27A Dell'Orto carburettor fitted, and the by now well-reputed Ducati handling from the single-loop open cradle frame, the Elite soon carved a niche for itself in the growing 250 cc market in spite of its undercapacity. It light weight and full-size brakes, with 2.75 front and 3.25 rear tyres, gained it a particular reputation for being a hard rider's bike in Italy at the turn of the decade, and it was the first Ducati model to become a notable sales success abroad.

A Super Sports version with uprated camshaft, larger carburettor and higher compression ration followed soon after, while for the US market the basic model was given high-rise handlebars and a slightly more laid-back styling treatment before being marketed as the 200TS America.

In 1959 the venerable Cucciolo pullrod design was finally dropped, and a smaller capacity 85 cc 45.5 × 52 mm version of the pushrod engine introduced to compensate, producing 5.5 bhp at 7200 rpm. Thus at the end of the 1950s the Ducati range consisted of the 85 and 98 pushrod machines, and the 125, 175 and 203 ohc line:

The 100 Sport had been dropped after only a year or so of production: the trend was away from small-capacity sports machines, and in an effort to keep their 700 employees fully occupied in the face of competition from all directions, Ducati would, in the 1960s, tread ever more firmly down the route of larger engines and a more sporting emphasis.

8

Racing parallel twins – a lost cause

The first Ducati motorcycle to boast more than one cylinder appeared in the 1957 Giro d'Italia, the last such stage event to be run on open roads. This 175 cc parallel twin was to prove the prototype of a range of designs to emanate from the Bologna factory using that cylinder configuration, none of which ever achieved the success in the showroom or on the track that the factory must have hoped for. Yet over the next 20 years they would constantly dally with the layout, even after achieving both competition and commercial success with the 90 degree V-twin design which became the firm's hallmark in the 1970s.

The 175 cc Ducati twin used exposed hairpin valve springs controlling two valves per cylinder and there were twin camshafts driven by a train of gears running up the centre of the engine. The design was, however, in all respects other than the cylinder heads similar to the later desmo twin racers which appeared in various capacities and at various stages over the next five years. It actually dated from 1950 when Taglioni had first sketched the valve-spring version of his parallel twin. It would be six years before he was to see it constructed, yet this was not the only case where an earlier product of his fertile mind would be taken out of the filing cabinet and dusted off ready to be employed when the time seemed ripe.

These first twins consisted of two separate light-alloy cylinders mounted vertically on a substantial, vertically split, common crankcase which was heavily finned at the front to cool the wet sump. The very strong seven-piece built-up crankshaft consisted of two separate flywheel assemblies (the flywheels were machined from the solid, as were the big ends) each pressed up individually before being clamped together to a central shaft carrying an integral spur gear by means of two pairs of radially-serrated Hirth couplings. This complicated and costly design gave great rigidity at the expense of

being time-consuming to strip down, and echoed a similar five-piece layout employed to good effect on the all-conquering NSU Rennmax 250 twins of the early 1950s. On these Ducatis which would be made in 125, 175, 250 and 350 cc versions, however, a single bolt with teeth formed in its head was used to clamp the couplings together, rather than three as on the German machines. The whole unit ran in four main bearings of the spring-loaded angular contact type which disassembled themselves upon removal, but which Taglioni employed in order to prevent high-frequency vibration at the very high engine revs which he intended the 180 degree units should run at.

The crankshaft pinion drove a jackshaft which in turn transmitted drive to the multi-plate oil-bath clutch (a dry unit was used on the 175 prototype with cooling slots cut in the outer cover) as well as driving the twin oil pumps, which in turn fed the camshaft bearings and head by external paired lines on either side of the engine, with gravity return. Twin crankcase breathers were positioned close together in front of the cylinders on the 125 and 175, then moved to the back of the engine on the 250/350. The jackshaft also drove a very large-diameter idler gear, which not only turned the shaft driving the twin contact breakers positioned behind the engine but also drove the camshafts by means of Oldham couplings and gears. This large idler pinion was rather fragile and prone to cracking on its spokes, with expensive results, since it was effectively the control gear for the upper part of the engine. A six-speed gearbox was fitted to all capacity models, with straight-cut primary gears which resulted in the engine running backwards. A single plug per cylinder (10 mm on the smaller engines, 14 mm on the larger ones) was all that could be squeezed in, on the outer side of each cylinder. Twin frame-mounted coils sparked the battery ignition system.

On all the engines a distinctive feature were the

converging inlet and exhaust ports, which enabled the exhaust pipes to be squeezed inside the twin front down-tubes of the factory frame. This was effectively a heavily beefed-up verion of the later double cradle design fitted to the 125 singles, employing a central single upper tube which divergd just before the seat to form a bifurcated rear sub-frame. The twin front down-tubes (curved on the 125/175, straight on the other machines) carried a single crossways bracing tube in front of the cylinder head, then carried on to run under the engine before rejoining the top tube just after it had split into two. A cross-brace ran between the rear sub frame and the rear part of the loop and the steering head was also braced under the tank.

A generator to power the compulsory horn and lighting set (but not a kickstarter, which was not required under the rules) was incorporated in the 175 version for its debut in the 1957 Giro d'Italia. The 49 × 46.6 mm engine followed what had by then become a Ducati tradition by being slightly oversquare; it ran a 11:1 compression, produced 22 bhp at 11,000 rpm, 6 bhp more than the 175 sohc version of the single-cylinder Gran Sport which it was intended to replace. But the twin's considerable

extra dry weight at 112 kg, as well as the narrower powerband, cancelled out much of this benefit, though its straight-line speed of around 110 mph once fully wound up was considerably more than the single.

In spite of this the 175 twin was unsuccessful on its only race appearance in Italy, rider Leopoldo Tartarini being forced to retire from the 1957 Giro with ignition and generator problems on the third of the eight stages, having failed to make an impression on the leader board. After that the machine sat around the factory racing department for a while until it was noticed one day by Joe Berliner on one of his regular visits. The upshot was that the dohc twin found its way to the USA, where it was raced with some success in 175 cc class road racing by loaned factory riders such as Francos Villa and Farne, who each spent a season at a time on the other side of the Atlantic helping to spread the message of Ducati's sporting image as the marque struggled for a foothold in this important new market. Ironically, their principal rival was the winner of the 1957 Giro, Joe Rottigni, who had himself emigrated to the States along with his 175 Parilla, to work and race for the US importers of that marque and Berliners' great compeitor, Cosmopolitan Motors.

After several successful seasons in the US the 175 twin was returned to the factory once interest in the 175 class declined. Again it was spotted, this time by

Two different drawings of the layout of the desmo twin racers

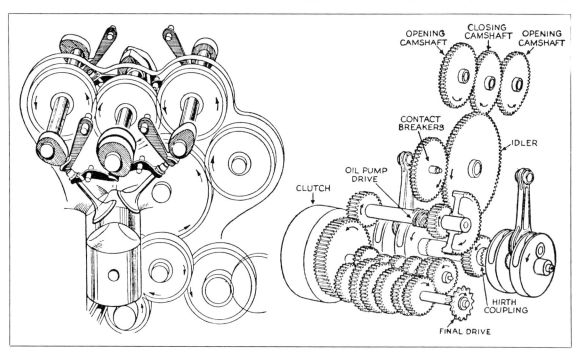

one of its former riders, Franco Villa. By now it was 1964, and with the factory out of racing there was no use for the machine; in any case its capacity class had died a death in Italy too. Villa, however, felt it had considerable potential as a 250, so working with his younger brother Walter – later to win four world titles on Aermacchi Harley-Davidson two-strokes in the 1970s – he persuaded Dr. Montano to let him have the machine in order to uprate and update it.

To bring it up to a full 250 the 175 cc valve-spring twin was bored and stroked to 55.3 × 52 mm – the same measurements as the successful 125 singles. Revised heads and barrels with reduced finning to save weight were produced, incorporating altered porting and squish combustion chambers. Detail changes were made to the clutch and gearchange mechanisms, while the new heads were cast in such a way as to permit a second 10 mm plug to be fitted to each cylinder close up against the camshaft drive train. Finally a new lightweight frame, vaguely resembling the original one, was built in the hope of handling what was expected to be substantial extra power as well as saving weight. Ceriani 35 mm forks were fitted with Oldani brakes, which were much larger than those originally fitted to the 175 machine, and 2.75 × 18 tyres. Total weight was down to 105 kg complete with fairing, less than the bike originally weighed in unfaired Giro form thanks to the substitution of a smaller fibreglass

tank for the original large-capacity alloy one, and so on.

Producing 39 bhp at 12,000 rpm, with a reasonable powerband from 8000 rpm upwards, the Ducati-Villa special seemed to be highly competitive for Italian championship racing for which it was intended, and which did not feature the exotic Japanese works machinery then dominating the Grand Prix scene. The similar 250 Paton twin, the pushrod Aermacchi single and the developing Bultaco two-stroke were well within its performance level, but two other machines probably accounted as much as anything for the fact that the bike never appeared competitively in the hands of the Villas: Provini's four-cylinder Benelli, then beginning the development cycle that would take it to a world title in the hands of Kel Carruthers in 1969, and the bike Provini had deserted to ride the Pesaro four, the incredible Morini single which Silvio Grassetti took over from him to good effect.

However, the real reason that the Villas did not persevere with the valve-spring Ducati twin was that at the start of the 1965 season in which it would have been raced they entered an agreement with Count Boselli of Mondial, for whom Franco had already won the Italian 125 title the previous year on a two-stroke single of his own design but bearing

The 175 cc Giro d'Italia valvespring twin at its debut at the Milan Show in November 1956 with brakes designed for use with a dustbin. It was raced only once in the Motogiro

the Mondial name. The contract was to design and develop a rotary-valve two-stroke 250 twin which was effectively a doubled-up version of the 125. The Ducati project was dropped, and until the debut of the twin-cylinder Mondial at San Remo later that year, Franco raced one of the dohc singles which Sandford and Provini had used to dominate the 1957 World Championship. The Ducati twin eventually found its way back across the Atlantic again, where it's now in a private collection.

Back in 1957, however, Taglioni had used the twin in 175 form as the prototype of a 125 Grand Prix machine, which duly appeared at the 1958 Italian GP at Monza, where it was ridden into 3rd place in the midst of the Ducati 1-5 sweep by, ironically, none other than Franco Villa. The new machine resembled the 175 valve-spring model closely, except that the cylinders were inclined very slightly forward by 4 degrees, and a three-camshaft desmodromic head was fitted, with the two closing cams sharing the central camshaft as on the singles. All three camshafts ran in ball bearings, and the positive valve control was effected in the same way as on the singles.

Taglioni's principal reason for producing the 125 twin was that the single had by now reached the limit of its development: smaller cylinders meant higher revs and greater specific power, just as Honda were to find later. Three machines in all were constructed, their 42.5 × 45 mm engines – unusually for a Taglioni Ducati, slightly under-square – producing 22.5 bhp at 13,800 rpm, running on 10.2 compression and breathing through twin 23

The 175 twin as prepared for the 1957 Giro d'Italia, with bigger fuel tank and other detail changes since Milan; note a horn!

mm Dell'Orto carburettors with specially made flat-sided float chambers to avoid frothing at high revs fitted after this problem had been experienced with the original single centrally mounted round chamber. A specific power of 180 bhp/litre was no mean achievement in 1958 especially for a four-stroke, and considerably more powerful than the previous class musclebike, the 1956 Gilera twin which produced a 'mere' 20 bhp.

With the engine safe to 17,000 rpm thanks to the use of desmodromics (though unlike on the singles, small hairpin valve springs were always fitted to the twins for ease of starting), the design offered an impressive safety margin, especially under braking. However, the increased power could only be achieved at the expense of a very narrow power band with effective urge only coming in at around 10,500 rpm. To keep it on the boil once fully wound up, the top three gears of the six-speed box were very closely matched (4th – 1:1.17; 5th – 1:1.10; 6th – 1:1.06) making clutchless changes a prerequisite of keeping the revs up. But a top speed of 118 mph was a good bit faster than the singles, and for this reason the twin was always most effective on fast, sweeping circuits such as Monza and Spa.

Another factor telling against the 125 twin on short tracks was its increased weight as compared to the singles. Though the factory only owned up to 202 lb dry, the actual ready-to-race weight was 218 lb with a gallon of fuel, and this affected its

BELOW *A piston and right-hand crank assembly from a 125 desmo twin – with small-size matchbox. The serrated face of the Hirth coupling can be clearly seen*

accleration out of tight corners. The handling too was less than perfect, in spite of massively braced fabricated front fork yokes and generous bracing too around the swinging arm pivot. A change from 17 in. to 18 in. rims improved stability, and the brakes, originally the same as fitted to the singles, were increased in diameter by 10 mm front and rear to good effect. Nevertheless, the model's only classic success in its two seasons of GP racing after that initial outing at Monza in 1958 were 3rd again in the same race a year later, this time in the hands of Luigi Taveri (who failed by only a length to win the race in the famous near dead-heat between winner Degner's MZ and the MV of Carlo Ubbiali), and 6th in the Belgian GP at Spa in 1960, ridden by Mike Hailwood.

There was a much-reduced scale of factory participation in competition in 1959 as efforts were made to stem the drop in road bike sales which threatened to drain the factory's life-blood. Outside Italy, involvement was restricted to backing certain key riders on factory-loaned desmo singles. Principally this meant Taveri, Spaggiari when he wasn't working at the factory in the test department, Australian Ken Kavanagh, who had settled in Italy and in due course became one of the 'locals', Alberto Pagani – son of former world champion Nello and then just starting on the road to a series of works rides culminating 13 years later in a partnership with Agostini on the MVs, and Mike Hailwood.

Mike's successful Grand Prix debut on the 125 dohc single the previous year, allied to father Stan's powers of persuasion, obtained for their Ecurie Sportive team the loan of one of the works desmo singles for the 1959 season. On it, Mike achieved his first GP classic victory in any class at the Ulster that year, which combined with three third places in the Isle of Man, Germany and Holland were sufficient to earn him third place in the 125 World Championship in his first full season of GP racing. Numerous victories on the British short circuits plus winning the 1959 ACU 125 Gold Star also came his way. The twin, on the other hand, was scarcely employed at all, especially after Villa fell off in the first classic of the season at the TT when, after a bitter race-long duel with former Ducati teamster Dave Chadwick's MV for fifth place, the two of them collided at the Morney Bends and the twin was quite badly damaged.

As always the final race of the season at Monza provided some useful pointers for the following season. The speed of the MZ and MV singles was such that Taveri's twin was the only Ducati to finish on the leader board. Hailwood was 8th on his trusty but now outpaced single, and it was this that decided father Stan to equip his son for the following season with a pair of that what seemed by now well-sorted desmo twins for the 125 class in 1960. This proved to be a mistake for Mike never enjoyed the same success with the machines as with the desmo single. He once wrote, 'Though incredibly fast for a 125, it had a very narrow effective powerband, poor acceleration and was far too small for me!' The twins were sold off, one of them passing to Aermacchi specialist Syd Lawton

for son Barry to cut his teeth on in British events, before both Hailwood machines eventually ended up in the USA, from where one of them returned to Britain in the late 1970s.

Meanwhile the third 125 twin had been retained by the factory before they sent it on loan to their Spanish Mototrans affiliate for use in the important 125 Spanish Championship events in the early 1960s, and here at last Taglioni's little two-pot desmo found its true niche. In 1962, after two years riding for the rival MV and Benelli teams when Ducati withdrew officially from all direct involvement in competition by the parent factory, the most inveterate *ducatisti* of all, Bruno Spaggiari, took the twin to a string of victories on the street circuits of the Iberian Peninsula, winning at Bilbao, Valladolid, La Coruna, Madrid and other venues to clinch the prestigious Spanish title for Mototrans. But an attack on the Italian title with the same machine the following season yielded less satisfactory results against stiffer competition and by season's end Spaggiari was back on an MV single for the lightweight classes. Meantime, Mototrans were working on updating the 125 twin, and with new cams producing a wider power band and now revving to 15,000 rpm, at which point it produced 24 bhp, the little machine reappeared with Spaggiari aboard once again at the opening events of the 1966 season in Spain and Italy, fitted with a new lightweight frame. A third place at Alicante behind Ralph Bryans's Honda four and Franco Villa's disc-

One of the ex-Hailwood 125 desmo twins, later raced by Barry Lawton and Dennis Trollope before finding its way to the USA; it's now back in Britain

valve Mondial single gave cause for satisfaction, followed up two weeks later by a similar placing at Modena in the first round of the Italian Championship behind the same machines. However, that same meeting saw the debut of the 250 desmo single-cylinder works Ducati in the hands of Franco Farne and thereafter Spaggiari was required to concentrate on developing this and the larger-capacity singles, to the detriment of the little twin, which was retired from competition and eventually found its way into the hands of a Benelux collector.

A brace of 125 twins were not the only machines which Stan Hailwood was able to persuade the Ducati factory to provide for his Ecurie Sportive for the 1960 season; in an attempt to rationalize his equipment and achieve the edge of what would in effect be a works machine, he successfully asked Montano and Taglioni to provide Mike with two similar machines for the 250 and 350 classes. The 250 twin appeared first and was revealed to the press in February 1960. It was similar to the 125, but scaled up in every respect so that really only the general outline was alike – there was no interchangeability between the two machines.

The 250 desmo twin used the same basic design with changes already noted, and measured 55.3 × 52 mm – once again the by now accepted Ducati 125 cc cylinder dimensions. Power output was

43 bhp at the crankshaft, translating to 37 bhp at the rear wheel, equivalent to a specific power of 173 bhp/litre at the crank – highly respectable compared to the 168 bhp/litre of the 250MZ of the same era, until a weight comparison is made. Ducati had claimed a dry weight of 112 kg prior to the

ABOVE *The 125 desmo twin prototype in the factory racing department in 1958, still in mock-up stage (Zagari)*

BELOW *The author on his 125 desmo twin, the same machine pictured on the facing page. Power comes in at 10,000 rpm, with a peak of 22.5 bhp at the rear wheel at 13,800 rpm*

machine's launch, but in fact this turned out to have been measured with a thumb on the scales, since the true weight with a gallon of fuel was just on 130 kg; far heavier than the 105 kg MZ and more too than the only slightly less powerful 250 MV Agusta twin which scaled in at 115 kg. The MV was to retain its 250 World Championship that season.

Testing at the Modena *aeroautodromo* with both Farne and Hailwood aboard showed up another problem. Though the engine had a respectable powerband, with peak power produced at 11,600 rpm and maximum torque at 10,800 revs – thanks to the desmodromics it was actually safe to 13,000 rpm – and the top speed of 135 mph compared favourably with that of the competition, the 250 desmo twin not only lacked acceleration out of corners thanks to its excessive weight but also, in the inimitable words of Mike the Bike himself, 'handled like the fastest five-barred gate in the world'! A series of long and very expensive experiments with modifications to the original frame – basically a slightly uprated version of the 125 chassis – were made, with several different types being tried and tested, all to no avail. Furthermore, the team was plagued with innumerable teething troubles ranging from broken gears in the six-speed gearbox to collapsed rear wheels and electrical problems, especially with the contact breakers, all

The 250 desmo twin built especially for Hailwood's Ecurie Sportive at its press unveiling in March 1960. The fairing was made of single-skin alloy

serving to illustrate only too well that even the most professional and best-equipped private team has neither the facilities nor the time to develop what is basically a factory toolroom special away from the mother nest. In the case of Ecurie Sportive, this problem was exacerbated by the fact that Mike was by now riding once and often twice every weekend, in every solo class, entailing between six and eight bikes being kept on the go. Under such circumstances it was hardly surprising that he generally rode his back-up machine in the 250 class, one of a brace of ex-works 250 dohc Mondial singles with which he'd won the 1959 ACU Star and which proved not only to be almost unbeatable in their class but a match for the 500s as well.

The 350 desmo Ducati twin, when it appeared later that year, proved to have all the 250's faults only more so, thanks to the 45 bhp at the rear wheel produced by the overbored engine. Hailwood scarcely raced the 350 at all, preferring to rely on his more controllable 7R AJS, but the team did manage to make the 250 steer well enough to win several races with it on the faster British courses such as Snetterton and Thruxton, as well as a record-breaking victory at the Silverstone Saturday meeting in 1960. At the beginning of 1961, a few weeks into the season and after Mike had scored a particularly noteworthy win on the 250 at the twisty Brands Hatch track, the whole set-up was sold to John Surtees, not for the ex-MV Agusta world champion himself, but for his younger brother Norman to ride under John's guidance.

Surtees immediately recognized that the Ducatis were indeed powerful and by now surprisingly reliable for a relatively undeverloped design, so attempted to solve the handling problems by commissioning Reynolds Tubes' frame-building wizard Ken Sprayson to construct a specially designed frame incorporating their own design of leading link, fabricated front forks. The finished product saved a considerable amount of weight and the bikes now handled properly for the first time, but unfortunately Norman was losing interest in bike racing and John too was deeply involved in four-wheel racing *en route* to a World Championship with Ferrari in 1964. Plans for Phil Read to ride the 250 in the 1962 TT fell through when the engine blew up at Jurby during testing, and in the end the 250s were sold to Dan Shorey, who himself had little fortune with them. In the 1970s they passed into the hands of a

ABOVE *Another view of the 250 twin at its first public viewing, this time unclothed. General outline is the same as for the 125 twin, scaled up*

BELOW *A 350 desmo twin came after the 250 in 1960, and was tested at Silverstone by Hailwood in May, when this picture was taken. Handling left much to be desired, however*

After John Surtees acquired the ill-handling 250 and 350 twins, he commissioned Reynolds frame wizard Ken Sprayson to manufacture a more rigid chassis, with Reynolds' own leading link front forks

Midlands-based research engineer and have not appeared in public running since the mid-70s. The 350s on the other hand were retained by Surtees himself, and when he resumed an active interest in motorcycling around 1980 one was restored and appeared at his testimonial day at Brands Hatch in 1981 ridden by Geoff Monty. Both machines and all the spares were subsequently sold to a German enthusiast, who appears with them on the Continent in classic events.

In spite of this flirtation with the parallel twin configuration for road-racing purposes, Ducati rather strangely did not immediately consider its application to road models. Strangely, because up until now all racing machines emanating from the Bologna factory had been directly related to the products the company manufactured for sale to its customers for everyday use on the highway. The twins, therefore, were the first Taglioni designs to be translated into metal exclusively for racing – indeed, they were the first pure-bred racers to come from the factory at all – and as such perhaps indicate the route he might have followed had he not been

obliged to work within the constraints of a production-based single in producing a Grand Prix racer. In the end, though, they proved not only something of a disappointment to all concerned – and there's no doubt that the factory were just as dismayed as the Hailwoods at the bigger twins' dismal handling performance – but also something of a dead end. Few lessons were learnt that had any relevance to the road model range except for one, which many years later when Ducati road-holding and handling abilities are generally taken for granted, seems almost absurdly obvious: there's no point creating an engine with excess power at the expense of excess weight and then mounting it in a frame that isn't up to the job of harnessing that power. It was a lesson that Ing. Taglioni would not forget, and indeed its implementation would become a focal point of his future designs for both road and track.

9

Ducati fours

Taglioni designed his first four-cylinder motorcycle engine as a graduation project while at Bologna University in 1948. It was a 250 cc V4 which he then developed into a horizontal 125 cc twin by the simple expedient of cutting off the rear cylinders of the 90 degree V-four design (sometimes pedantically called an L-four by those with calligraphic handwriting). It was, however, simply a drawing project which never reached the stage of being constructed.

The 1950s were the last decade of single-cylinder supremacy, when any motorcycle with more than one pot was exotically termed a 'multi', and the age of the Japanese with their superbly conceived four-, five- and even six-cylinder racers had still to come. Even twin-cylinder designs were rare in the smaller capacity classes, and a four unheard of. To Taglioni, though, breaking new ground was a familiar challenge which he seized eagerly, and in 1958 he designed a four-cylinder, in-line 125 cc racer that had the capability of being bored and stroked out to 175 or 250 cc. At a time when the smallest capacity fours were the 350 cc MV and Gilera racers (apart from various home-made devices achieved by bolting up a row of 50 or 75 cc engines), such a step seemed particularly audacious, and when news of the design leaked out from the Bologna factory at the start of the 1959 season, the racing world waited with baited breath for the appearance of such an exotic machine.

They waited in vain, for in light of Ducati's policy reversal and subsequent scaling-down of their racing activities the hoped-for Ducati four did not appear, and instead Honda became the first to race a small-capacity four-cylinder engine, in 1959. Some castings were made, and a test cylinder run up on the brake, but that was all.

There the project might have foundered but for the enthusiasm of the Spanish Mototrans affiliate, who by the mid-1960s had attained the position of the third largest Spanish motorcycle manufacturer behind Montesa and Bultaco. This had been achieved largely by means of their success in road racing rather than at the country's national sport of trials, in which their two two-stroke orientated rivals excelled.

Mototrans were eager to maintain their excellent record in the important 125 cc racing class, achieved with the help of guest riders such as Bruno Spaggiari and Franco Farne, who were assigned to them for a season at a time to compete with Spanish licences in the national championships, with great success. Spaggiari in particular excelled there, spending two seasons riding for Mototrans in 1962 and 1965, winning the Spanish title the first year on their 125 Desmo twin but losing out to the increasingly competitive water-cooled Bultacos in the latter year, in spite of some useful back-up from the second Mototrans works rider on a 125 Desmo single. His name? Angel Nieto.

At Mototrans' request, therefore, Taglioni brought out his late-50s four-cylinder design and used it as the basis for a brand-new 125 multi, which first appeared after exhaustive brake tests in March 1965. A beautifully executed and extremely compact design whose width from one side of the fairing to the other was only 2 in. more than the 125 Desmo twin, the 125 four was, however, of more conventional dohc valve-spring format, with transverse in-line arrangement of the four separate, deeply finned cylinders, inclined forwards at 40 degrees on the crankcase, which was also heavily ribbed at the front for cooling purposes.

The most significant aspect of the engine was Taglioni's use for the first time publicly of a four valve per cylinder configuration, which Honda had in the previous five years shown to be desirable, particularly in small-capacity engines, for reasons already discussed in the chapter on desmodromics. Even so, Taglioni would still have liked to fit desmo

valve gear to the four, but was prevented from doing so for two reasons: ease of maintenance by Spanish mechanics relatively far away from the parent factory and the designer's guiding hand, and the need to keep the engine as compact as possible. Later, he would design a four-valve desmo head for the 250 single which Spaggiari did race with on a couple of occasions before the idea was dropped only to resurface on the 1971 500 cc GP bike, whose 2-valve sister proved more reliable.

Another modification, tried out by Mototrans themselves in 1966, was another 250 four-valve head for the Mach 1 production racer, this time with coil valve springs, twin 18 mm Dell'Orto carburettors feeding a bifurcated inlet tract, and separate exhaust ports and pipes: it produced very little more power than the two-valve head, and proved Taglioni's long-held theory that a two-valve head, if carefully designed and ported, can be almost as efficient as a four-valve one, without the added

The four-carb sports version of the Ducati Apollo V4 engine. Note the car-type distributor driven off the camshaft and the awkward throttle slide cables

complication and with the possibility of desmodromic valve action to narrow the difference even further.

For the 125 four, however, he resorted to conventional coil springs for the 16-valve engine, having been persuaded by Honda's success with this format that it was worthwhile exploring. Unlike the Honda, though, the twin overhead camshafts were driven by a train of gears running not up the centre of the engine but behind a Y-shaped cover on the left side. Included valve angle was 90 degrees – already then considered too wide for maximum retention of the incoming charge.

Ignition was by four coils strapped to the front down-tubes of the twin-loop cradle frame, fed by a battery mounted under the front of the seat, behind the cylinders, and firing a single specially made 8 mm plug per cylinder: the fact that Taglioni had to resort to these tiny spark plugs is an indication of how cramped the space was in the hemispheric combustion chamber of each 31 cc cylinder. A set of points incorporating four separate contact breakers was driven off the bottom pinion of the camshaft gear train, behind which sat the large-diameter multi-plate wet clutch, running at half engine speed. The compact wet-sump cases contained an eight-speed gearbox with gear primary taken off the centre of the crankshaft. A spur gear off the bottom of the camshaft gear train drove the high-capacity oil pump.

The practically square engine dimensions of 34.5 × 34 mm each cylinder permitted a safe engine speed of 17,000 rpm, with peak power initially 23 bhp at 14,000 rpm. The forged pistons had deep valve inserts and a pronounced squish band, giving a compression ratio of 12:1. Cycle parts featured 32 mm Ceriani front forks and Oldani brakes, with a mechanical Veglia rev-counter reading to 18,000 rpm driven off the exhaust camshaft. Eighteen-inch rims with 2.50 section tyres were fitted front and rear, and the claimed weight was a staggeringly low

85 kg without fairing – practically the same as the 125 Desmo single of the late 1950s. Four 12 mm Dell'Orto carburettors, each pair sharing an oblong separate float chamber, fed the engine, their slides controlled by a linkage system of rods with a single throttle from the twistgrip: unlike on the Hondas, however, there was no 'desmodromic' or positive throttle closure!

It was never seriously considered, much though the press may have championed the idea at the time, entering the 125 cc Ducati four in World Championship events, since the factory was realistic enough to recognize that inserting themselves into the titanic, no-costs-barred struggle then being waged between Honda, Suzuki, Yamaha and – on a much more impoverished basis – MZ would be financial suicide. But the protected nature of the Spanish market meant that the Japanese had yet to tread there, and the four made perfect sense provided its competitive appearances were restricted to the Iberian Peninsula.

Initial tests were conducted with Franco Farne

The Apollo prototype with mid-Atlantic styling and whitewall Pirelli tyres which were, however, to prove the achilles heel of the project. The bike was finished in a metallic bronze colour

aboard at Modena in the spring of 1965, and were encouraging enough for further development work to be carried out during the course of the next 12 months. But power output, though eventually raised to 24 bhp at 16,000 rpm, was not considered adequate for the degree of complication presented by the four-cylinder layout. Both two- and four-valve cylinders were tried, but the four never much exceeded the by now well-proven 125 twin's 22.5 bhp, and after further tests in the first part of 1966, this time with a specially designed Marelli ignition system running off the intermediate pinion in the camshaft gear-train, feeding two 6V coils instead of the four 3V units previously fitted, development was discontinued. The difficulties of providing adequate ignition had been one of the principal difficulties, and though it was never intended that the two machines should race against each other, it will be seen how far Ducati had still to go when their four's ultimate 24 bhp is compared with the Suzuki RT65, which won the 1965 World Championship for Hugh Anderson, and produced 31 bhp with a dry weight of around 90 kg. The 125 four disappeared from view after 1966, and was reputed to have found its way to the USSR, where it may apparently be seen on display in a Leningrad museum.

One would have thought that after the disap-

The official completion ceremony at Borgo Panigale in 1964, when the Apollo V4 prototype was delivered to the Berliner Corporation. Shaking hands is Dr. Montano (in the white jacket), with to his right Dr. Cosimo Calcagnile, the Ducati sales director. Ing. Taglioni is second from the right

pointments of the 125, Mototrans would have had their fill of multis, but this was evidently not the case, for in March 1967 they revealed the existence of an in-line 250 cc four, which, unlike the 125, they had designed and manufactured entirely in Barcelona. Though not a true Ducati – it was dubbed the MT 250 when it finally appeared in public later in the year – this Spanish-made four was unfortunately no more successful than its Italian cousin. The engine was beautifully made, and again featured separate finned cylinders, but here the similarity with the 125 ended, for they were arranged vertically, and drive to the double overhead camshafts and two-valve per cylinder head was taken by a large pinion, Honda-style, from the middle of the crankshaft between the 2nd and 3rd pots.

The squared-off crankcase was again ribbed at the front, though more for additional strength than for cooling purposes, and contained three litres of oil in the wet sump design, with a seven-speed unit gearbox, drive to which was taken off the central crankshaft primary pinion. This also drove the contact breaker for the points ignition, mounted on top of the gearbox, with the twin coils fitted on the top frame rails of the duplex frame, which bore a strong family resemblance to the 125 four, scaled up. A dry multi-plate clutch was fitted on the left of the engine, but with its cooling airflow partially obscured by the width of the crankcase: clutch slip was apparently a problem even in early testing.

The 125 four on its initial appearance at Modena for testing in early 1965. The engine produced 23 bhp at 14,000 rpm, and here fitted with four 3v coils (Zagari)

With oversquare engine dimensions of 44.5 × 40 mm, the MT 250 four produced a claimed 50 bhp at 14,000 rpm, with maximum safe revs of 16,000, running on a 10.5:1 compression ratio. Four 15 mm Dell'Ortos were fitted, again sharing a pair of oblong float chambers, and the white-faced Veglia rev-counter this time driven off the inlet camshaft.

With 35 mm Ceriani forks, Oldani brakes and Girling rear units (later replaced by Cerianis) mounted vertically, the MT 250 looked well thought out and set to provide much-needed European interest in the important 250 class. Unfortunately, its debut at the Spanish GP at Montjuic – a stone's throw from the Mototrans factory in Barcelona – on 30 April was simply embarrassing. Clutch slip was so bad after just a few laps of the tortuous park circuit that in spite of repeated efforts to cure the problem, Spaggiari was about to park the bike in favour of his more dependable 250 single when he fell off it; just to complete a day of gloom, the single too let him down in the race.

Further efforts were made to cure the MT 250's inherent problems, but a complete redesign of the bottom end was in order, and this was beyond the factory's resources. As the first Spanish-designed four-cylinder racer, it had brought them a deal of prestige, but unfortunately not accompanied by success on the track. The bike was pensioned off in favour of the new desmo-headed 250 single, and did not appear again apart from a couple of desultory laps in practice for the 1968 Spanish GP.

At the other end of the capacity scale, earlier in the decade Taglioni had produced the largest-capacity motorcycle made in Europe since 1945: the 1257 cc V4 Apollo. Once again, one of the company's overseas affiliates was responsible for the machine's inception, this time their American distributors, the Berliner Motor Corporation. Berliner had, as already recounted, assumed the Ducati concession in 1957, but before that they were already importers for a number of European marques, including the German Zundapp; in 1960 they also began to distribute the British AMC group's Matchless and Norton machines. Zundapp were notable primarily for a BMW-like 600 cc flat twin, the KS601, a shaft-drive tourer descended from their Second World War *Wehrmacht* machine, which was also available in military and police versions.

Joe Berliner, the president of the company, was astute enough to recognize the potential of the important police motorcycle market in the USA, then firmly in the grip of Harley Davidson after the demise of the Indian marque. American anti-trust legislation required that police departments across the country at least consider alternative sources of supply, even if this meant evaluating foreign machines, to the resultant Harley monopoly, and this gave Berliner his chance. Selling a batch of KS601s to a string of cities for the nominal price of one dollar in order for them to be evaluated as possible future police department equipment, he tried to break Harley's stranglehold on this lucrative market.

Two problems surfaced: first, Zundapp ended production of their large-capacity twins in 1958 in favour of concentrating entirely on small 50 and 80 cc two-stroke mopeds. They'd been losing ground continuously to BMW, and decided to call a halt. This left Berliner without a suitable bike, a fact made all the more unfortunate by the fact that several of the departments to which he had sold Zundapps had reported favourably on them and were keen to take matters further.

They were prevented from doing so, however, by the second key problem. US police department construction-and-use regulations were practically the same all over the country, and outlined in some detail the specification called for in official equipment, including patrol motorcycles. These naturally favoured the overweight, large-capacity behemoths which the American industry had concentrated on building since its earliest days, and specifically required engines of at least 1200 cc, a wheelbase of minimum 60 in. and, worst of all, tyres of 5.00 × 16 section: no other covers were acceptable.

Berliner was not easily daunted, and with Zundapp now a spent force he contacted Ducati to see if they were interested in producing a special machine for this large potential market. After considering the design of the 1340 cc Harley, which was then effectively standard issue to US police forces and whose side-valve engine dated back

nearly to the Great War, Montano and Taglioni readily agreed, certain that they could produce a better, more efficient and much more modern design which Berliner could sell at reasonable cost even after payment of the then quite stiff import duty. Though the company's largest-capacity model in 1959, when Berliner first approached them, was the 200 cc Elite, this was not regarded as a problem, and indeed it was natural that Taglioni eagerly accepted the opportunity as a technical challenge.

At the same time, Berliner was in negotiation with AMC in Britain with a view to taking over their US distribution, which had ironically been held by the Indian Motor Corp. before they went under. His intention to attack the police market, one which AMC were already heavily involved in both in the UK and abroad, and for which they had a number of suitable models, was an important negotiating point in his favour, but though he ended up securing the concession, he was amazed when the AMC board told him that they would only consider building a vertical twin for the US police market (as they did elsewhere), which effectively meant a maximum capacity of 800 cc if vibration was to be kept within manageable levels – too small to satisfy the specifications. In other words, tell the customer what he ought to want, rather than what he's decided you can try to sell him: the classic reason for the demise of the British motorcycle industry.

Fortunately for Berliner, Ducati were much more flexible, but Montano had run up against a major problem in the form of the bureaucrats in Rome who controlled the company's finances. They were reluctant to underwrite the substantial development costs of a bike aimed at so specialized a market, and which was so completely different from any of Ducati's existing models. It would mean too, a substantial expenditure in new tooling if the model should go into production, with no guarantee of recouping the capital investment: it was, in short, a risky financial gamble at a time when all Italian bike manufacturers, including Ducati, were under attack from a combination of a shrinking home market and increasing competition from the newly arrived Japanese abroad.

After extended haggling, an agreement was finally struck whereby Berliner would share the development costs of the new model, code-named Apollo. In return, Berliner was allowed to dictate its specifications, but would be expected to make a further contribution towards tooling costs should the model gain acceptance. The Apollo thus became a joint venture between Ducati Meccanica and the Berliner Motor Corp.

ABOVE AND RIGHT *The sixteen valve version of the 125 four, pictured in January 1966 (Zagari)*

BELOW *Another view of the 125 four in its inaugural 1965 form (Zagari)*

Berliner wanted a four-cylinder machine with shaft drive and as simple a specification as possible for ease of maintenance, but which at the same time would be superior in all departments – speed, handling and manoeuvrability – to the Harley-Davidson. As a committed V4 exponent, Taglioni plumped immediately for this format, which moreover would permit him to build a pushrod ohv design with a single cam positioned between the cylinders just as on the V8 car engines which US police mechanics could work on in their sleep.

The agreement to proceed was struck in 1961, two years after negotiations had began, when Joe Berliner visited the factory with a group of his dealers in October 1959. Taglioni worked on the project throughout the following year, and the prototype was ready for testing in the spring of 1963, prior to being shipped to the USA for further testing by Berliner before its display to potential buyers. One complete bike, plus a spare engine, was made.

In spite of its massive cylinder capacity, the Apollo engine was a compact unit thanks to its 90 degree V4 configuration, effectively two V-twins side by side. The four separate cylinders measured 84.5 × 56 mm, the most extreme adoption yet of Taglioni's oversquare format, yielding a 1257 cc displacement. The forward-facing pair of cylinders had longitudinal external finning, with conventional circular fins on the rear pair: Taglioni had at one time considered the benefits of water-cooling but dismissed it on the grounds of unnecessary additional complication and weight. The crankcases measured a quite slim 19 inches across, and featured unit construction with two pairs of cranks each supporting a pair of rods running on a single caged roller big end.

A central pinion drove the single camshaft while also providing the power take-off to the five-speed gearbox; a kickstarter was provided for the brave to use, while for more normal mortals a Marelli electric starter, similar to the one used on a Fiat 1100 car, was fitted. The gearbox case was designed to accept the Sachs variable-speed automatic transmission, as later fitted to the Moto Guzzi 1000 Convert V-twin, if desired. Final drive was at Taglioni's insistence by duplex chain, a tried and proven alternative to Berliner's preferred shaft-drive layout which the Ducati engineer mistrusted for reasons of reliability.

Valve adjustment was simply effected by dint of removing the rocker covers on each cylinder via a single nut and checking the screw-type tappets with a feeler gauge. Ignition was by means of a 12V battery fitted under the seat, with four contact breakers, two running off each end of the camshaft, and four coils feeding the single 14 mm spark plug per cylinder. A massive 200W generator was fitted, opposite the seven-plate oil-bath clutch, in order to cope with the additional load imposed by various police paraphernalia such as sirens, radios and ancillary lights.

It was always intended that the police Apollo should form the basis of a touring line of highway (or rather freeway) cruisers, which would provide an additional means of recouping the outlay spent on development. The prototype engines were therefore in two stages of tune: one was a 'cooking' version running on 8:1 compression and fitted with a single 24 mm Dell'Orto carburettor for each pair of cylinders, front and rear. This produced 80 bhp at 6000 rpm with a softer cam also fitted, while the Sport version (not that they had races for 1260 cc monsters in those days!) yielded around 100 bhp at 7000 rpm running on 10:1 compression and four 32 mm Dell'Ortos. Maximum safe engine speed was 8000 rpm.

The engine was fitted in a beefy set of cycle parts consisting of a giant-sized version of the Norton Featherbed frame, built around a massive fabricated steering-head from which two tubes also reached down to meet the engine above the camshaft: it would have been necessary to detach the front cylinders in order to remove the engine. Each set of exhaust pipes met below the rear cylinder to form a single tube exiting through a quite small cylindrical silencer: noise was apparently not a problem, however. With telescopic Ceriani suspension front and rear, the handling and ride were certain to be streets ahead of the equivalent from Harley, who had only recently discovered rear suspension, but Ducati decided to go for broke on the comfort stakes by fitting a huge American-style dual seat with chrome grab bar: all that was missing were the tassles and fringes. The resultant mid-Atlantic styling looked curious in the extreme, not helped by a ritzy metallic gold paint job and 'semi-peanut' steel tank perched atop the front frame tubes which looked as if it had been taken from the parts stock for one of the 175 roadsters. High-rise 'ape-hanger' bars, deeply valenced mudguards and fat, specially designed and built 5.00 × 16 Pirelli whitewall tyres not only completed the Italo-American styling but also met the police specification, as did the surprisingly short 60.5 in. wheelbase. The overall styling was so heavy, not improved by the fat car-section tyres, that the Apollo looked much bigger and heavier than it really was: dry weight was just 270 kg thanks to the light alloy engine – just under 600 lb, a comparable figure with today's superbikes and quite a bit lighter than the Z1300 Kawasaki and Munch, the only machines of equivalent capacity since made outside the USA. More important in 1963, the Apollo was also lighter than its iron-barrelled Harley-Davidson rival, though having twice as many cylinders.

Initial tests proved the machine to have an abundance of power, and to meet the performance specifications easily. The prototype was handed

over to Berliner in an official ceremony at Borgo Panigale, and the Ducati development team gave themselves a metaphoric pat on the back for a difficult and unusual job well done. But then alarming stories came filtering back across the Atlantic of test riders nearly killed on high-speed test sessions on banked ovals and long straightaways. What could possibly be wrong? The culprit was the Pirelli tyres, unique to the Apollo. In those days, 20 years ago and more, well before the advent of today's hyperbikes and four years even before the arrival of the Honda 750 four, speeds of 130 plus mph such as the Apollo was capable of were quite beyond the ken of motorcycle road tyre designers, especially when the machine was as heavy as the V4 Ducati. The rear cover in particular would not stand up to the power, and would throw its tread swiftly at sustained speeds over the ton, with imaginable results.

The solution was to detune the engine still further, reducing the compression to 7:1 and

LEFT AND BELOW *The 125 four in its final form, with specially-made Marelli ignition driven off the idler gear in the camshaft drive train. The design had originally been pencilled out by Taglioni in 1952!*

installing softer cams. This lowered the power output to 65 bhp, still quite adequate to meet the requisite performance specifications, and superior to the Harley thanks to the lighter weight.

But this step effectively ruled out the Apollo being sold as a luxury tourer, since its power-to-weight ratio was inferior to the British twins which then dominated the US market, as well as to the BMW range. It had been hoped to market the Apollo in the States at around the $1500 mark for the touring version and about $1800 for the Sport. At that price level, substantially more than the top-of-the-line British twins, the Ducati would have had to boast an additional performance edge to justify its multi-cylinder engine: in detuned version it would not do it. With the V4 set up to deliver the right kind of power, power it was capable of, it would be lethal until tyre technology had caught up with it.

This situation provided the perfect opportunity for the government-controlled bureaucrats in Rome to kill the project off, citing as an excuse the fact that with the machine now only suitable for the specialist police market, its sales would be insufficient to justify the immense tooling costs involved in gearing up the Ducati factory for its production. Berliner, who had already privately demonstrated the prototype to certain selected police chiefs, was appalled. He had promised that production would begin of the reduced-performance version at the start of the following year – 1965 – yet now the project seemed in danger of collapse.

So it turned out to be. In that period at the end of 1964 Italy was in the throes of yet another of its interminable political upheavals which have been a depressing feature of the postwar period. Bologna was then and is now the headquarters of the Italian Communist Party, who as the largest political force in the country have traditionally been the sparring partners of the successive centre-right coalitions led by the Christian Democrats. The latter have since 1945 been the governing party, at eternal log-gerheads with the Communists, with Bologna frequently the battleground. When the government department refused to allocate further funds to the development of the Apollo, citing the tyre problems and the smaller market the bike would now have to be aimed at, there seemed little doubt that political loyalties played a large part in the decision. Montano was reluctantly forced to cancel the project, and today the solitary prototype sits in the Berliner warehouse in New Jersey, a sad reminder of a motorcycle that was killed off by a mixture of government infighting and its own advanced

specification. As an indication of how proud he was and is of the design, the other engine is today on display in Ing. Taglioni's office in the factory, a silent testament to his versatility and farsightedness. For 20 years later, the 90 degree V4 is suddenly in vogue, as each of the Japanese manufacturers fills their model range with variations on that theme. Taglioni and Ducati have cause for wry amusement, as they too work on the new generation of Borgo Panigale product, themselves powered by a V4 engine; it's never a good thing to be *too* far ahead of your time.

Despite its abortive conclusion, the Apollo project had many significant ramifications for Ducati, in both the long and short term. The factory had shown itself capable of designing a large-capacity motorcycle successfully, and the mid-1980s smaller-engined V4 would bear a striking re-semblance to the 1260 cc monster. Before then, as a prophetic article in the Italian *Motociclismo* magazine had suggested a wise move when the existence of the Apollo was first revealed in 1963: one half of the engine in a more European set of cycle parts would make a superb V-twin roadster. Five years after the Apollo's demise, Taglioni proved how right the suggestion had been when the first of the magnificent line of 750 V-twins, based loosely on the Apollo, was unveiled. And it had demonstrated once again the remarkable technical viruosity of Fabio Taglioni.

There was, however, one major penalty: the Apollo project, in spite of Berliner's contribution to the development costs, had cost Ducati dear at a time when they could little afford it. With a large chunk of their investment capital abortively spent without any direct return on the machine's design and the building of the prototype, at the same time that their sales of smaller capacity machines were shrinking, the company was placed in a severe financial bind. Whereas before the government had acted solely as a principal shareholder, leaving the day-to-day operation of the company in the hands of a board of directors who in turn appointed Montano and supervised the running of the company through him, by 1969 the financial situation of Ducati Meccanica (and ironically enough, at the same time, of its great rivals MV Agusta) had become so precarious that financial aid had to be requested from the government in the form of an additional injection of capital. This was forthcoming, but at a price: *direct* government control, with the company henceforth forming part of the giant EFIM organization (Ente Finanzaria per gli Industrie Metalmeccaniche) through which other similar companies in the same branch of engineering were run direct from Rome. Montano retired, having done more than anyone else with the exception of Taglioni to create the world-respected reputation of the Bologna marque, and was replaced by a government-appointed administrator.

There were various political reasons as to why and how this move came about, which are too convoluted to go into here. Suffice it to say that once again it was Bologna's position as the centre of PCI (Italian Communist Party) power that accelerated the government's decision. At the same time, the fact that the company was saved from going under, or falling into the hands of an entrepreneur such as de Tomaso – a fate which later befell the rival Benelli and Guzzi concerns, with greatly differing consequences – was thanks to the PCI's influence and desire to protect the loyal workers of their stronghold.

The move indeed did not have any great immediate effect other than to give the company's employees and its customers a greater sense of security for the future. The V-twin range, then under final development, was still announced and ushered in another golden era on road and track for the Ducati name. But the fortunes of the company would from now on be inextricably linked with political events in the country as a whole and especially in Rome, and the calibre and enthusiasm of the succession of government administrators, appointed in four- to five-year cycles to manage the company, would play a vital part in the future development of Ducati Meccanica SpA. If they were good, the company prospered; when, as we shall see in the disastrous episode of the mid-1970's parallel twins, they were poor, its fortunes ran at a low ebb. It was the Apollo project which more than any other single circumstance contributed to the creation of this situation.

The Spanish-designed MT 250 cc four which Mototrans struggled to develop in the mid-60s. It was a conspicuous failure in spite of the workmanlike manufacture

10

The 1960s – highs and lows

The conscious efforts by Calcagnile and Montano to broaden Ducati's sales horizons in the late 1950s were to dramatically affect the company's future direction and model range in the 1960s.

Though the Italian home market was still of great importance, new vistas began to unfold, particularly in North America, where motorcycling had suddenly become respectable. The 1950's image conveyed in films and magazines of motorcycle gangs terrorizing whole townships under the snarling leadership of Marlon Brando lookalikes mounted on oversize American V-twins festooned with tassles and fringes whose very appearance looked mean and evil, was replaced by a general realization that motorcycle riding was fun, and was by no means a pursuit liable to lead to an early demise at the hands of the National Guard. Led by the Japanese companies, motorcycle manufacturers throughout the world suddenly discovered that North American presented an enormous new market for their products that had hardly been tapped.

The type of product that this new market required was moreover quite different from the traditional American motorcycle which Indian, until its demise in the 1950s, and Harley-Davidson had made for so many years. People who had never ridden a motorbike before were daunted by these monsters, quite apart from the fact that in the eyes of many newcomers to two-wheeled transportation, the big V-twins were irreconcilably stamped with the Brando image: they'd no more be seen dead on one than in a Russian-built car. Both were equally un-American, therefore unacceptable – even though such machines were ironically the sole US-made product of America's last surviving motorcycle manufacturer!

Instead, these newcomers to motorcycling, as well as those more experienced riders looking for more nimble handling and better performance than

that offered by the big Harleys, turned to foreign manufacturers for their purchases. Even Harley were forced to acknowledge this trend by acquiring first a controlling interest, then full ownership of, the Italian Aermacchi factory, whose range of lightweight pushrod roadsters was marketed in the USA as Harley-Davidson Sprints in order to plug the gaping hole in H-D's model range which the new interest in 250 cc and smaller machines had exposed.

The Sprints sold well in the US against their principal competition, which not surprisingly consisted of the Japanese manufacturers, led by Honda; in those early days of the swinging sixties no Oriental manufacturer had yet decided to move up the capacity scale to attack the British twins and singles which dominated the intermediate 500–700 cc class, or the large-capacity Harleys; such a move was inevitable, but had yet to come. Instead, the Japanese concentrated on the smaller classes, where their eventual domination was challenged by the host of smaller European manufacturers who also entered the American market in an effort to grab a slice of the cake for themselves.

Prompted by the Berliners, who were eager to have a 250 cc machine with which to try to carve a niche for themselves in this lightweight market, Ducati at last took the step of introducing their quarter-litre road machine. Since taking on the Ducati franchise in the late 1950s, the Berliner Corporation had come to play an increasingly important role in the direction the Bologna company was heading, highlighted by the saga of the V4 Apollo described in the last chapter. Much of the reason for this had to do with the personalities of the Berliner brothers themselves: of Eastern European immigrant stock, their fast-talking, big-dealing, sharkskin suit and alligator shoe image contrasted vividly with the urbane and courtly manners of Dr. Montano and the shy and retiring

ABOVE *The 200 Super Sports was sold in Britain for £199 0s 0d
in 1964, and was the first model to be imported by Vic
Camp after he took over the British Ducati agency*
LEFT *Dr Giuseppe Montano, key figure in the factory's
success in the 1950s and 60s – urbane and courtly*

have disastrous consequences in the long run for all
concerned, though in the short term, at least, the
Berliners' aggressive marketing techniques secured
for Ducati a much larger slice of the US market than
they would otherwise have acquired. This enabled
them to stand out from the horde of other small
European companies all trying to tilt at the Japanese
windmill.

Ducati's other major export market at the time
seemed set to be Great Britain, where in the wake of
Stan Hailwood's discovery of the firm at the 1958
TT, and son Mike's first appearance on the 125
Ducati at Assen soon after, Hailwood Senior's retail
firm, King's of Oxford, had set up a new British
importer appropriately named Ducati Concessionaires Ltd., round the corner from the
company's Manchester shop. The new enterprise
began trading in 1959, replacing the previous Britax
arrangement which had really only covered the
Cucciolo and anyway had lapsed in 1956, and some
informal interim distribution by amongst others the
sporting dealership of Geoff Monty and Alan
Duley-Ward.

For the first time Ducati motorcycles were
available on an established basis in the UK, and a
range of the factory's home market products was
introduced, most of which were, however, re-
labelled for British buyers. Thus the 125 Monza was

loftiness of Ing. Taglioni. When the Berliners
appeared at Borgo Panigale on one of their periodic
visits, it was, according to one employee of the era,
'as if a team of Las Vegas gamblers had just marched
into the factory'. Such high-rolling, big business,
US-style, blustering ways eventually resulted in
Ducati's US distributor effectively calling the shots
with regard to the company's model line-up and
future development. It was a situation which was to

in fact the Italian market's 125 Sport, while the Monza Super was a sort of stage 2 version with high-compression piston, modified camshaft offering greater lift and dwell, a slightly larger SS1 Dell'Orto racing carburettor and a straight-through exhaust. This version was specially created for the British market and not sold in Italy, and though as expensive as most British 350 cc machines, provided startling performance for so small a bike and made a useful basis for a production racer. A similar exercise was performed with the 175 Sport, which became the Silverstone in Britain and was complemented by the Silverstone Super high-performance version. However, for the serious racer, King's also imported the 125/175 Formula 3 racers, which at a time when the G50 Matchless 500 was available for just under £450 ready for the Isle of Man or Grand Prix racing, went on sale for over £500 to a market that was much less committed to small-capacity racing than was the case in Italy: not surprisingly few of these sohc valve-spring racers were ever sold outside the Latin countries. King's completed their intial range with the 200 Elite, plus its Super Sports version, but neither of these was as fast as the 92 mph 175 Silverstone Super, which was in every way the forerunner of the fabulous 250 Mach 1 – a road-equipped single-cylinder racer with a superior performance to most British 500s.

King's too were pressing Ducati for a full 250 cc machine to complete their range and present effective competition to the British and Japanese factories. Accordingly, as was rapidly becoming standard Ducati practice, Taglioni first designed a racing 250 to provide a testbed for the new model range which would follow. He bored an sohc 175 Gran Sport out to 248.59 mm with the aid of a special 74 mm cast-iron liner. The resultant bike produced 32 bhp at 9000 rpm, and was sent to the USA for trial in local road racing events with Franco Villa aboard. Having won most of its races, many of which were run in conjunction with 500 cc events, which resulted in the little Italian bike beating most of the larger-capacity machines to finish well up in overall placings, the prototype 250 Ducati returned to Italy to be turned into a production roadster. Villa's development abilities had made him an ideal choice to carry out the project and in an astute publicity move, the little bike, though otherwise sporting Gran Sport cycle parts, was fitted with a prototype 250 Diana tank which would later enable the factory to point to its success in improving the breed through competition.

Thus the first Ducati 250 was announced at the Milan Fair in April 1961, beginning the line of narrow-crankcase machines, originally fitted with a four-speed gearbox, that would run through to the introduction of the wide-crankcase version in 1967. True to form, a number of different variations on the same theme were offered, with the basic model known as the 250 Monza, fitted with high bars and a dual seat. Aimed primarily at the US market, it was

Taken from an American advertisement, this Diana has the high bars for that market. Date is 1965, which means 5-speed

The 160 Monza Junior, in 1967 form: a mismatched collection of parts that made a surprisingly peppy little motorcycle

not sold in Britain until the following year, which was just as well, as the model name would have caused some confusion with the 125 Monza already available! The 175 range, incidentally, was discontinued by the factory to make room for production of the new larger-capacity bike, and the 125s went too in the mid-1960s.

The Monza's appearance also marked the introduction of a previously eschewed policy of exaggerated factory power claims which hitherto had been reasonably truthful. Thus the Monza's output, running on standard 8:1 compression with a 24 mm Dell'Orto carburettor, was initially claimed to be 22 bhp at 7200 rpm, rising in 1963 to 24 bhp at 7500 rpm. If true, this would have made it easily the most powerful 250 production bike of the era. (The Mach 1 version was to earn this crown truthfully in future years.) Several magazines fell for the factory's boasts initially before they were forced to modify their figures in the light of harsh realities: the true Monza output was 16.4 bhp at 7500 rpm, measured at the rear wheel and with the carburettor breathing through an air cleaner mounted in the right side

panel. This was sufficient for a top speed of 74 mph for the high-barred American-type version, though it's an interesting example of the confusion surrounding the Ducati range at the time that the 250 Monza tested by *Cycle World* in the USA in 1963 was fitted by Berliner with a 30 mm SS1 Dell'Orto in a presumed effort to cook the test figures, but could only manage 77 mph, a disappointing performance considering the 24 bhp reportedly on tap!

The Monza was complemented in Europe by the Diana, a sportier version of the same 74 × 57.8 mm basic model with a similar mechanical specification, apart from the fitting of a slightly less restrictive silencer, which was actually the result of a styling move, but with the adoption of a slimline fuel tank and narrow clip-ons. This machine was marketed in Britain as the Daytona, continuing Ducati Concessionaires' theme of naming the majority of their models after racing circuits, and was good for a top speed of just on 80 mph (128 km/h in Italian tests of the time). Though it was never actually designated as such by the factory, it will remove some confusion if we refer to these models as the Diana Mark 1 (the high-barred Monza, the slowest of the range), and the Diana Mark 2 (the clip-on version,

ABOVE *A 250 Daytona GT on test for* Motor Cycle *in June 1965. Note the swan's neck clip-ons and typically Italian rocking pedal gearchange*

BELOW *The 98 cc Cadet with fan-cooled engine; this bike formed part of the shipment of Ducatis with which Bill Hannah flooded Britain in the late 60s*

known as the Daytona in Britain).

The 250 range sported a new bottom-end assembly and revised crankcases, though maintaining the same general layout which had characterized the previous range of four-stroke Ducati singles. This revised design had actually been introduced in 1960 without any fanfare on the 'B' series 204 Elite, and featured a longer crankshaft and wider flywheel on the left-hand (generator) side, whereas before the flywheels and crankpin had been the same size on either side. A revised clutch housing for ease of removal of the clutch bearings during an overhaul was also incorporated and the all-alloy engines by now featured polished end covers on all models. The new 250 also required new head and barrel castings to accommodate the wider bore, with a longer camshaft fitted as a consequence. Thus for the first time the chunky, heavily finned look which characterized the later Ducati singles as mean and purposeful machines came into being, once leading the engine to be colourfully described as like a gnarled giant's fist clenched in anger! The 250 Ducatis did inspire that kind of romantic hyperbole. . . .

Ignition was by means of a 6V Ducati Elettronica flywheel alternator, feeding a battery and coil to the single plug. The four-speed gearbox as usual featured unit construction, with a helical gear primary, and was actuated by the traditional Italian rocking pedal on the right. The multi-plate (13 in all) oil-bath clutch was externally adjustable via the usual oval cover on the left, and just above it and to the rear a substantial crankcase breather ventilated into the left-hand side cover, which also contained a tool box. The single overhead camshaft was once again driven by a vertical shaft and bevel gears off the crankshaft, which used roller and ball bearings throughout. Though coil spring conversions were sometimes fitted later to permit use of lumpier cams for competition use, the Ducati road singles always employed hairpin valve springs. A left-foot kick-start was a bone of contention throughout the singles' production run, not least in the USA, where the right foot was traditionally employed for this purpose.

The 250 frame followed the same basic format as the earlier singles, consisting of a curved main single-tube backbone running from the steering head to the rear of the engine, where it met the swinging arm pivot and was heavily braced at that point. Another down-tube ran from the gusseted steering head down to the front of the engine, gripping the crankcase by a pair of lugs. The result was a light and rigid assembly that was effectively a single-loop frame employing the engine as a semi-stressed member, and whose excellent handling properties became legendary on road or track, even with highly tuned engines turning out 50 per cent more power than the original Monza version. Eighteen-inch rims with 2.75/3.00 tyres were fitted, with full-width sls brakes more than adequate to stop the light 292 lb machine whose 52 in. wheelbase ensured finger-light steering.

It was inevitable that the new 250 would appeal to the sporting owner, and indeed Ducati had intended this from the beginning. Accordingly an uprated version entitled the Diana Mark 3 was introduced in 1963, initially for the US market only, where it was at first known as the Diana Mark 3 Super Sport before the resultant mouthful was abbreviated. Though nominally a road model complete with quickly detachable front and rear lights, this was clearly intended as a dual-purpose machine. Its standard equipment also included not only clip-ons for the first time on a US model, but also a 30 mm Dell'Orto racing carburettor, 10:1 lightweight piston, an uprated camshaft, megaphone exhaust, a separately mounted rev-counter (the road bike's speedometer was mounted in the headlamp, so automatically discarded along with the lights), racing tyres, quick-release fuel cap, abbreviated mudguards and, as a standard fitment, competition number plates. A flywheel magneto replaced the previous battery and coil, and 30 bhp was claimed at a maximum 8300 rpm. This was sufficient to propel the 265 lb bike to a top speed of 104 mph in a carefully monitored *Cycle World* track test, which also saw the four-speed machine cover the standing $\frac{1}{4}$-mile in 16.5 seconds with a terminal speed of 79.5 mph. Even a TD-1 Yamaha racer tested by the same magazine that year was unable to match the Ducati's top speed, and no other road-legal bike could compare with its performance: it was now indeed the fastest 250 cc street bike in the world.

An optional racing kit with 9.2:1 piston, 27 mm carburettor and megaphone exhaust had been marketed in the UK since the 250's launch in 1962, but it was to be 1964 before a European version of the US-specification Diana Mark 3 was to become available as a complete bike. This situation was remedied in September that year when the legendary Ducati 250 Mach 1 was introduced, offering the same sort of specification as the Diana Mark 3 of 1963, but with heavier valve springs, solid rockers with shim adjustment, a 29 mm carburettor with matching inlet tract, larger 40 mm inlet and 36 mm exhaust valves and the priceless advantage of a

five-speed gearbox. This had actually been introduced in May 1964 on the Monza 'touring' and Scrambler versions, a surprising move in view of the fact that the Mark 3 Diana would have benefited from it more.

The Mach 1 offered Europeans a genuine 100 mph 250 for the first time, and its raw-edged performance, hairline handling and raucous exhaust note marked it as one of the great street motorcycles of all time. A 1960s equivalent of the BSA Clubmans Gold Star of the previous decade or the Inter Norton of the pre-war or immediate postwar era, it shared with these British street-racing singles the same reluctance to idle at less than 2000 rpm without continual blips of the throttle at standstill, thanks to the lumpy cams, whose overlap was actually greater than that of a standard Manx Norton of 7R AJS! Yet the Mach 1 achieved with only 250 cc the same sort of performance that the bigger bikes did with increased cubic capacity, aided notably by the light weight – only 255 lb with oil but no fuel – and skinny profile: top speed on standard gearing was 94 mph with the rider sitting up, but 106 mph with him lying prone on the tank. The five-speed box was a great boon in improving acceleration, with 4th and 5th particularly close at 6.10 and 5.38 respectively, giving a drop in revs of only 500 rpm when changing up. Indeed, the same top and bottom gear ratios were employed as on the four-speed version and the increased acceleration this afforded put the little machine on a par with others of twice its displacement. Claimed power output was 27.6 bhp at 8500 rpm (Berliner boasted of 30 bhp at 8300!), but a more realistic figure appears to have been 24 bhp at 8200; whatever the case, there was no doubting the Mach 1's appeal.

With the decline in the personal connection between Stan Hailwood and the Ducati factory, once Mike began riding for Honda and MV Agusta, Ducati Concessionaires gradually lost interest in promoting the marque's sales on an active basis, and in the winter of 1965–66 the firm was wound up. Into the resultant breach stepped their most successful dealer, Vic Camp of Walthamstow in East London, who took over the Ducati distributorship for the UK and ran it on a most enthusiastic basis, together with his wife Rose and foreman Bert

Throughout the 1960s and early 1970s, Ducati produced a bimonthly news sheet which dealt with all their activities. This issue from May 1967 shows not only their motorcycle involvement, but also their role as Triumph car importers for Italy, and their activities in the light industrial engine and outboard motor field. The 'new' Cucciolo was actually a two-stroke marine engine

Furness, till he was unceremoniously dumped by the factory in 1973. Camp was largely responsible for the dedicated following which Ducati built up in Britain, and while appreciating the need for a larger organization than his to handle what it was hoped would be the greater sales of the big V-twins, his treatment on the part of the Ducati factory's government-appointed administrators was on occasions shabby in the extreme.

Vic Camp made Britain the Mach 1's leading market by an ingenious combination of customizing and enthusiasm. He became actively involved in racing, and the sight of the little 250 singles humbling much larger machines in long-distance racing, as well as dominating their classes in short-circuit events, swayed many potential buyers towards purchasing one for themselves. Camp also offered a large variety of extras which the speed-conscious owner could fit to his bike. These included alloy rims, wider section, grippier tyres (standard covers were only 2.50 and 2.75 section front and rear), racing seats with raised backs, a single-pedal gear lever to replace the Italian rocking one, rubber-mounted rev-counters (only a speedo was fitted as original equipment) and folding footrests, which went some way towards reducing the size of the indentation every Ducati owner displayed on his left leg as a result of rapping his shin on the footrest when kick starting the 10:1 engine.

The Mach 1's modifications were carried over into the Diana Mark 3 for the US market, and the five-speed gearbox made the model even more competitive in North American club racing than had been the case to date. However, curiously, the US model was now fitted with high-rise bars instead of the clip-ons, and a 27 mm carburettor instead of the European version's 29 mm unit. Other aspects of the specification were the same, and most owners simply junked the bars anyway and fitted larger carbs if they were going racing. The Monza continued as the basic model in the USA, but for some reason it was felt necessary to introduce an even softer degree of tune to the 250 range for Europe, in the form of the 250GT. Fitted with high bars American-style, this had the 8:1 engine with a 24 mm carb, and thanks to a very timid camshaft yielded 18.4 bhp at 7200 rpm; its principal aim was presumably the ride-to-work market.

At the same time Ducati had made long overdue inroads into the booming offroad scene with a Street Scrambler model that first appeared in 200 cc form in 1959. The 200 Motocross, as it was known, was a true forerunner of today's dual-purpose machines, though slanted towards tarmac use with its street frame strengthened for off-road use, conical 180 mm brakes, a sump guard, high bars, a 2.75 × 21 front tyre mated to a 3.00 × 19 rear, both fitted with knobbly tyres, and an upswept exhaust with minimal lip service paid to silencing. The engine was actually not that of the Elite, in spite of the model designation, but a detuned version of the 175 Sport with a scrambles cam which gave excellent low-down torque and yielded 18.5 bhp – more with some attention paid to tuning. At least one was converted to trials use in Britain, where it performed with credit against Tiger Cubs and the like.

The Motocross was offered in Britain for a very short time in 1959 only, but in Italy and the USA it

A publicity photo from the mid-60s, featuring the Piuma moped and disastrous Brio scooter. Many would have felt that the best thing to have done with the latter would have been to heave it into the water!

achieved a degree of popularity that led the factory to realize that they had somewhat inadvertently touched on a segment of the market with strong potential. Berliner realized this too, but felt the US market demanded a more serious, larger-capacity machine, and the announcement of the 250 model line in 1961 was the prelude to such a bike. This was the delightful Ducati Scrambler, employing a modified version of the 250 road frame fitted with 19 in. wheels, alloy guards and slightly longer-travel suspension. The engine was a half-way house between the Monza/Diana and Diana Mark 3, running on 9:1 compression and using a scrambles cam, with modified internal gearing on the standard four-speed box giving a top speed of 82 mph; Berliner claimed the magical 30 bhp figure again, but in reality this was around 22 bhp at 7500 rpm, and a 27 mm carburettor and flywheel magneto ignition were fitted as standard rather than available as optional extras. None the less, a wide range of extras was available to prospective owners, including in the US a pair of rigid frame members to replace the suspension units for flat track racing. In truth, the 250 Scrambler was much more of a competition bike than a road one, in contrast to the 200 Moto Cross and the later Street Scramblers which followed. The five-speed gearbox was introduced on the model in 1964, and the larger valves of the Mach 1 followed soon after. The only drawback to the bike from the point of view of serious competition use were the large-diameter road brakes which the Scrambler shared with the Mach 1. They were much too big to get thoroughly warmed up in dirt use, and many owners replaced them with smaller units to avoid grabbing problems associated with overbraking: of course, the flat trackers removed them altogether! Vic Camp went so far as to commission a short run of special Hagon frames for grass track use in the late 1960s, and with 250, 350 and 450 engines fitted the Camp-Hagon Ducatis enjoyed much success for a number of years in British events, with the engines fitted with high-compression pistons and running on methanol.

Ducati's success in North America, and to a lesser extent in other export markets such as Britain, Australia, Germany and so on, provided the basis of an expansionist policy at Borgo Panigale, and not only concentrating exclusively on motorcycles. Remarkably by 1965 Ducati Meccanica SpA was the Italian distributor for Standard-Triumph cars and Leyland vans and trucks, and a mid-1960s publicity photograph shows a fleet of Triumph Herald vans lined up outside the factory gates painted in red and white livery and lettered with Ducati

A well-restored Mach 1 seen on the Isle of Man in 1983. Note the bolt-on Smiths rev-counter, standard equipment for the British market

Meccanica's emblem. These were the service vans, carrying spares and technical assistance to the two dozen or so dealers in Italy whom the firm had appointed to sell Triumph Vitesse and Herald saloons and convertibles. Another profitable line was the range of Penta outboard engines, for which again Ducati were Italian agents, and this tied in with an increasingly important sector of the company's own manufacturing plan, covering industrial engines and generators, mostly of the small to medium diesel variety. In due course this side of the firm would not only overtake the motorcycle manufacturing area but would save the company from financial self-destruction, and end up subsidizing the continued production of complete two-wheeled vehicles.

Those days were still relatively far off in 1965, but the seeds of destruction were already being sown. Mention has already been made of the 50 cc two-stroke line, with the same piston-port 38 × 42 mm 47.6 cc engine producing anywhere from 0.92 bhp at 4600 rpm in the basic single-speed moped called the Brisk (which must have been some kind of in-joke, because it wasn't) up to a claimed 4.2 bhp at 8600 rpm in the three-speed 48 Sport Piuma, a quite attractive little boy racer with clip-ons, knobbly tank and racing seat. These Ducati two-strokes were indeed raced with some considerable success in their homeland, but though the company's concessionaires, especially Berliner, tried hard to sell them abroad, it was next to impossible: the market just wasn't there. The engine was even bored out to 80 cc for a short time, without any resultant success in that form either.

Even more disastrous was another attack on the scooter market, as if the experience of the ill-fated

The first Ducati Street Scrambler – the 1959 200 cc model was in style and concept years ahead of its time

Cruiser of the early 1950s had been completely forgotten. Perhaps Ducati felt that their name was now so well established that it would be sufficient to sell the new model on its own: they were to be proved sadly wrong. When the Brio was introduced in November 1963 even the normally sycophantic sections of the Italian press were hard put to make suitably laudatory noises, for the simple fact of the matter was that the thing was a stone. A slightly modified version of the Brisk/Piuma unit, produced a miserly 1.3 bhp at 4300 rpm yet this tiny output was considered adequate to drag along a fully enclosed scooter – fitted with a pillion seat – weighing 63 kg dry. No wonder the top speed was but 24 mph; even getting the snail to crawl that fast on its 7:1 compression ratio was a major feat, and acceleration off the traffic light grid, always a strong selling point in the home market, was termed 'disappointing' by the few magazines who bothered to road test it. The full enclosure of the engine required the use of a fan to cool the cylinder, driven by an alloy plate bolted to the flywheel magneto rotor. The same engine was also used somewhat more successfully in a roadster motorcycle and a trail bike, called the Cacciatore (hunter), though for what reason it was felt necessary to fit the fan cooling on a machine where the engine sat clearly exposed to the slipstream is unclear. All three machines had a hand change to the three-speed gearbox, located in the left twistgrip.

In short order the failings of the 50 cc Brio's power-to-weight ratio were recognized. Almost none at all had been sold resulting in a stock of undelivered machines that enabled the model to be offered until 1968; the engine capacity was doubled in 1965 to 100 cc. This produced 6 bhp at 5200 rpm and fitted to the scooter gave at least a respectable performance, and the Cadet roadster and Mountaineer trail model similarly benefited. But the fact that both 50 and 100 cc versions of the same bikes were featured in the Ducati catalogue during the middle 1960s at the same time, as well as the 50 cc air-cooled/non-fan range, *and* the four-stroke road singles, indicates a lack of rationalization that was bound to spell disaster. Instead of concentrating on a well-developed line of sporting four-strokes, the factory allowed themselves to be deluded into mounting attacks on market sectors of which they had little recent experience and no chance of success. Far better to have concentrated on what they could do as well as anybody and better than most. Taglioni obviously thought so: he refused to have anything to do with the two-strokes and instead busied himself with future plans that would shortly bear fruit.

The first such harvest arrived in 1965, when the largest-capacity Ducati yet made first appeared in

99

March that year: the 350 Sebring. Once again a racing 350 was constructed first, and tried out in competition before the road version was released to the public. The theatre for the bike's inaugural appearance was again the USA, since this was supposed to be the principal market for a bigger machine, and Berliner had been instrumental in persuading the factory to move up the capacity scale. Originally it was intended to produce a 350 single and a 500 pushrod twin (dealt with in a separate chapter), but once the latter's failings had been mercilessly exposed at a sneak preview to the press and dealers at Daytona in March 1965, it was shelved for the time being, and all efforts, both technical and marketing, concentrated on the 350 single. Happily, the week after Daytona Farne obliged by giving the 350 racer a class win first time out at the FIM international races run in conjunction with the 12-hour car event at Sebring, in Central Florida; the AMA, who ran the Daytona 200, were not then affiliated to the FIM, who sanctioned a different club to put on a contrasting event. It did not posses a fraction of the charisma of the banked speedway's races. A book could be written about the politics of American motorcycle sport during that period, but suffice it to say that the 350 class was not usually well supported in the USA, only in Canada, and hence the few bikes around were forced to run with the 500s and 750s for a separate award. Thus it was that Franco Farne, who'd returned to America especially for the Sebring race with the new bike, found himself finishing 11th overall in an event catering for 251–750 cc machines, but the fact of his winning the 350 class handsomely enabled Ducati, and particularly Berliner, to name the new road model the 350 Sebring.

The 350 engine was not, as might have been expected, achieved by simply overboring the 250 single; instead the new engine had a different bore and stroke of 76 × 75 mm, measuring 340.2 cc. The almost 'square' dimensions were uncharacteristic for a Taglioni design, and showed that his intentions for the new unit lay in touring and off-road use rather than creating a high-revving roadburner. Indeed, the Sebring was only available for the first few years of its run in a very soft state of tune; running on 8.5:1 compression, it produced a claimed 20 bhp at 6250 rpm, which combined with a dry weight of 270 lb, slightly heavier than the 250 single, yielded less than sparkling acceleration and a top speed of only 125 km/h – just under 80 mph. The 350's performance was just about equal to the 250 Monza, and some way inferior to the Mach 1.

At the same time another new model was

Actually photographed in Bologna but for the Americans. Mach 3 on the left, Mach 1 on the right

160 Monza Junior ready for the American college kids for whom it was created

introduced, almost entirely at Berliner's insistence, and indeed it was only ever really marketed seriously in the USA at first: the 160 Monza Junior. This effectively replaced the now defunct 175, and was supposed to represent an economical run-around catering for the novice rider, though one might have considered the 250GT to represent all that was required in this field. here was yet another example of unnecessary model proliferation, whose only purpose seemed to be to allow Berliner to claim in its advertising of the period that 'Ducati has a model for every rider!' Maybe so, but were there riders for every model? A soon-to-be-enacted scenario would appear to indicate not.

The 160 Monza Junior was announced at the same time as the Sebring in early 1965, and effectively consisted of a small-scale version of the 250GT engine in the same frame as the larger-engined bike. The unit measured 61 × 52.5 mm, for a total displacement of 156 cc, but apart from a lack of finning on the sump and rocker covers, and the use of the old-type four-speed gearbox, there were no other differences from the 250 engine. The smaller unit looked rather lost in the open frame, which was clearly too big for it, especially when mated to 16 in. wheels front and rear and 30 mm front forks from the 98 cc pushrod Bronco. In a final act of mismatching, the mudguards were clearly designed for 18 in. rims, so that the whole bike was a real 'committee' job, whose members were the storeroom staff rather than the company's engineers. It looked as if it was built out of spare parts, and it probably was.

The 16 in. wheels fitted to a frame designed for 18 in. rims produced an odd steering effect, particularly when matched to the standard American-spec high bars; replacing these with a set of flat bars (the fork shrouds didn't permit the use of clip-ons) improved the feel greatly. And the 160 was indeed economical, its 22 mm concentric Dell'Orto yielding over 90 mpg, not bad for an ohc engine fitted in a bike weighing just under 250 lb dry.

In 1967 Ducati revamped the 250 model line by producing a wide-crankcase version, whose improvements were also incorporated into the Sebring. Before this some attempt at rationalization had taken place, but ludicrously it was the one model which had any distinction which disappeared: the Mach 1. This was phased out at the end of 1966, having only been made for two years, and was replaced by a Europeanized version of the Diana Mark 3, called simply the Mark 3, but fitted with the battery and coil ignition off the Mach 1. An increase in compression ratio to 10.25:1 and an extra 1 mm lift on the camshaft raised the 250 valve-spring's output to just over 28 bhp at 8500 rpm, with a corresponding increase in performance, but sadly the Mark 3 European version did not have the Mach 1's racy seat and rearset footrests.

The new-style wide-case engine appeared at the end of 1967, and was introduced to iron out some of the design defects which had become apparent over

ABOVE *Mike Berliner posing on a 450 Scrambler prototype in the late 60s*

RIGHT *Spaggiari about to set off for a lap of the Modena track on a prototype 450 Street Scrambler in July 1968 (Zagari)*

the years on the older narrow-crankcase models. Chief amongst these was the kickstart mechanism, especially on the five-speed version, which broke its gears with regularity and was responsible for several gearbox warranty claims. Also, it was deemed necessary to increase the sump's oil capacity from 4 to 5½ pints, as well as to redesign the bottom end slightly for increased rigidity, though the crankshaft still ran in two ball bearings, but with the drive-side bearing slightly enlarged with a caged roller big end of increased diameter. The frame too was beefed up slightly with a twin loop rear section replacing the single rear down-tube for extra strength, and tyre section on the Mark 3 increased over the Mach 1 and narrow-crankcase Mark 3 from 2.50/2.75 to 2.75/3.00. The wheelbase was still 53 in., but the weight had increased dramatically, the Mark 3 sports model now scaling 280 lb dry. Apart from this penalty, which naturally took the edge off the performance, the redesigned 250 was a great improvement over the previous models, both from the point of view of handling, which was not quite so knife-edge, and reliability; the electrics particularly had come in for some attention, and were now if not exactly perfect, at least acceptable. On the competition side, though, the new machine was over-engineered compared to the Mach 1, which continued to be the first choice of the racing *Ducatisti*.

First deliveries of the new engine began in early 1968, though as an indication of market trends of the time it was not the road version which comprised the first batch but the 350 Street Scrambler, consisting of the five-speed Sebring engine fitted in a new, more street-than-scrambles-oriented set of cycle parts with long-travel rear suspension and 19 in. front rims. A 250 version followed soon after, and then the road bikes, all with the new-style engine whose crankcases were claimed to have been directly developed from the Formula 2 racers of 1964, though in truth this was not so. The North American press release heralding the new range also was at pains to point out that 'a number of Berliner-inspired changes, aimed directly at the American motorcycle market, are incorporated in the '68 Ducati presentation'. Maybe, but these were most assuredly not of an engineering nature, but consisted of a variety of styling exercises on the same theme, such as the Street Scramblers and the poor old Diana Mark 3, which now looked distinctly ill at ease with a racing number plate bolted in front of the headlamp, contrasting awkwardly with the semi ape-hanger handlebars clamped to the top of the fork stanchions.

But as usual Ing. Taglioni was about to resolve the identity crisis that the range of 250/350 singles was experiencing with an engineering coup: the first

The 450 SS in final production form: at one point in the early 70s it was Ducati's best-selling model

production road motorcycle with desmodromic valve-gear. Whereas in the 1950s such a concept would have resulted in a horrendously expensive product which could never have been sold economically – hence the confinement of the desmodromic principle to the factory's own racing machines and those built especially for the Hailwoods – by the mid-1960s production techniques had advanced to the point that a road desmo could be seriously considered, since the fine tolerances necessary for successful desmodromics could be achieved on a series production basis with the new generation of machine tools.

A hint that something of the kind was in the wind was given by the appearance of Farne in the 250 race at the early Modena meeting in April 1966 with a factory-entered prototype racer fitted with an experimental desmodromic head. The engine was identical to the Mach 1 from the cylinder head down, with a wet clutch and five-speed gearbox, and though fitted in a racing frame not dissimilar to the abortive 125 four, which was also being developed at that time, was evidently capable of slotting straight into the current road bike frame. The remarkably light weight of 87 kg was claimed, with a power output of 32 bhp at 10,500 rpm, and though Farne retired from the race with unspecified problems after failing to make much of an impression, the word was out: Dr. T was up to something again.

A year went by without further developments before the desmo single reappeared at Modena exactly 12 months later in 1967, with Roberto Gallina and Gilberto Parlotti aboard 250 and 350 versions. A more intensive season of development racing followed, described more fully in the next chapter, with the factory telling interested parties that the desmo head would be available on an over-the-counter basis for fitment to customers' valve-spring bikes as a racing modiciation. This may indeed have been the intention at one time, but Taglioni was intent on seeing a production road bike put on sale with a desmodromic head – the ultimate affirmation of the principle of positive valve control he had espoused since his earliest days as a qualified engineer in the late 1940s. Dr. T, as he was by now becoming known on the other side of the Atlantic, even though his correct qualification is *Ingenere* rather than *Dottore*, had his way and in January 1968 plans were announced to build and market the Mark 3D – D for Desmodromic.

However, as was to be the case even more frequently in the future, a long time lay between promise and fulfilment – almost exactly one year, in fact. Ducati were being particularly cautious in perfecting the new engine, since with such a revolutionary concept in production terms being made available for the first time to the everyday rider they could even less afford to have the design develop any post-delivery snags. Another development season of racing, this time with Spaggiari aboard, took place in 1968, and for the first time the Ducati name appeared in the list of 500 cc class runners, with a 450 cc single-cylinder desmo prototype making its appearance to good effect against the MV and Benelli multis and the Linto and Paton twins.

At last at the beginning of 1969 the long-awaited desmos were to be seen in noticeable quantities on the roads of Europe and America, sharing the same set of cycle parts as the valve-spring Mark 3, which continued in production in both 250 and 350 wide-crankcase form; the Sebring denomination had been largely dropped, though it was retained in some markets by the local importer. In contrast to the ultra-lightweight singles and desmo twin racers of yore, the new desmo single used a single overhead camshaft to control the actuation of the two valves, rather than the triple-camshaft arrangement Taglioni had employed previously. Thus all four closing and opening lobes were mounted on the same shaft, in a similar system to the Mercedes-Benz racing car one but with the rockers mounted on separate shafts rather than scissor-type ones. Lightweight hairpin springs were fitted to close the valves the last couple of thou for ease of starting, a practice which had been dispensed with for the 125 desmo singles but retained on the twins. The only obstacle therefore to kickstarting a 250 road desmo was the 10:1 compression ratio, slightly detuned from the later Mark 3 valve-springers (9.5:1 on the 350 desmo). Surprisingly, the same 80 degree valve angle which had been employed by Taglioni ever since the Marianna had first appeared was retained

for the desmo roadsters, even though this was by now recognized to be less than ideal in terms of cylinder filling and combustion.

The Mark 3 had been somewhat detuned by the time the 250 desmo arrived on the market, so that there was a much greater distinction between the two types of machine. Most notable was the rev limit, which with positive valve control was 9500 rpm on the 250 but only 7800 rpm on the valve-spring bike. But it was the 350 version which benefited most from the desmo head, transforming a previously rather sluggardly machine into a much more sporting one, but not without some work on the owner's part. Once again the factory were less than accurate regarding output figures, claiming 35 bhp for the 350 desmo at 7500 rpm. In fact, the true power figure was 30 bhp at the crankshaft at 8000 rpm, translating to 24.5 bhp at the rear wheel, but this was insufficient to pull top gear in standard form with the silencer fitted. An open or cored exhaust worked wonders, giving peak revs of 8500 rpm and a top speed of 109 mph: little wonder that many owners got to work on the exhaust in the search for the bike's real performance. Maximum torque was achieved at only 4000 rpm, making the bike a real delight to ride and recapturing much of the Mach 1's old charm.

Though not announced at the same time, a larger-capacity version followed shortly after, when the wraps came off the 450 Ducati range in January 1969. Based on Spaggiari's racing prototype, this was theoretically an overbored 350, measuring 86 × 75 mm for a total capacity of 435.7 cc, but in practice few major parts were interchangeable with the smaller bike. Some surprise was registered that Ducati had not gone the whole hog and produced a full 500, but there were two reasons for this. Firstly, it was still hoped to introduce the 500 pushrod twin, which made its reappearance in rethought form at the same US dealer get-together at Bologna in late 1968 at which the 450 was shown for the first time;

LEFT *250 Mark 3 (or as often as not Mk III) of 1965–66. Note large bore crankcase breather and awkward kickstart*

RIGHT *One of the 350 Sebrings imported into the UK by Hannah. In spite of its extra capacity the model was not as perky as the 250 Mach 1*

and secondly the single-cylinder design could not be taken out any further as the throw of the crankshaft only just missed the gearbox pinions in 436 cc form. For this reason it's impossible to increase the capacity of a 450 to appreciably more than its standard dimension. Because of the theoretically impending twin, Ducati could not afford to redesign and retool the single-cylinder engine to make a full 500, though in retrospect it is generally considered that this was a big mistake. Taglioni at any rate had already prepared the necessary drawings for such a model.

The 450's principal reason for existence was not, however, for use in the street bikes but to power Ducati's most successful dual-purpose motorcycle yet – the 450 Street Scrambler. Though the 450 desmo was a true 100 mph bike in standard form with silencer fitted (reaching 111 mph with a megaphone) and with a dry weight of only 291 lb it was every bit as much fun to ride as the smaller bikes, the increased sales tax that it attracted in many countries, not least its home land, as well as higher insurance premiums and greater thirst which its owner could expect made it a less attractive proposition than its smaller brothers, and it never

ABOVE *The head of a 250 Monza with the covers removed. Hairpin valve springs were employed on all non-desmo singles till the end in 1974*

sold as well. There was the feeling that it just wasn't a 'real' 500, and though it could out-perform many bikes of up to 650 cc, including most of the legendary British singles, the *ducatisti* just didn't take to it.

The Scrambler was a different story. Originally conceived as a US-market model aimed four-square at the British dirt dinosaurs such as the Matchless 500 singles and Triumph twins, its most direct competitor was in fact the 441 cc BSA Victor. But an even more surprising fact was the way that other markets, and particularly the Italian home one, took the 450 Street Scrambler to their hearts. In the 1970–71 period it was Ducati's best-selling model, and though it was never as effective a dirt tool as it was at home on the tarmac, it was in every way the most successful forerunner of the modern trail bikes which every Japanese manufacturer offers today with great success. Indeed, it is unlikely that Ducati would have survived into the 1970s without the success of the Street Scrambler, which was soon available in Europe in both 250 and 350 versions as well as the bigger 450.

The reason for the company's financial decline in the latter half of the 1960s was its near-absolute dependence on the strength of the US market for its corporate health. While that market was still relatively unsophisticated, both from a product and marketing standpoint, Berliner and Ducati prospered. As the market changed, Berliner became confused, and started peppering off shots, in the form of new models and different versions of the same machine, in all directions, hoping that some at least would hit the target. The fact that some did, to a lesser or greater degree, was insufficient to compensate for all the duds like the Brio and Cadet, with the result that stocks of unsold and unsaleable models mounted on both sides of the water, tying up precious capital and preventing the development of new models. It was a vicious circle which it seemed impossible to break and stay in business, and with the Japanese companies intensifying their sales efforts with an ever-widening range of models, the future looked grim indeed.

The British scene was completely different, and provided an object lesson on how the North American operation should have been run. Instead of dreaming big dreams, Vic Camp concentrated on attacking a narrow section of the market, which in due course he made Ducati's own, though unfortunately he was not permitted to reap the full benefits of this astute plan. Recognizing that Ducati was an enthusiast's motorcycle in the sporting mould, he concentrated on the performance versions of the 250/350 singles (and later the 450), and in doing so not only laid the basis for Ducati's future reputation in Britain but also sold a lot of motorcycles into the bargain. What's more, he made money on every one of them, and only brought in the occasional example of one of the other models as a curiosity to spice up interest in the marque. Berliner should have paid Camp's way to America to give them an object lesson in market awareness.

Instead, they did their best, together with the parent factory, to put him out of business. By 1967 the results of a proliferation of unsaleable models, coupled with increasing Japanese market penetration, brought both Berliner and Ducati to the edge of a financial abyss. The 160 Monza Junior had proved to be a predictable flop in the US market for which it was designed, and yet another large shipment totalling 3400 bikes was about to leave Italy. This comprized a mixture of 160s, 100 Cadets and Brio scooters, as well as of Camp's staple diet of 350 Sebrings, 250 Monzas and 250 Diana Mark 3s. The Berliner Corporation was now experiencing cash-flow problems, with large unsold stocks of many models, but they tried hard not to let this fact become apparent to the Ducati factory, and especially not to lose face by being forced to admit that they'd misread the market and had got Ducati to produce models that nobody would buy. Though the shipment should have been paid for before sailing from Genoa, it was in the middle of the Atlantic on the high seas before the alarm bells started ringing at Borgo Panigale.

The official version later became that Berliner had refused shipment of the bikes because of market saturation; the simple fact was that they just couldn't pay for them. The situation had repercussions far beyond the USA and Bologna, for Berliner were also US distributors for Associated Motor Cycles of Plumstead, E. London, then manufacturers of Norton, Matchless and AJS machines. In the spring of 1967, when this scenario began to be acted out, Berliner informed the British board that they no longer required any further supplies of their motorcycles. Since AMC was itself in a parlous financial state and had already called in the receiver before becoming part of the Manganese Bronze group in September 1966, this was bad news indeed. The reason Berliner gave was that they were first committed to disposing of the unwanted Ducati shipment before they were able to resume receipt of the British products. In these circumstances, the AMC (or to be strictly accurate the Norton Matchless Ltd) board were vitally interested in

ABOVE *The valvespring singles all became known as Mark 3s in the 1970s, in the standardised colour of mid-blue with a gold panel. This is a 1973 model*

BELOW *By contrast, the desmos were all finished in yellow in 1973–74, with lean styling thanks to Tartarini. This is a 1974, with disc front brake to use up components left over after an early run of 750 V-twins (Nutting)*

finding a buyer for the Berliner Ducati shipment.

That buyer turned out to be British, in the shape of Liverpool entrepreneur Bill Hannah, who negotiated a deal with Berliner to relieve them of their embarrassment. He had the 3400 bikes shipped to Liverpool, and even though Vic Camp was the official Ducati importer for the UK, set up a rival sales organization to dispose of the US-specification bikes. Having recently begun to sponsor the Italian Paton team in GP racing, Hannah's name was well publicized in the motorcycle press of the time, and though he had no retail motorcycle experience was smart enough to employ people who did. A fast-talking high-roller in the Las Vegas mould, Hannah soon had the British market flooded with cheap Ducatis, and Camp's sales sunk to a very low ebb. In fact, the whole Berliner deal would be only one of several Hannah transactions later investigated by the British tax authorities, of whom Hannah ran afoul in the 1970s.

How did Hannah get to hear of the bikes? The most likely means has been recently identified by British Ducati expert Mick Walker, thanks to some correspondence he possesses between Berliner and AMC, and seems to be that Norton Matchless Ltd set about finding a buyer for the unwanted shipment. Whatever the case, the whole saga was to undermine the sales of Ducatis in Britain for some years, and since Hannah's organization had no direct links with the factory, spares for some of the

models (especially the Brio and Cadet) were literally unobtainable in the UK. Hannah had bought only complete motorcycles, without spare parts. The only way he could satisfy the demand for these was either to buy them wholesale in Italy or else to break up unsold examples of the model in his Liverpool warehouse. His minions usually chose the latter – but when there were no more Brios left, for example, with cooling fan rotors, that as far as the unlucky owner was concerned, was that. It was a most unsavoury and unsatisfactory situation, which the Ducati factory studiously refrained from becoming involved in directly.

One reason they did so was that they had been edging ever closer to the abyss themselves, and with the abrupt decline in the American market were facing a major financial crisis which threatened to engulf the company terminally. The situation could only be resolved by the creation of the EFIM government holding company already referred to previously, which meant in effect direct government control over the day-to-day operation of the factory, via a government-appointed administrator whose independent powers were a fraction of what Montano's had been. Sadly, Dr. Montano retired from the company he had been so instrumental in building up from scratch with its financial balance sheet in tatters and its future uncertain; his only mistake had been to put too much faith in the potential of one market, and to depend too greatly on one distributor for advice on the evolution of new models.

In return for this direct control, the Italian government pumped in sufficient funds not only to

The unloved 24 Horas made by Mototrans and in 1971 imported into Britain by Vic Camp after a dispute with Ducati Meccanica. Note the perspex window on the top bevel cover

tide the company over its present cash crisis, but also to develop a new range of models, the bevel-driven ohc V-twin. The pushrod 500 twin was scrapped and the single-cylinder range rationalized to include a valve-spring roadster, desmo roadster and street scrambler version of each of the 250/350/450 capacities. Until 1973 though there might be minor cosmetic differences from one year to another, such as chrome mudguards on one or a different coloured tank on another, the Mark 3 and Desmo models were effectively the same bike with a different head and transfers. In 1972, the Desmo's styling was amended to feature silver metalflake tank and seat bodywork for the 1973 model year, to identify with the Imola-winning 750s, and a double-sided front brake was fitted for the first time as standard. Later that year, Vic Camp was replaced as British distributor by a new company again called — Ducati Concessionaries, not this time an offshoot of King's of Oxford but of a company which had taken their place as one of the largest retail dealers in the country, Coburn and Hughes. Camp was permitted to continue was one of the new company's dealers, and because Coburn & Hughes could see no future for the desmo singles, preferring instead to import only the Mark 3 valve-springers and 750 twins,

There can't be a single motorcycle sport in which Ducati engines have not been employed. Londoner Fred 'Oily' Wells (father of present-day road racer Jim Wells), used a 450 engine with magneto ignition (on the right) in this sprinter. This is the 1968 version, dubbed 'Oilybird I'!

Camp was also allowed to import the desmo singles himself direct from Italy at first, as he had done in the past. Coincidentally, the two types of single-cylinder model received quite distinct styling one from another, with the Mark 3 standardizing at blue and gold on all capacity models, while the Desmos fell under the stylish spell of Leopoldi Tartarini and emerged in their distinctive yellow livery with tank shape and seat based on the 750 Sport.

By now improvements had been made to the electrics yet again (though these still remained as 6V systems to the end of the model's run) as well as a raise in compression, 29 mm carburettors standardized and refinement to the tuning resulting in even more performance and improved handling. The final major change took place in 1974, when the last run of desmo singles were fitted with a single disc front brake mated to 38 mm Marzocchi forks, which seemed particularly out of place on the 250! The reason was that these were 750 parts left over when some of the V-twin range was converted to twin front discs, so rather than waste them it was

decided to cut the forks down and use them on the Desmos; the result was a very stiff fork action, and the last of the drum-braked bikes was a better bet.

By now the dead hand of bureaucracy had settled over Borgo Panigale, resulting in the unfortunate decision to phase out the single-cylinder range at the end of 1974; in fact sufficient bikes had been made for them to continue being catalogued well into 1975, at which point the quintessential Ducati roadster finally died a death. Now that not so much later the Japanese manufacturers have 'discovered' the merits of the single-cylinder four-stroke anew, it seems particularly unfortunate that Ducati, who produced the ultimate such motorcycle in the 1960s, should no longer be in a position to respond to this new awareness of the single's values. The decision to stop making them was a crass and shortsighted one: the world oil crisis of 1973–4 should have been fresh in the minds of the government appointees who took the decision, advised by certain distributors who could only think in terms of bigger and better V-twins. The time for an economical, sporty four-stroke single with 12 V electrics and modern switchgear and instruments, that was also fun to ride, had already dawned: the Ducati directors were unfortunately too blinkered to see it. With tooling long since paid for, the design was relatively trouble-free apart from irritating little faults that could easily have been taken care of by an inexpensive updating programme, and an image

Fred Wells also built a 250 cc sprinter for son Jim: this is 'Oilybird 2', on show in the winter of 1967–68

had been painstakingly built up over the last 20 years. But the bureaucrats for whom motorcycling was a numbers game, who by now ruled the many full-blooded motorcycle enthusiasts in the Ducati factory with an iron hand, dictated otherwise, and with production space at a premium when the new factory was begun in 1975, it was deemed that the singles should be scrapped. The fact that they were effectively replaced by the disastrous 350/500 parallel twins, that product of a non-motorcyclist's hand, made their loss particularly hard to bear.

Thus the unbroken line from Marianna to 450 Desmo was finally ended, though for a while longer a cousin of the family lived on; the Mototrans factory in Barcelona continued to make its version of the bevel-driven single for some years to come, but alas not for general export. A half-hearted attempt was made later in the 1970s to replace the old range with a belt-driven ohc model that was effectively one half of a V-twin Pantah: we'll take a brief look at it in a later chapter. But it was like trying to replace an E type Jaguar with an XJ-S, Elvis Presley with Neil Diamond, a '59 Beaujolais with a litre bottle of Eurowine. The end of the Ducati single's production meant for many enthusiasts of the Bologna marque a betrayal of the values that had been espoused by its products for

over 20 years: it was a sad day for lovers of efficient motorcycles – and doubly sad if you'd ever had the thrill of riding a Mach 1. . . .

There are a couple of interesting postscripts to the tale of the Ducati singles. In the early 1970s a 239 cc version of the Mark 3, achieved by reducing the engine dimensions to 72.5×57.8 mm, was produced for the French market so as to take advantage of a much lower rate of TVA sales tax applicable to motorcycles of less than 240 cc. Otherwise almost identical to the Mark 3 sold elsewhere, it was not a great success in a market than infatuated with Japanese machines, and the resultant unsold stocks later found their way after the end of the singles' production into other countries such as Britain and Germany who were more deeply committed to the single-cylinder four-stroke theme.

Similarly, at the same time the 125 sohc engine was resuscitated and fitted in a special Scrambler frame that featured a single front down-tube bifurcating into a double cradle running under the engine, and thus quite different from the bigger

ABOVE *Vic Camp's colleague Bert Furness was a keen trials man, so he built this mudplugger in 1968 using a 160 Monza Junior engine*

BELOW *Vic Camp built a series of Ducati-powered grass racers with 250, 350 and 450 engines which met with great success. One even found its way on to the speedway track*

street scramblers. Indeed, the 125 Scrambler as it was known was a much more serious competition motorcycle than the bigger bikes, and though the little engine produced a relatively low output (which the factory were too coy to publish) in comparison to the two-strokes then dominating the class, running on 8.5:1 compression up to 8500 rpm and employing a 20 mm Amal Mark 1 carburettor, it was an excellent enduro mount that was really ahead of its time, for it would have sold well in the 1980s. Sadly, it was felt necessary to replace the machine after a short time by the ill-fated two-stroke 125 Regolarita, dealt with later on.

Then of course there was the 24 Horas . . . or 24 Horrors as it became ubiquitously known in Great Britain. This was not strictly speaking a Ducati at all, being a Mototrans product that celebrated the Ducati wins in the Barcelona endurance classic over the years. It employed the narrow-style crankcases and was actually based on the 200 Elite mechanically, since the power unit was quite different from the Italian 250 singles. The 24 Horas measured 69 × 66 mm for a total capacity of 247 cc (compared to the Bologna 250's 74 × 57.8 mm), but like the latter was fitted with a five-speed gearbox – it was really a five-speed overbored version of the 'A' series 200, employing the early camshaft and gear design but the later clutch. Almost no parts were exchangeable with the Bologna machines, as was common practice with the products of the Mototrans range,

which were rarely seen outside their native shores.

The 24 Horas did, however, voyage abroad. In 1971 Vic Camp had been having problems with the Bologna factory's new management over prices, and in a desperate measure cancelled his order with them for that year's supply of singles, instead arranging with Mototrans to import the 24 Horas valve-spring bike as a replacement. Not surprisingly the Ducati directors were livid, and this whole episode was to tell heavily against Vic in 1973 when the question of his continued representation was reviewed.

At any rate, Camp imported between 200 and 220 24 Horas from Spain for the 1971 season, and must have spent the rest of the decade wishing he hadn't. The quality of manufacture left much to be desired, with the most common faults relating to the rivets on the Motoplat alternator working loose and scoring the flywheel and crankshaft irreparably. The Spanish metal finishing too on the camshafts and rocker faces was quite inadequate for the job, with the result that these wore out very quickly with imaginable results. The consequences of this disastrous episode both for the name of Ducati (which is what the bikes were sold as) and Vic Camp's reputation were far-reaching, although Vic tried gamely to do his best by the inevitable dissatisfied customers. It was one of these who first coined the name '24 Horrors', which he did in an advert in *Motor Cycle News* inviting anyone who was interested to witness the stripping down of one of these motorcycles, on which he'd covered less than 1000 miles before striking terminal trouble, to meet up on the pavement outside Vic Camp's Walthamstow shop the following Saturday morning. Not surprisingly, quite a large crowd gathered, who were entertained by the increasing desperation of the unfortunate owner, as he discovered yet another of the 24 horrors his engine had been waiting to reveal to him!

The Ducati singles were by no means perfect bikes – anyone who's been stranded in a downpour with inoperative electrics, or tried to pick their way along a winding road with the dubious aid of the 6V headlamp, will attest to that – but as enjoyable, sporting machines which epitomized the fun of motorcycling, they will take some beating in the future. Fortunately, a bigger and more powerful brother, for those who could afford it, was just around the corner.

LEFT *Dutch enthusiast Bert Bels with his 500 desmo special in 1982, after it had scored a second place on its first-ever outing at Zolder. The bike represents what many feel the factory should have produced instead of the disastrous parallel twins. The engine employs a 450 bottom half with reworked gearbox, and the rear cylinder from a 900 SS*

BELOW *In fact, an excellent bike in spite of the factory's obvious last ditch stand; the date is 1971*

11

Sporting sixties –
racing improves the breed

Meccanica Ducati retired from official factory representation in Grand Prix racing at the end of 1959, but though the company's resources were now to be channelled into developing its road bike range to meet the needs of the 1960s, works machines continued to appear in selected events and championships throughout the next decade. At certain times, however, it was deemed necessary to cloak this involvement for political reasons, hence the factory racing department was wound up and the works 125 desmos sold off to private owners (some after having valve-spring heads fitted). A few of them received direct factory assistance in their racing programme from the technical department under the pretext of 'development work'. Initially it was nothing of the kind, but later the new generation of larger-capacity singles were indeed exhaustively race-tested before being marketed as road bikes. By the end of the decade Ducati would justifiably be able to point to their range of valve-spring and desmo roadsters with pride as a classic instance of a breed improved by racing.

Initially, however, in 1960 the factory remained involved officially in just the Italian 125 Championship, with Farne mounted on a 125 desmo single. Things got off to a good start when he won the first round at Cesenatico on his return from a successful series of races the previous year in North America, where he'd spent the season contracted on loan to Berliner to give technical advice and earn the marque some recognition in local events. He did so with such success that the idea was repeated in 1960, this time with Franco Villa competing in the 200 cc class on a 175 Formula 3. It was no contest against the Triumph Cubs that packed the grids in this category at the time, but stiff competition came from his old adversary Joe Rottigni on a Parilla. Nevertheless the Ducati rider won four of the six races he contested during his four-month stint in the USA, finishing second on the

other two occasions in events run on tracks such as Thompson, Mosport, Daytona and Laconia.

Meantime Farne's encouraging start in the Italian 125 series was unfortunately not maintained in the second round at Imola, where he failed to score in a race won by Ubbiali's MV. The long trek down to Sicily for the third and final round on the Siracusa street circuit yielded third place, enough to earn Farne the runner-up slot in the championship behind the MV ace, who then retired from racing at the end of the year after a long and glorious career. Ducati, however, did have the notable satisfaction of winning the manufacturers' crown, which assured some useful publicity.

Having achieved some sort of a winning note, the factory decided to pull out altogether at the end of the 1960 season, instead offering 'assistance' to two notionally private teams, both coincidentally based in Bologna: the Villa brothers' Scuderia Due Torre and Farne's Scuderia Farne-Stanzato. Of the two the latter was the effective factory team, since the Villas also raced Mondials under a similar arrangement (Mondial having officially retired from racing after their clean sweep of the 125 and 250 cc world titles in 1957). Franco Villa must have regretted doing so after the first round of the Italian 125 series at Modena in 1961, for with MV now absent, having withdrawn from the small-capacity classes, Farne won on his desmo single with Villa second on a Mondial followed by no less than 11 other Ducatis in line astern. The second round at Cesenatico along the promenade produced the same result, and Farne was now looking good for the one title he so badly wanted personally to win.

Instead, though, it was the international Coppa d'Oro meeting two weeks later at Imola which provided Franco Farne with his finest hour, and one which was to provide a dramatic dress rehearsal for one of the great days in Ducati sporting history 11 years later. Farne rode his 125 desmo against a star-studded field which included the works Hondas of Phillis and Redman, the latter a former 125 Ducati owner who had finished 13th in the 125 TT in 1960. But in spite of the speed advantage of the twin-cylinder Honda, it was Farne who streaked into an immediate lead and drew away from the pack to win comfortably from the two Japanese bikes, lapping the entire field up to and including the fourth place man, who to provide additional satisfaction was none other than the Mondial-mounted Villa! Only Degner's MZ offered any resistance, before expiring with a seizure while in second place behind the flying Ducati single.

Farne's performance in this race had interesting technical repercussions, for Honda were frankly taken aback by the performance of the desmo single, then effectively an obsolescent five-year-old design. Forced to consider an alternative to their dohc four-valve cylinders with tiny paired valves controlled by coil springs permitting astronomical revs, Honda actually went so far as to design and build their own 125 desmo twin, which duly appeared in public at Modena in 1962, ridden by Luigi Taveri. Though no details of the engine were, in best Honda tradition, ever released, it appears to have utilized a four-camshaft layout, one for each set of opening and closing cams, and presumably also adopted Honda's usual four-valves per cylinder arrangement as well. However, the desmo Honda

did not apparently produce appreciably more power than the valve-spring 125 twin and it did not reappear in future; Honda instead pursued the path towards increased power at higher revs by means of ever smaller and ever more numerous cylinders, that eventually resulted in the five-cylinder 125 and 250 six of hallowed memory.

Sadly, Farne was unable to continue his drive towards the Italian 125 title, Villa winning both the following two races to clinch the title for himself and Mondial. However, to even things up, Villa also comfortably won the Italian 125 constructors' championship, which was run that year as a separate four-race series for Formula 3 bikes, and which was dominated by Ducati Sport and Gran Sport machines: in the final race at Monza on the morning of the Italian GP in September, all but two of the 22 starters were Ducati-mounted, and Villa won comfortably to land the Bologna factory this important title on his works-supported Scuderia Due Torre 125 Sport.

Unfortunately, as the factory concentrated more and more on making road bikes and the North American market's potential, so its successes in Italian competition, geared to a different set of requirements, became fewer and further between.

Franco Farne at speed at Modena in March 1961 on his 125 desmo in a test session (Zagari)

Franco Farne dons the winner's laurels after the 125 race at Valladolid in Spain in September 1963. To his left, leaning on the screen of the bike on which he finished second to Farne that day, is Ricardo Fargas

Even in Junior and Novice racing, traditionally Ducati-dominated since the mid-1950s, other marques were overtaking them in performance and a whole new breed of Italian riders who would become household names in the next few years were beginning their racing careers on machines other than Ducatis. Thus, for instance, the first meeting of the 1962 season at Monza was for Junior riders, and saw not a single Ducati on the track the entire day. Instead, the 125 class was won by a certain Roberto Gallina on a Motobi, while the 175 event saw a bitter duel between eventual winner Renzo Pasolini on a four-speed Aermacchi and a promising beginner named Giacomo Agostini on a Morini Settebello. It was the shape of things to come.

The introduction of the 250 Ducati in 1961, itself developed from a racing prototype debuted before the launch in America, went some way towards redressing this situation, though not at first in Junior racing, which only catered for the 125 and 175 classes. But the 250 Formula 3 was a genuine 100 mph production racer which did much to build the hitherto somewhat neglected 250 class in local Italian racing up to its present importance. The F3 was marketed in Britain as the Manxman, and though very few were sold as a result once again of the very high price, one customer was Irishman Campbell Donaghy, who used his bike to good advantage to earn the first World Championship 250 cc points ever gained by a Ducati single when he finished 5th in the 1962 Ulster GP behind the three works Honda fours and Arthur Wheeler's Guzzi. Though nominally the same specification as the 'cooking' Monza model, the F3/Manxman was in fact a genuine replica of the 250 factory prototype, and produced 23 bhp at 8200 rpm, translating to 19.8 bhp at the rear wheel running on 9:1 compression and fitted with a 27 mm SS1 Dell'Orto racing carburettor and open megaphone.

In due course the Diana Mark 3 street racer appeared in the USA, and was enthusiastically adopted by club racers on the other side of the Atlantic. Riders such as Frankie Scurria, Yvon Duhamel, George Rockett and Syd Tunstall earned many successes on tuned versions of the production bike, and Rockett even managed fourth place in the inaugural 250 US GP at Daytona in 1964 behind winner Alan Shepherd's works MZ. But the valve-spring bike was no match for the two-stroke TD1 Yamahas then beginning to flood the US racing scene, nor somewhat suprisingly for the pushrod Aermacchi single, aka Harley-Davidson Sprint, which throughout the closely parallel competition careers of the two machines always seemed to have the beating of the ohc Ducati. Nevertheless the Ducati provided a good sound ride for the aspiring GP star, and was usually reliable enough to earn place money, as with Rockett's Daytona effort, or a Singapore rider's third place in the 1963 Malaysian GP on his Diana Mark 3 behind the works Yamahas of Fumio Ito and Hasegawa.

If outright speed was not the Ducati's forte, durability was, and the increasingly popular world of long-distance racing was tailor-made for the 250 single. The Spanish Mototrans factory was particularly alive to this fact, for the single most important motorcycle event on the Iberian Peninsula was the annual Barcelona 24-hour race, the results of which had a vital bearing on the buying public's choice during the next twelve months. Though permitting prototypes, the race in practice catered almost exclusively for modified road machines fitted with a generator and lighting equipment for the night section, and was thus precisely the type of event in which Ducati had made its mark in Italy in the mid-1950s. However, the demise of the Milano–Taranto and Motogiro meant that such endurance events would henceforth be run on closed tracks like the twisting Montjuich Park circuit in the centre of Barcelona, and Ducati thus transferred their attentions to the 24 *horas* to good effect.

Their Barcelona debut had taken place in July 1957, and was rewarded with immediate success

ABOVE AND BELOW *A well-restored and rare Mach 1/S 250 cc racer of 1964 – but with incorrect seat and tank. Note the* 19 in. rims and large Grimeca brakes, betraying the model's endurance racing heritage

Phil Read on the San Remo street circuit in October 1971 aboard the 500 V-twin Ducati. He finished 2nd behind Agostini's MV, ahead of team-mates Giuliano and Spaggiari

when Gandossi/Spaggiari won the race outright on a 125 Gran Sport which had been prepared for the abortive Milano–Taranto, cancelled in the wake of the Mille MIglia tragedy. The winners covered 586 laps at a speed of 57.66 mph for the 24 hours including stops, a distance of 1385 miles, to lead a triumphant 1-2-3 for the Bologna marque in their first attempt at the gruelling race: Farne and Mandolini finished second on an identical works bike, with locals Relats/Roda third, also on a 125 Gran Sport. This unexpected result gave the Mototrans company, founded that year, a great send-off, and it was little wonder that their sales boomed from the very first month of the firm's existence. In 1958 an even more impressive result was obtained, this time with Mandolini/Maranghi leading home four other Ducati riders to sweep the first five places overall, all mounted once again on sohc 125 Gran Sports. Exactly the same distance was covered in the 24 hours as the previous year, namely 586 laps, while 11 laps down in second place came fellow factory riders Farne and Villa, with third place going to Ricardo Fargas, later to become the man behind Ducati's great run of success in this event, teamed with a refugee from the Montesa camp, Jaime Caralt. Five Ducatis started the race, five finished, in the first five positions!

Success eluded the marque in the 1959 event, which was won by Britons Peter Darvill and Bruce Daniels on a 500 cc BMW. But the following year Ducati mounted a massive effort for overall victory, entering a team of no less than eight sohc 175 Sports, running in the 250 class, and with a mixed squad of Spanish and Italian riders. This very strong effort resulted in the tables being turned on the bigger, faster but thirstier machines, and Franco Villa and Amedeo Balboni led from start to finish to win at 59.25 mph, covering 603 laps in the 24 hours; they actually broke the BMW's distance record at the end of 23 hours, such was the speed and reliability of the little machine. Darvill/Daniels could only finish second, with two more Ducatis third and fourth, with Ricardo Fargas crewing with Neapolitan Enzo Rippa for another top three finish.

Ricardo Fargas at last achieved his cherished ambition of winning his country's most important race in 1962, when he teamed once again with Rippa on an experimental Mototrans 250, which in fact proved to be the prototype of the later 24 Horas road machine, fitted with hefty Grimeca brakes and an evidently much more reliable engine than the

Someone had some fun. This striking zebra-coat 900 SS didn't last the distance but everyone remembered

production models! His speed of 58.42 mph did not set a new record, but previous winners Villa/Balboni on an Italian factory 250 had seemed set to do so before retiring when in the lead at half-distance. Once again the fleet little singles outpaced the bigger bikes, for though a 175 Bultaco two-stroke was second, the best 500 cc machine was Howard German and Peter Darvill's Velocette, which could only manage third place.

A Montesa won in 1963 to register a return to the 1950s, when the Spanish two-strokes had been invincible in this event, but in 1964 Ducati once again reversed the result with Spaggiari and Mandolini winning outright on the first Ducati ever to appear with an engine larger than 250 cc. Their 284 cc factory prototype was in fact an overbored 250 measuring 79 × 57.8 mm, and was like the Fargas/Balboni 250, which finished 5th overall and second in the 250 class, as well as a couple of the other team bikes, fitted in a special twin-loop frame with massive 220 mm diameter Grimeca brakes, a 4ls front and 2ls rear. The winning pair set up another new distance record of 635 laps, breaking the 1500 mile mark for the first time and winning a special trophy for the first-ever 100 km/h-plus average speed in the history of the event, in spite of a 20-minute stop after 16 hours to change a piston.

Darvill was second once again, this time back on a BMW twin and paired with Norman Price.

This latest Barcelona victory prompted the Italian factory to construct a short batch of production racers based on the endurance bikes. It was effectively a means of using up the copious supply of spares which had been built up to support the Barcelona effort. Though based on the 250 Diana/Mach 1 engine, these in fact had special sandcast crankcases much wider than the standard bike but still with a wet clutch, and offered increased bottom-end stiffness and superior clutch location. True to form it was the forerunner of the later wide-crankcase road singles which Taglioni had been first testing under racing conditions. This crankcase modification made the bikes ineligible for the Italian Formula 3 production-based category, and were thus the first outright production racers to be available from Borgo Panigale since the 125 Grand Prix. Though eligible for the Italian Formula 2 class, this was not the model's correct designation, as some people later claimed, but instead they were referred to on the instruction sheet which accompanied each one as the Mach/1S.

Two versions were made and put on offer in January 1965; the 250 and a 350 version, which thus became the prototype of the 350 road bike announced three months later, and indeed it was a 350 Mach/1S which Farne rode at Sebring and thus gave the roadster its name. Both ran on 10.8:1 compression and delivered a genuine 34 bhp at 8500 rpm in the case of the 250, and 39.5 bhp at 8000 rpm for the 350, both figures measured at the crankshaft. Why genuine? Because Taglioni himself put his name to the output quoted on the instruction sheets, and Dr. T – whose title at the time was interestingly enough 'Project Department Manager' – does not exaggerate. Both engines had five-speed gearboxes and ran 40–42 degrees of ignition advance, with battery and coil ignition and twin-plug heads: the second 10 mm plug was tucked down beside the bevel shaft housing on the right side and in due course this modification became a standard one for go-faster private owners on all Ducati singles. The head was a standard hairpin valve-spring unit employing the usual 80-degree valve angle, but the desmo head when it came along fitted readily on to the engine in best Taglioni tradition. In fact the factory retained some machines which, suitably lightened for shorter races, provided mobile testbeds for the positive valve control system in the 1966–68 period.

The phrase 'suitably lightened' gives the clue to the reason why these machines, of which only a dozen were built in addition to the five works bikes, did not become successful. They had been over-engineered on the chassis side in an effort to ensure reliability at Montjuich – hence the robust duplex frame with quite long swinging arm featuring eccentric wheel adjusters all resulting in a comfortable 56 in. wheelbase, and especially the huge Grimeca brakes which may have been invaluable in anchoring up countless times at the many sharp corners on the Barcelona track but which were far larger, and heavier, than necessary for short-circuit racing. This, plus the heavier engine and steel Mach 1 fuel tank combined in a dry weight with fairing of just on 280 lb. All of it was far too much for the 250 class and was on a par with the ruggedly built British singles in the 350 class, where the 240 lb Aermacchi single was already pointing the way to the future. Curiously, too, the Ducatis were fitted with 19 in. rims front and rear, since it was believed there was a better choice of racing tyres in this size.

Not surprisingly few of the production racers were readily sold, but three did end up in Britain, one of which achieved some success on the Isle of

Ricardo Fargas (right) and Italian Enzo Rippa enjoy victory after the 1962 Barcelona 24 Horas on an experimental Mototrans 250

Man, whose rugged racing conditions held few terrors for such a strong bike. The first person to buy one was a British rider named Ken Watson, who while serving his National Service in the RAF in Aden became attracted to the Ducati marque, thanks to a combination of the fanatical enthusiasm of a fellow airman named Mick Walker, later to become one of the marque's leading dealers in Britain, and the local motorcycle shop in the colony, which believe it or not was a Ducati dealer. Before being posted to Aden, Watson had become a leading British short-circuit rider on Manx Nortons, but was now planning to acquire something more modern with which to resume his racing career after his impending demob, and a 250 bike to match the 125 CR93 Honda he already had would be ideal. Persuaded by Walker to invest in one of the new Ducatis, he journeyed overland to the Bologna factory after being discharged from the service at the beginning of 1965, and turned up one morning with a fistful of lire looking for a racing motorcycle.

Watson's surprise when he discovered that his racer was fitted with Barcelona-type lights and a generator can be well imagined, but after it was explained that this, together with the kickstart, could be removed for shorter events, he completed the deal and took the bike back to England with him. Once there, he ran it in and entered for the Manx GP on the Isle of Man, where he'd had three lowly finishes on 500 Nortons from 1959 to 1962 before being called up. His delight at finishing 9th in the 1965 Lightweight MGP on the Ducati was matched by the silver replica he earned – his first ever in the Island. But the bike was too heavy for short-circuit events, and Watson eventually transferred to a lighter Mach 1-based racer which he rode to 2nd place in the 1966 Manx GP, entered by Vic Camp.

Camp himself had imported the other two Ducati Mach/1S machines into Britain in March 1965, intending to campaign them in British short-circuit events that season with none other than Derek Minter and Dave Degens aboard. Minter refused to ride them after a Brands Hatch test session, citing them as much too heavy to be competitive and incapable of being lightened. After urging his riders to rev the engines to as high as 10,000 rpm in an unsuccessful effort to blow them up, so that he could then return them to the factory in a trade for something better, Camp discovered how truly bullet-proof the engine was. Both bikes held

together in spite of this abuse, but the factory took them back anyway in a swap for a Mach 1 and Sebring, which Camp's foreman Bert Furness then converted to outright racing specification and provided successful mounts in British events for a variety of riders, including Reg Everett, Paul Smart, Tom Phillips, Chas Mortimer and many others.

Ducati racing involvement during the 1964–66 period was sporadic, since it was evident that a two-stroke was necessary to have any success in the smaller racing classes unless your company's name was Honda: thus although, as detailed in the chapter on the racing parallel twins, Spaggiari strove manfully on a lightweight, updated version of the 125 desmo, the two-stroke Bultacos and Villa-Mondial were more than a match for the high-revving twin. In the Junior classes though, where production-based machines were *de rigueur* in a sensible effort to cut down on costs for beginners, Ducatis were still competitive. Nevertheless Giacomo Agostini won the 175 title in 1963 on his pushrod Morini; the runner-up was Walter Villa mounted on a 175 Ducati Sport breathed on by his

This 350 prototype was developed as a possible production racer, employing the standard die-cast 350 road engine, here at Modena in January 1967 (Zagari)

then more famous elder brother. Villa, then beginning the career that would take him to four world titles in the 1970s, was joined in 1965 by another future champion, who finished runner-up in the 125 Junior series on an sohc Ducati – Eugenio Lazzarini. *His* greatest rival for the honour of finishing on the first Bologna-made bike that year was invariably another star of the future, Gilberto Parlotti, who in due course would become a works Ducati rider in his own right.

Indeed, Parlotti made a considerable impression in his first season as a Senior in the following year, 1966, finishing in the top six in each of the early-season street races on a converted 250 Mach 1 which he'd heavily modified himself. His successful efforts were enough to get him recognized by Taglioni as exactly the sort of rider-engineer he liked to work with. Though it was Farne who had debuted the 250 desmo at the 1966 Modena meeting in March, a year later Parlotti and another youngster, who was to achieve a certain degree of success on the racing development side, were charged with continuing the job of sorting out the desmo heads' wrinkles on the track. His name was Roberto Gallina, later to win two 500 cc world titles not as a rider (though he did indeed gain much success on the track in the early 1970s) but as the team manager and development engineer responsible for the RG500 Suzuki-mounted victories of Marco Lucchinelli and Franco Uncini.

Gallina it was who debuted the prototype 350 desmo in its first race at Modena in March 1967, finishing 7th in the 500 race and 2nd in the 350 class. Just behind came a machine that was to prove the Ducati's great rival then and in future years, Gilberto Milani's works Aermacchi. The 350 desmo had the same cylinder dimensions as the Sebring roadster, and produced 41 bhp at the gearbox, revving to 10,500 rpm. Meantime a revised version of the 250 desmo yielding 35 bhp at 11,500 rpm had been sent to Daytona for Farne to ride in the 100-mile Expert Lightweight event supporting the famous 200-miler, but thanks to a protest from a rival team and the AMA's crazy rule structure, was prevented from starting. The desmo head was found to be a 'non-standard component constituting a change in basic design'; in those days the fiction still persisted that AMA racing bikes had to be derived from standard road-going models, so the TD1A Yamaha was legal, for example, because it retained a tenuous relationship with the YDS roadster. Having come all the way from Italy with two mechanics in order to ride, Farne had to sit the race out, and this

incident was unquestionably the reason why Ducati did not run the F750 bike at Daytona or Ontario in 1972–73, when it might have had an excellent chance of victory.

Back in Italy, however, Gallina and Parlotti, who had now also begun to appear on a second 350 desmo, were producing steadily encouraging results in the early-season street races, capped by Parlotti's 3rd in the 350 race at Rimini behind the four-cylinder machines of Pasolini (Benelli) and Hailwood (Honda). Parlotti was now also out on the 250, and a fourth place at Cesenatico was particularly satisfying, since for the first time a Ducati beat Milani's fleet Aermacchi in a straight race.

Meanwhile, in Britain two Mach 1 production bikes entered by Vic Camp had finished second and third in the 250 class (and 6th and 7th overall) in the prestigious 500-mile race for production bikes at Brands Hatch. Ducati's biggest moment of the year. came later on, though, when Gallina actually led the 500 race at San Remo on the 350 desmo, in front of the works MVs and Benellis. Sadly, however, it was too good to last and he crashed spectacularly, breaking his collarbone and bringing down no less than six other leading riders when his fuel tank burst, flooding the racing line!

Though Ducati did not contest any further events with the desmos that season, testing continued at Modena, and in due course it was officially announced in April 1968 that a road version would be produced. It was, however, not to be until the following year that deliveries began, for 1968 was to be another development year on mainly Italian tracks. This time the rider selected was the faithful Spaggiari, who appeared for the first time on the desmo singles at the Alicante road races in southern Spain – one of his old stamping grounds – at the end of January. The performance of the two bikes raised many eyebrows, for Bruno finished a solid third on the 350 behind Read's Yamaha V4 and Ago's MV – the first of many occasions during the next four years that he would find himself in this position – and would certainly have occupied the same position in the 250 race behind the Yamahas of Read and Ivy had he not suffered a flat battery. The bikes had been the subject of much modification during the previous six months since their last outing, and though nominally entered by Spaggiari's own team were very much a works effort. Both now had dry clutch housings fitted to the standard Mark 3 crankcases, and the 250's output was now up to 36 bhp at 11,000 rpm, breathing through a 36 mm Dell'Orto, while the similar 350 produced 46 bhp at 9500 rpm, fitted with a 40 mm carb. Top speed achieved in testing had been 130 mph for the 250 – an incredible figure if true – and 134 mph for the bigger bike: their performances at Alicante and indeed throughout the season which followed would certainly seem to support this sort of claim, especially since both bikes weighed in at just 245 lb in spite of the use of a standard Mark 3 frame complete with lugs for the centre stand. A notable modification over the previous bikes was the reinforcement of the rocker arms, which had shown a tendency to crack under sustained high revs: this improvement was incorporated into the production bikes when they finally appeared, and was but one of many examples of how the racing development programme benefited the roadsters.

When the Continental Circus reassembled at Rimini in March 1968 for the first of the Italian

RIGHT *Farne testing the 350 prototype at Modena in February 1967 (Zagari)*
BELOW *Vic Camp was also an active road racing sponsor: Tom Phillips at Brands Hatch in 1968 en route to one of many victories he obtained in British events with this 250 (Greening)*

meetings, Spaggiari was seen to have a third mount, a dry-clutch desmo version of the recently announced 450, fitted like the 350 racer with a 42 mm carburettor. Running on 10.5:1 compression an output of 50 bhp at 9000 rpm was claimed for the new bike, Ducati's first entry in the blue riband 500 class. Like the smaller desmo racers the 450 boasted twin-plug ignition and oversize valves, with a straight-cut primary to obviate power loss to the five-speed gearbox. Like the standard 450 frame, the racers were all gussetted along the upper frame tube on either side for added rigidity, and 35 mm Marzocchi front forks were standardized on all three bikes, with a lightweight 210 mm 4ls Oldani front brake and 2ls rear stopper; Marzocchi rear suspension units were favoured, though Ceriani were also tried.

The 450's race debut at Rimini could hardly have been more encouraging, Spaggiari catching John Hartle's G50 Metisse for third place behind Ago and Hailwood on MV and Honda respectively before slowing as he was shaping to pass the British rider on the last lap and pushing home with a dead engine to finish 6th. In the 350 race though it was a different story, the desmo Ducati blowing off all the other singles to take a comfortable third place behind the multi-world champions, 30 sec ahead of Milani's Aermacchi, which, however, turned the tables on the Ducati single in the 250 race. Spaggiari was forced to settle for fourth place in a race won by Pasolini's Benelli four followed home by Bergam-

onti on the incredible and fast four-valve Morini single. Ducati were so shattered by the short-stroke Aermacchi's performance that they had it measured – unsuccessfully. Nevertheless, the performance of the desmo singles had set the racing world humming, and the factory had to field several enquiries during the next couple of weeks from privateers who wanted to know when they could buy replicas of the Spaggiari machines, especially the 450.

Two weeks later at a sodden Cesenatico, Gallina joined Spaggiari on a 250 desmo, finishing 6th after a race-long duel with John Cooper on the Padgett Yamaha; Spaggiari had been involved too, but retired near the end, though an untroubled third place in the 350 race to lead the 'banger brigade' home made amends. The 450 was not entered, since further work was being carried out after its initial race at Rimini. The big bike was absent too from the next meeting the following week at Imola, run in similar damp conditions, at which Spaggiari claimed 4th on the 350 desmo behind Paso, Agostini and Read; he retired from the 250 while scrapping with Milani, when the engine blew all its oil out through the breather pipe. A fourth with the 350 at Riccione completed the run of Italian spring meetings.

The large-capacity bike appeared next at the

Long before his famous 1972 Imola victory, Paul Smart was a successful Ducati rider. Here he takes a Vic Camp-entered 250 to another Brands Hatch win in 1968

Spanish GP at Montjuich at the beginning of May. It was entered at 386 cc, measuring 81 × 75 mm, thus was an overbored version of the 350. Spaggiari led the first lap after a demon start, but had to give way to the inevitable Agostini and Aussie Jack Findlay on the McIntyre Matchless before eventually retiring at half-distance. It was not a happy day for the Italian rider as he also withdrew from the 250 race on the desmo single after trying out the Spanish-built MT four once again. After a couple of desultory laps in practice, during which he failed by some margin to match his times on the single, he quit.

The next motorcycle event at Montjuich saw a change in Ducati fortunes, however, for in the 24 hours in July Reg Everett teamed with a rider who would later bring dramatic success to the Ducati marque – Paul Smart – to capture third place overall and win the 250 class. Coincidentally, as he would do some years later at Imola, Smart came in as a last-minute replacement on the Vic Camp-entered bike, a near-standard Mach 1 roadster which had already finished third in the Brands Hatch 500-miler in the hands of Charles Mortimer and Tom Dickie. This combination of results was enough to secure for the British Ducati concessionaire the coveted FIM Coupe d'Endurance – another feather in the Bologna factory's hat. Ironically, the race was won outright once again by Ricardo Fargas – but this time he was mounted on a 750 Norton Atlas!

Spaggiari had one final outing that year at

Monza, finishing fifth in the 350 Italian GP behind three fours and the CZ twin, but ahead of Stastny's Jawa. The 350 desmo was evidently highly competitive, and was good enough to have earned Spaggiari third place in the Italian championship that season.

For the 1969 season Gallina and Parlotti featured less heavily in the factory's plans, though once again both they and Spaggiari, back again to ride just the 250/350 (not 450) bikes in the Italian meetings, were entered notionally as privateers. The first meeting of the year at Rimini saw Spaggiari involved in a first-lap pile-up which forced him to retire, while the other two *Ducatisti* battled each other for fifth place with the verdict just going to Gallina. But neither was within remote range of the two works Aermacchis of Bergamonti and Milani, whose ultra short-stroke pushrod engines revved to 12,000 rpm with evident reliability, and seemed quite a bit faster than the 250 desmo. Spaggiari was a lone entry in the 350 race, in which he uncharacteristically crashed for the second time in a day.

The cold and wet Modena meeting which came next was scarcely more rewarding at first, for Spaggiari retired with ignition problems while in second place in the 250 race. His faithful 350 carried him to a secure runner-up finishing spot behind Pasolini's Benelli four, and ahead of the fleet of

The 1970 version of the 450 desmo racer. With standard roadster crankcases it produced 50 bhp at the rear wheel. Spaggiari rode the bike in early-season Italian events

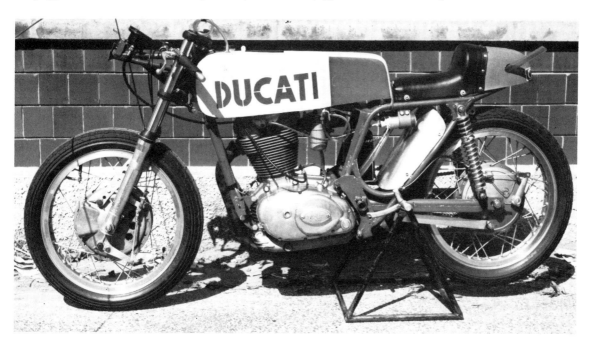

Aermacchis; it was evident that even the short-stroke 350 version of these could not live with the desmo, while the positions were reversed in the 250 class. Yet in the very next meeting at Riccione, along the seafront, Spaggiari rode like a tiger to lead not only the Aermacchis but also Read's Yamaha and Bryan's Honda for three laps of the 250 event, before a rocker broke and he was forced to retire; he later owned up to revving the bike to 12,000 rpm in an effort to keep in front! Third in the 350 race behind the Ago/Paso duo was some consolation, followed up by fourth at Imola in the next event thanks to the appearance of Grassetti's Yamaha. Bruno had to work for it, though; he was never more than 10 yards ahead of the two Aermacchis and Cooper's new Seeley 7R. He retired from the 250 race once again, however. The following weekend at Cesenatico, though, the 250 desmo finally came good, with Spaggiari finishing second behind the Benelli four after pipping Bergamonti's Aermacchi screamer on the line after a race-long dice. To cap his best result so far, he also finished fourth on the 350 again behind the same riders as at Imola, but comfortably ahead of the other singles. Sadly, he and Grassetti collided during practice for the next meeting at Cervia, ending up in hospital with minor injuries. They were, however, serious enough to sideline Spaggiari from the final round of the Italian championships at San Remo the very next week. Salt was rubbed into the wound when Milani won the 350 race on the Aermacchi, with Pasolini also sidelined through injury; it was an event that in the absence of the Benelli four Spaggiari and the Ducati would have been almost certain to win.

The Italian spring season of races followed each other in close order, and while the names may be largely unfamiliar even to students of Grand Prix racing, the fact is that the meetings were all international events, attracting the cream of riders from all over Europe as well as Italy. Run for the most part on street circuits either round the houses or up one side of an Adriatic seaside town's promenade and back down the other, with a twisty section at either end, they were at least as demanding a set of tracks as anything else in Europe. They even rivalled the Isle of Man for the special combination of man and machine that was required for success. Spaggiari was an old hand at such events having cut his teeth on them in the 1950s, but even so the performance of the near-veteran rider on a modified production machine was highly creditable. It not only yielded Ducati much useful publicity but also enabled Taglioni,

Farne warms up the 450 desmo prototype at Modena in February 1970. Scuderia Speedy Gonzalez was the 'private' team formed by Farne, Spaggiari and others, most of whom worked in the Ducati racing department! (Zagari)

who attended most of the races himself to keep an eye on his toys, to develop the desmo design on roads not so very different from those on which his customers would ride the street versions – admittedly at somewhat lower speeds! The Italian street circuits played a vital part in the development of the Ducati range.

A final outing of the season once again took place in the Italian GP at Monza in September, confined as before to the 350 event, in which Spaggiari, now recovered from his injuries, finished sixth, surprisingly beaten by Bertarelli's Aermacchi. Meantime, however, two much more significant events had taken place in terms of Ducati success, one of which entailed the marque's first major off-road victory ever, when Dave Douglas and John McClark teamed up to win the Baja 1000 race in Mexico aboard a modified production 350SSS Scrambler. In later years the Baja would become the king of desert races, but even in those days it was a hard and difficult event, success in which proved the durability of both men and machine. This victory had much to do with the later sales success of the Scrambler range in the USA, but the second major victory simply served to confirm what the market it affected already knew: Ducati made the fastest and best-handling 250 road bike than available from any manufacturer.

The race which underlined this truism was the Production TT in the Isle of Man, run for road-legal

Another view of the 450 desmo racer: note the gusseting on the frame (Zagari)

bikes with silencers and full lighting equipment, and which in 1969 provided Ducati with their first-ever TT victory. Even more remarkable was the fact that Alistair Rogers's 250 Production TT-winning bike was a five-year-old Mach 1 dating from 1964, on which he averaged 83.79 mph fore the three-lap race to beat the Japanese and Spanish competition. Chas Mortimer, on the Vic Camp-entered Mark 3 Ducati, had been the pre-race favourite to win, but a loose footrest and intermittently inoperative ignition dropped him to third place in the class at the end. Clive Thomsett was fifth on another Ducati.

For the 1970 season Parlotti continued to ride the 250 and 350 desmos occasionally, but also had his own bikes with wet-clutch engines that were effectively converted roadsters with a few factory parts. With them he did well enough to be selected to ride the promising 125 Morbidelli twin, on which he would go on to make his mark on the world scene before tragically losing his life on the Isle of Man. Spaggiari, on the other hand, did not ride the smaller bikes at all, concentrating instead on a new racing version of the desmo 450 which appeared at the beginning of the year, now fitted with a Fontana front brake and Ceriani forks. Closely based on the production road bike, the new Senior Ducati employed a set of die-cast roadster crankcases complete with oil-bath clutch; doubtless this was one reason why in future years almost any clutch malady on a Ducati twin or single could be cured by

fitting 450 clutch springs! Power output was again claimed to be 50 bhp, as on the 1968 bike, but this time measured at the rear wheel instead of at the gearbox, an effective increase of about 6 bhp, still at 9000 rpm. At the same time rumours abounded of a four-valve head for the smaller bikes, still with desmodromic valve operation, which naturally entailed no less than eight rockers in the one head, but though a prototype was certainly made, it appears never to have been used in anger.

Once again a new Ducati racing model made an impressive debut, Spaggiari holding second place in the first spring meeting at Rimini behind the MV but ahead of the several Linto and Paton twins, until engine trouble forced him to retire at three-quarter distance. His next appearance on the big bike was at Cesenatico, one of his favourite circuits, where he finished fourth, followed by fifth the next week at Cervia. The new 450 desmo racer evidently had the beating of the British singles, since it was only ever headed by the Italian fours and twins. Work was, however, already proceeding on the new V-twin 500s and the promising desmo 450 racer was shelved while still in its development stage. Many non-Ducati riders were highly disappointed at this decision, which seemed to have been made without a careful analysis of the current racing market. There was still considerable potential for a fast, reliable and torquey unit-construction single-cylinder 500 to replace the ageing British bikes. Many privateers would willingly have paid a good enough price for a 450 Spaggiari replica for the factory to have made money out of a small production run, but instead they were forced to purchase expensive, troublesome Lintos or Kawasakis that were the financial ruination of more than one shoestring competitor.

So instead it was the non-racer who benefited from the factory's involvement in road racing in the late 1960s, those who bought the road bikes which were derived from the works desmo racers. More than in any other period of Ducati's history, the sporting sixties were the time when the Bologna factory raced what they sold, and sold what they had raced. As ultimate proof of that, Chas Mortimer won a second 250 Production TT for Ducati in 1970, aboard the Vic Camp Mark 3, on which he averaged 84.87 mph to secure victory by less than six seconds from John Williams's Honda after being trapped at over 100 mph through the Highlander on his little four-stroke single. Success in the Isle of Man is the ultimate test of a road machine; Ducati passed the exam with flying colours – and would do so again later in the decade.

12

Road parallel twins – more lost causes

By 1964 Ducati had achieved a position of some apparent security, thanks chiefly to their successful penetration of the growing North American market with their expanded range of sporting-orientated singles. The Berliner Corporation had successfully established the Bologna marque's name amongst enthusiast circles, and the startling performance of the Diana Mark III 250 single in particular made it a favourite with performance-orientated riders, not only in the specialist Californian market but throughout the USA.

This success seems even more laudable in retrospect when it's considered in the context of the times: for the early 1960s saw a massive sales drive in the USA on the part of the Japanese manufacturers, led by the milestone slogan that 'You Meet the Nicest People on a Honda', which did much to legitimize motorcycling in general in the eyes of the American public as a whole. Not only did motorcycle dealers, whose numbers increased by leaps and bounds every month, get to meet these nice people, they also started going to the bank more often. The boom period of 1960's motorcycle sales had arrived, and for Ducati as well as their European contemporaries it did much to cushion the effects of the late-50's slump on their home market as traditional bike buyers transferred their affections to the motor car. The pay-off came later. The Japanese at that time concentrated their attentions entirely on the lightweight end of the market. With the exception of a few curiosities such as the BMW-inspired Marusho Lilac, no Oriental company offered a machine larger than 350 cc to the US buyer. This in turn gave the British industry, who, except for small companies such as Greeves and Dot, saw the North American market exclusively in terms of their larger-capacity machines, delusions of security, and even the advent of the CB450 Honda in 1965 sent few warning flares into the British motorcycle industry boardrooms.

While the British seemed disinterested in contesting the small-capacity US market, the Italians were quite the reverse; their lightweight motorcycles were their staple product. Though never able to compete in terms of sheer volume or advertising power with the Japanese, several Italian companies and their US distributors put up a stout defence on the North American battlefield: the leader was Ducati.

Berliner, however, realized that market conditions were changing; people who started out riding a Honda 100 might transfer to a Ducati once they got hooked on the joys of sporting motorcycling and became more adept mechanically. In time they might be looking to move up the capacity scale, where apart from the Harley-Davidson behemoths and the specialist BMW tourers, there was little alternative to the British twins and singles. Berliner's ties to the British industry – they were US distributors for Norton and Matchless also – made them realize that it was in too bad a shape and unlikely to survive in its current form for very long. New models were becoming ever scarcer, with facelifts of the by now elderly 1950's (and even older) designs the rule rather than the exception. It would only be a matter of time before the Japanese would begin to move on up the capacity scale themselves, and that spelt dire trouble for anyone not similarly prepared to match them. New models and up-to-date styling with mechanical specifications which satisfied the changing needs of the market were the formula for survival.

The same problems were being carefully studied elsewhere in Italy, and in the mid-1960s a whole range of what would now be termed medium-capacity machines, but which in those days were considered to be heavyweights of 500 to 750 cc capacity, were being developed. The young Massimo Laverda's lengthy sojourn in the USA had convinced him rightly that it would in future become a big bike market. His return to Italy soon saw the appearance of the Honda Hawk-inspired 650 (later 750 cc) parallel twin, at first marketed Stateside by a distributor as the American Eagle and then quickly under Laverda's own name. Similarly, Cosmopolitan Motors, Berliner's chief importer rival, were trying to persuade their contacts at Benelli to produce a large-capacity twin to supplement the lightweight range: after a five-year gestation period, the 650 Tornado – originally sold under the Montgomery Ward department store chain label – came about. Gilera too were working hard on a 500 parallel twin, with the additional aim of producing a police version which might rival the established Triumph and Norton models outside North America.

Ducati's response to Berliner's request for a larger-capacity model than the range of singles which continued to do well in the US market was surprisingly ambivalent. Taglioni had sketched out numerous exciting 500–750 cc twin-, triple- and four-cylinder designs, with valve gear varying from triple-camshaft desmo to pushrod, any one of which, if produced, would have made the 1968 appearance of the Triumph Trident/BSA Rocket and the Honda CB750 four much less revolutionary. The problem, as always, was the company's

political control from Rome. As detailed elsewhere in the chapter on the Apollo (which saga it should be remembered was being acted out during precisely this period), the bureaucrats who controlled the purse-strings of the State-owned company were for all sorts of reasons, both rational and otherwise, extremely reluctant to invest new funds in a development project which they saw as only benefiting one particular market and one particular importer. A wider application was more desirable, even necessary.

It's easy to imagine being a fly on the wall at one of the many meetings which must have taken place to thrash the whole matter out. 'You want to construct a 500 cc single-overhead-camshaft desmodromic three-cylinder motorcycle for sale to the American public? Isn't this a very complicated type of engine? Does anyone else offer such a machine? No? Well then it must be because it's too revolutionary a design, so we can't possibly do so. So now tell us please, what type of motorcycle is it that presently sells best in this capacity class in the USA? A pushrod parallel twin-cylinder, you say?

Ducati's second try at a 500 cc parallel twin: this is the 1968 ohv model, an improvement over the first, overweight prototype but nonetheless abortive

Well then, that's what we'll give you the money to make!'

Taglioni and Montano were powerless in the face of this type of outside interference, which must sound familiar to students of the British industry of the era. The upshot was that the machine they finally received permission to construct was a 500 cc 360 degree pushrod ohv parallel twin, which was unveiled to the public as a prototype at the Daytona Show in March 1965. The dimensions of 72 × 58.8 mm seemed promising, but the massive alloy crankcases on which they sat contained not only the four-speed gearbox but also an electric starter positioned in front of the crankshaft, with a hefty oil sump underneath. This meant not only a very long wheelbase, which in turn suggested the machine lacked the nimbleness of the British models it was theoretically, for the time being at any rate, competing against, but also a weight of well over 420 lb. Ducati claimed to anyone who asked that its power was 52 bhp at 6500 rpm, but in fact a figure of 36 bhp was nearer the truth, resulting in sluggish acceleration *en route* to a claimed top speed of 'over 100 mph'. Compare these figures with the first of the modern era of superbikes, the Royal Enfield Interceptor, which in a test the very same month as the 500 Ducati first appeared registered a top speed of 114 mph, produced 52.5 bhp at 6000 rpm from its 736 cc engine, and thanks to a kerb weight of only

ABOVE AND RIGHT ABOVE *The Taglioni-designed dohc 700 cc parallel twin prototype dating from 1967. Unfortunately outside pressure from State controllers and Ducati's own lack of financial resources meant that no version was fully developed (above Zagari)*

RIGHT BELOW *The police version of the same 700 cc parallel twin. In spite of impressive test figures and obvious suitability it failed*

430 lb was able to cover the standing quarter mile in 13.8 secs.

Selected journalists and dealers were permitted to ride the Ducati twin briefly in the parking lot of the motel, and all give it a less than enthusiastic reception. Though quiet and smooth, it was sluggish and unresponsive: 'Though I've ridden snappier machines, it is a most interesting entry', said one, trying not to be ungrateful to the Berliners for buying him breakfast at the launch, but in truth the machine was a disaster. Attempts at sporting cornering almost fetched the rider off, so low did the twin exhaust pipes have to run to clear the massive engine cases, and the machine's excess weight dictated the use of large-diameter 220 mm twin leading-shoe Grimeca brakes (which grabbed badly when cold) as fitted to the factory's 250 racers. (To complete a disastrous week for the company they were completely outpaced in the Daytona 100-miler by their Yamaha and Aermacchi competition.) At

the end of Cycle Week it was quietly packed up and shipped off back to Bologna for all concerned to think over again. Two months later the dohc CB450 Honda was announced, and the rules of the game were changed.

Though Taglioni, who had been against the whole project from the start, wanted nothing more to do with it, and Berliner too became convinced that both they and Ducati had missed the boat, the bureaucrats thought otherwise and dictated that development should continue. One bright hope was that, like Gilera's similar design, a properly-thought-out police version would have considerable sales potential world-wide. Accordingly, the machine was completely redesigned into a much more workmanlike and more compact model which was shown to an incentive group of Berliner dealers during the course of their visit to the factory at the end of 1968.

The new machine featured completely redesigned, heavily ribbed crankcases that were far smaller than the original design thanks to the placing of the electric starter behind the cylinders and above the gearbox, which now featured five speeds; a supplementary kickstarter was also fitted on the left. Two Honda/Laverda-like heavily finned light-alloy cylinders surmounted the bottom half, with plug inserts cut into the finning on either side. Unlike the inspirations for the cylinder styling the valve gear was pushrod operated, but the same standard 250 cylinder dimensions were retained. A

A parallel twin engine undergoing development in the factory testbed in 1975

single 32 mm Dell'Orto carburettor with separate float chamber indicated that the machine's purpose was not a sporting one, though overall appearance displayed a close kinship to the 250/350/450 singles of the same period. Closer attention to weight-saving had brought the kerb weight down to 390 lb with a much shorter wheelbase and smaller, 180 mm 2ls, Grimeca brakes fitted as a result. The frame was particularly well though out, of a full double-cradle tubular design with a bracing tube running up under

An early styling exercise on the parallel twin in the mid-70s, probably inspired by Tartarini's studio. The white exhausts would have been somewhat impractical!

the well-padded dual seat to enclose the generous tool and battery box. The exhaust problem had been solved thanks to slimmer cases and a narrower frame, and the bike in general seemed a much more workmanlike project altogether. A top speed of 103 mph and a power output of around 38 bhp at 6500 rpm was adequate without being startling.

Unfortunately the dealer group were not as impressed as the factory had hoped they might be, and were much more interested in getting hold of supplies of the planned 750 V-twin, which would enable them to compete effectively with the recently announced Triumph triple and Honda four. Though the British would insist (and to a certain extent prove) otherwise, the time was past in North America for pushrod vertical twins to make any reasonable impact on the market. Faced with this less than enthusiastic response, and a refusal by Berliner to commit to minimum orders, the pushrod 500 ohv Ducati twin was finally dropped. Too little, too late – it was a classic instance of those outside the factory and indeed the motorcycle industry as a whole believing wrongly that they knew better than the people whose lifeblood was motorcycles what the public wanted.

A much more likely contender in the parallel twin stakes had been developed simultaneously, but with similarly abortive resuts. This was a 700 cc design inspired once again by the Roman bureaucrats who had been under some considerable pressure from the Italian Carabinieri to ensure that one of the

Italian factories produced a large-capacity parallel twin with which they could equip their patrol riders, then clamouring to have their ageing Moto Guzzi Falcone singles replaced with British Norton or Triumph twins. Since Ducati was the only factory under government control the order came down to construct such a machine, which in contrast to the American market version was to be at least 650 cc in capacity, and be capable like the Apollo of being sold in civilian trim to offset development costs.

This was the sort of engineering challenge Taglioni relished, so two variants of the same basic model were run up, one with a pushrod engine designed for the police bike, the other a sporting version with dohc valve gear, driven by a chain up the right side of the engine and running off a spur gear from the five-bearing built-up crankshaft. Both 360- and 180-degree version were produced; no answer to the vibration endemic in such a cylinder layout was found without resorting to the use of power-sapping balancers which Taglioni regarded as an engineering abhorrence, but both machines were very powerful. The pushrod version produced 70 bhp at 6500 rpm, while the double-knocker unit, which was intended for both touring and sporting trim, churned out just over 80 bhp at 7500 rpm. Both prototypes employed the same sturdy Norton-like twin loop frame, fitted with Grimeca brakes which in the case of the much heavier police version were of 220 mm front/ 190 mm rear as opposed to the 210 mm/190 mm combination of the Mark 3 single-

The 500 GTV parallel twin as it eventually appeared in production form

styled dohc machine. Both bikes featured a 5-speed unit gearbox with massive polished side covers behind which a hefty oil-bath clutch lurked on the left of the engine. Mark 1 Amal Concentrics were employed in testing, though for publicity purposes the only previously published photo of the machine showed it as equipped with Dell'Ortos to further the all-Italian image.

Though the 700 prototype was in Taglioni's estimation an excellent bike, with low fuel consumption of over 60 mpg one of its many attributes, it died a death at the end of 1967 for the simple reason that the home Italian market was not considered by the Roman bureaucrats to hold much promise for this type of machine – even though they had commissioned its design and the construction of the prototypes under the same market conditions as pertained when the decision was taken to cut off funds for its continued development. Less than a year later Laverda proved the fallacy of this belief by their success both at home and abroad with a similar size and type of bike, with the added irony that Moto Guzzi stepped into the void left by the cancellation of the Ducati 700 project to supply not only the Carabinieri but also foreign police forces as far afield as California with a police version of their 700 cc V7 pushrod V-twin, a bike which eventually gave rise to the successful Le Mans range of today. Yet another lost opportunity for the men who controlled Borgo Panigale at this period, who had once again refused to listen to the voice of the motorcycle world.

Unfortunately, this particular lesson was not learnt by those in control of Ducati's fortunes in the following decade, for in the early 1970s the spectre of a parallel twin hung once again over the Ducati development department. This time the reasoning behind the project was a European one: Ducati's big twins had proved highly successful in their particular market segment, but the oil crisis of 1973 brought in its train an added awareness of fuel economy and a growing interest in smaller, lighter and more efficient machines. As well, there was a need to reduce manufacturing costs, for the bevel-driven ohc mechanism of the big V-twins was expensive to produce and, in the case of the desmo versions, required such close attention to tolerances that the machines could scarcely be made to sell at a profit. Consequently the burgeoning industrial engine and diesel manufacturing side of the business was increasingly tending to subsidize motorcycle production.

An interim answer to delay the phasing out of the trusty singles, but these were by now felt to be somewhat long in the tooth and in any case no single-cylinder motorcycle revival was yet in view; in 1974 they were considered practically vintage even by certain sections of the enthusiast market. The solution, therefore, was to produce a middleweight Ducati twin – but the decision as to what type provoked much discussion and ultimately dissension within the company's hierarchy.

Taglioni had already intended to develop a downsized version of his big V-twin, and had

The 350 cc version of the desmo-headed Sport model, little seen outside Italy: it was designed to take advantage of local tax laws, but was overweight and underpowered in comparison to such as the Morini V-twin

ABOVE(BOTH) *Two views of the good-looking 500 Sport desmo, with styling by Tartarini. Though it handled well, it vibrated badly and leaked oil severely thanks to the vertically split crankcases*

several ideas as to how production costs could be saved – such as the substitution of toothed belts for camshaft drive, already proven in the car world and tested on the 500 GP racer of 1973. The government-appointed controllers wanted something more conventional with which to compete against the parallel twins of 400 and 500 cc then beginning to appear from Kawasaki, Suzuki and Laverda, not to mention Honda. Ing. Milvio, then in charge of the company, decided that Ducati would construct its own vertical twin.

The decision appalled Taglioni, who refused to have anything to do with the project and threatened to take early retirement unless he was permitted to continue his work on parallel lines on a mid-sized V-twin; fortunately his stock was such that he had his way, and the Pantah was the result. Meantime, though, his number two Ing. Tumidei took on the task of producing the parallel twin-cylinder contender, with help from Milvio who fancied his talents as a *progettista*.

The result of their efforts eventually appeared at the Milan Show in November 1975 after two major redesigns had taken place on the original prototype. This had initially begun life as a 360 degree vertical twin (in fact the cylinders were inclined forward by 15 degrees) with twin balance shafts incorporated in the design to smooth out the vibration endemic in such a design. However, these contra-rotating shafts absorbed too much power to be viable, a discovery which was also being made at the very same time by Norton-Villiers in Britain as they struggled to develop their Cosworth-powered Challenge machine. Additional demerits of the system were increased fuel consumption and lubrication problems associated with the increased oil drag promoted by the heavy shafts as they circulated in the unit-construction engine. The design team was forced to drop first one balance shaft, then the other, turning finally in desperation to a 180 degree crank throw and its attendant rocking couple as a means of countering at least some of the vibration problems.

Thus when the model finally appeared – on

schedule, it should be said – it was already a compromise. Three versions were offered initially; a 350 cc 'cooking' model, the GTL, measuring 72 × 43 mm, and producing 35 bhp at 8500 rpm, and a 500 of 78 × 52 mm, but owing nothing to either of the previous 500 parallel twin prototypes. The larger bike produced 40 bhp at 8000 rpm, and both it and the 350 employed single ohv valve gear with springs, with the camshaft driven by a single-row chain running off the gearbox up between the siamezed cylinders. There was, however, also a 500 Sport version which featured desmodromic valve gear, still with the chain-driven ohc but with the camshaft carrying twice as many lobes as for the valve spring versions. The benefits of the extra reciprocating weight and complication seemed hardly apparent with only an extra 500 rpm available compared to the 500 GTL, though other modifications including a sharper cam with an extra 6 degree of overlap resulted in a greater power output of 44 bhp; maximum torque was achieved at 5800 rpm. Though the new model series had been created primarily as an economy product, it was the 500 Desmo Sport which captured most attention, a fact which caught the factory rather on the hop, as it had only been conceived at the last moment as a means of adding spice to the range. It was not until 1977 that it became readily available even in its homeland. The problem was provoked by two other factors: Ducati Meccanica was undergoing one more serious financial crisis at the time, and was severely strapped for cash with which to set up production of the new model. Conversely the world-wide demand for diesel engines had stepped up dramatically in the wake of the fuel crisis and the industrial engine side was in full swing and bursting for space in its share of the crowded Borgo Panigale factory, which to exacerbate the situation was in the process of being rebuilt. Even if the new parallel twin range had been a roaring success – and it was far from that – the question of space in which to build the required numbers of motorcycles would have presented a ticklish problem.

In the end a solution to the difficulty was found close at hand. Leopoldo Tartarini had maintained close ties with Ducati since his days as a works rider in the 1950s, while his fledgling Italjet company on the other side of Bologna had grown steadily from an assembler of bought-in moped components to a fully established manufacturer in its own right. At the same time, Tartarini had acquired an industry-wide reputation as a styling genius whose talents were much in demand on a consultancy basis, and

indeed he had already been responsible for the transformation of the big V-twin from raw-edged, clumsily-styled prototype to lean and purposeful greyhound before its production launch in 1972. He had been in on the parallel twin project from the beginning but originally only in a styling capacity; whatever the merits or otherwise of the mechanical specification, there were few arguments that the bikes looked good, and indeed the 500 Sport's smooth and elegant red and white lines would shortly be repeated with renewed success on the 900 Darmah.

Tartarini had recently constructed a new and spacious factory in the eastern suburb of San Lazzaro di Savena, which the growing Italjet firm had yet to employ fully. As a long-time adherent to the parallel twin cause – he was and is a British bike fan enjoying recognition in the late 1960s with the Velocette-powered Indian and, more relevantly, an Italjet roadster powered by a 650 cc Triumph twin engine – Tartarini was reluctant to see the Ducati project with which he'd been so closely associated founder. He therefore arranged to take over the manufacture of the range, receiving the engine units from Ducati and installing them in Italjet-built cycle parts for sale under the Ducati label through their dealer network.

This arrangement enabled the model to be built reasonably economically and not at the expense of other more profitable activity at Borgo Panigale. Having made the commitment, both parties were nevertheless disappointed that sales did not take off as hoped, and though the range, with the addition of a 350 desmo version, producing 37 bhp at once again 8500 rpm, gave the companies an important foothold in the vital 350 class for the home market (where machines over this engine capacity are subject to greatly increased taxation), it was never anything of a seller.

The principal reasons were inherent in the design of the engine, for all models handled very well, especially the 500 Desmo with its beefed-up chassis. To start with the engine still suffered badly from vibration, especially in comparison with the turbine-like smoothness of the V-twins, and this coupled with the vertically split crankcases and wet sump resulted in the traditional British problem of oil leaks now spreading to the Ducati range. In addition, the whole bike, thanks mainly to the massive engine unit, was much too heavy, ranging in a dry weight from the 168 kg of the stripped 350GTL model up through the 175 kg of the 350/500GTV versions introduced in 1977 to broaden the range with a better-equipped version of the valve-spring model, to the 185 kg of the 500 desmo. The result was reflected in sluggish acceleration out of corners and from a standstill and, ironically, a disappointing fuel consumption of 55–60 mpg.

The all-alloy engine unit featured steel liners with a forged one-piece crankshaft running on only two plain main bearings with a massive central flywheel. Though a wet sump engine, the oil reservoir was separated from the crank after the problems encountered with drag on the balance shafts by means of an internal horizontal wall incorporated in the engine casting. This, therefore, necessitated the use of a gear-driven pump which not only fed lubricant to the various parts of the engine but returned it to the sump as well, instead of relying on gravity as would normally be the case. The plain bearing crankshaft design, with split shell big ends, demanded careful attention to the oil level and regular changes of lubricant every 2000 miles; many owners unaccustomed to taking such care in maintaining their engines suffered terminal engine disasters in consequence. Two oil filters were fitted in recognition of the importance of keeping the lubricant clean, a fact made even more difficult by the fact that, in accordance with normal Ducati practice but not that of the other manufacturers of plain-bearing engines, the five-speed gearbox not only ran in unit with the engine, linked to it by a helical gear primary drive, but also shared the same oil supply.

Though he's never admitted to it publicly, there exist good grounds for belief that Taglioni was unable to resist bringing some influence to bear on the design, since the included valve angle of 60

The parallel twin's first appearance in 'cooking' form at the 1975 Milan Show. Note the dated tank styling

degrees was the same as fitted to the 1973 Imola V-twin racers and would later see service on the Pantah. Though an eight-valve head was considered at one stage all the production bikes had two-valve combustion chambers, fed in the case of the 500 Sport by twin 30 mm PHF Dell'Orto concentrics with accelerator pumps. Both the chamber and the semi-slipper flat-top piston with large valve inserts featured accentuated squish bands; compression ratio on all models was 9.6:1. A good feature was the light-action clutch, possible in view of the relatively low power output of the range, and as on all Ducati road models a multi-plate oil bath type which could be adjusted by removing a triangular (rather than oval, as on the singles and V-twins!) cover on the right engine case.

As so often was the case with Italian machines and especially Ducatis at one time, one of the parallel twin's Achilles heels were the electrics. A 200 W crankshaft-mounted alternator, manufactured by the Motoplat affiliate to the company's Spanish Mototrans subsidiary, charged a 12 V/12 Ah battery, with the current controlled by a transistorized regulator and ignition by a set of contact-breakers mounted behind the rear of the left cylinder. Not only was the system inaccessible, it was also unreliable, and did as much as anything to give the model a bad reputation. Electric starting only was standard on all models.

Instead of the Marzocchi units fitted to the big twins, these Ducati middleweights were equipped with less expensive suspension components front and rear from the smaller Paioli company, which proved nevertheless to be entirely satisfactory, and together with the twin-loop frame, open at the bottom and using the engine as a stressed member, gave exceptional road-holding. Likewise, the use of twin cast-iron Brembo discs at the front and another at the rear on all models, even the valve-spring 350s, ensured more than adequate braking performance, and indeed the only unsatisfactory aspect of the cycle parts was the lack of padding on the thinly covered Sport seat which, allied to the extremity-tingling vibration, made journeys of any length a daunting experience. The use of Lanfranconi exhausts, better known for their appearance on the Moto Guzzi Le Mans on which they achieved a similar reputation to the dearly-loved Contis of the Ducati V-twins, gave a typically Bolognese exhaust note, for the 180 degree crankshaft throw resulted in an off-beat engine note not dissimilar to the 90 degree V-twins.

With a top speed of just over 110 mph for the 500 Sport, down to 92 mph for the whole 350 range

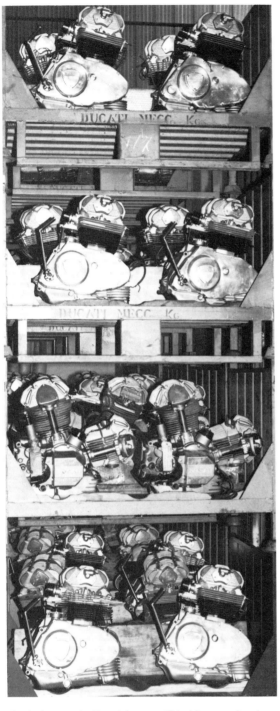

(including the desmo version), the sohc Ducati twin's performance was on a par with the pushrod Guzzi twins of equivalent capacity but inferior to the Laverda 350/500 twins as well as to the Japanese middleweights now beginning to make an impact on the Italian market in spite of hefty tariff barriers. Though a few brave souls stripped the 500 Sport down for road racing, it had no worthwhile success in the sporting arena. For the majority of Ducati enthusiasts, as well as most assuredly for Ing. Taglioni, who has never in the wake of the machine's disastrous sales record refrained from making the point that he was implacably opposed to its development from the start, the model has never qualified as a 'real' Ducati.

Instead, the motorcycle that most observers felt should have been built all along to the exclusion of the parallel twins appeared only two years after them at the 1977 Milan Show; the Pantah.

By the late 70s the Ducati factory still had large stocks of unsold parallel twin engines. After assembly had been farmed out to Italjet for a period, it was started up again in a desultory fashion at Borgo Panigale and by 1983 the final batch of 50 machines was being assembled

13

Road V-twins – bigger, and better?

In the summer of 1970 a very strange motorcycle was spotted on several occasions on the *autostrade* near Bologna. It appeared to be an ingenious hybrid consisting of a wide-angle V-twin engine set lengthways in the frame, with the front cylinder an Aermacchi one converted to bevel-drive ohc to match the rear pot, which was obviously off a Ducati single, the pair mounted on a specially made common crankcase. The frame looked like nothing else in the world and was apparently home-built, and the various ancillary components were all off-the-shelf items fitted as practically standard wear to thousands of Italian bikes over the last two decades. It was obviously, to those who saw it, a cleverly constructed one-off special; after all, no motorcycle manufacturer could possibly consider building such a weird-looking bike – could they?

Efforts to ascertain the motorcycle's provenance only resulted in an impressive display of its remarkable performance, for attempts to engage the rider in conversation were frustrated when he simply hooked a lower gear – there seemed to be five available – opened the throttle wide and disappeared into the distance, leaving the enquirer struggling in his wake. Though the age of the modern superbike had indeed dawned, Honda fours and their ilk were still rare birds on Italian roads, and this strange special repeatedly demonstrated to those who came on it that it had the legs of most street motorcycles it encountered.

It also handled well too, as one rider of a coveted new CB750 Honda found to his disgust when the well-used, ratty-looking hybrid cleared off from his powerful but 'hinge-framed' Japanese multi one evening returning to Bologna from Florence through the serpentine, switchback curves of the Autostrada del Sole, where it rises high over the Apennine Mountains before plunging down into the flat Emilian plain to which Bologna is the gateway. He was so impressed and yet mystified by the bike's

Tests of the 750 V-twin prototype were carried out not only on the roads around Bologna, but also at the Modena Aero-autodrome. Here in August 1970 the machine is nearing final development: Spaggiari is the rider, with Farne checking the fuel level and Ing. Taglioni receiving feedback from the tester. Note the drum front brake (Zagari)

performance, he actually sat down and wrote a letter to his favourite bike magazine; had they any idea, he implored, what the mystery special could be?

Indeed they had, for whispers had been rife in informed circles of the Italian press for the best part of that year about the new 750 V-twin that Ducati were developing to give the now wholly State-directed and financed company a stake in the increasingly important superbike market. Since the shelving of the abortive 500/700 cc parallel twins, Taglioni and his staff had been working full speed ahead on the new design, taking as their rough outline one-half of the equally ill-fated V4 Apollo.

True to form, Taglioni had considered and actually designed no less than four different versions of the same engine, which was to be a wide-angle 90 degree V-twin for the very reasons he had adopted the same included cylinder angle on the Apollo. These were a reduction in vibration due to the cancelling out of primary inertia forces (at the expense of an acceptably small degree of secondary vibration) and the superior cooling of the rear cylinder, partially masked on narrow-angle V-twins by the front pot, offered by such a layout. As well, the slim profile presented by a V-twin engine permitted a reduced frontal area of the machine as a whole, yielding reduced fuel consumption and increased performance due to more efficient air penetration. And then finally – though Dr. T himself could never be prevailed on to admit to this – there was the indisputable fact that like his other designs, whether road or racing, it was just *different*!

All four versions offered various advantages in strict engineering terms: a pushrod engine would be economical and easy to maintain, though hardly in the tradition of a Taglioni Ducati; a single ohc valve-spring version would on the other hand combine a fair degree of performance with acceptable manufacturing costs. But in the minds of many of the bike's potential customers Ducati meant desmodromics, so it made sense to design and consider a desmo version as well. Taglioni actually drew up two, one a single-cam development of the ohc valve-spring version, just as the desmo single then in production was related to the Mark 3, and the other a full-blooded triple-camshaft throwback to the days of the 125 racers which he estimated would in 750 cc form comfortably exceed 100 bhp and 150 mph.

The triple-ohc V-twin desmo would sadly remain a glimmer in its designer's eye, transcribed onto paper in a set of drawings that would be consulted again in the future, for when the time came to begin work on the 90 degree V4, which first took shape in 1981, Taglioni would once more design the same four types of engine in the new configuration before making his final choice. Yet in 1968, the days when it might have been possible to make the grand gesture of producing a triple ohc desmo 750 for the road market were already long gone, drowned in the ruthless tide of economic reality that had swept in from the East. The decision was made to follow the path already trodden by the single-cylinder

A side view of the 750 V-twin prototype at Modena in 1970 (Zagari)

ABOVE *A studio shot of the first V-twin, with rakish-looking stance and 18 in. front wheel filled with the large-diameter 4ls front brake – possibly a Fontana?*

TOP *Farne at speed at Modena in February 1972 on a 750 V-twin fitted with experimental fuel injection. Sadly, this feature was never adopted in spite of Ing. Taglioni's strong belief in its value (Zagari)*

LEFT *The first V-twin Ducati to enter Britain, displayed on Vic Camp's stand at a show in the winter of 1970–71. The tank has been changed from the prototype, and twin front discs are now fitted, of British parentage*

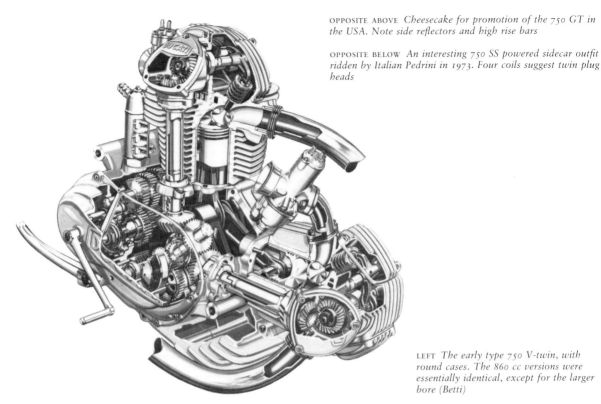

OPPOSITE ABOVE *Cheesecake for promotion of the 750 GT in the USA. Note side reflectors and high rise bars*

OPPOSITE BELOW *An interesting 750 SS powered sidecar outfit ridden by Italian Pedrini in 1973. Four coils suggest twin plug heads*

LEFT *The early type 750 V-twin, with round cases. The 860 cc versions were essentially identical, except for the larger bore (Betti)*

range and to produce an sohc valve-spring basic model, with a desmodromic version available for the sporting rider as a top-of-the-line model.

Thus when the mystery prototype was spotted on the Bologna *autostrade*, it was not long before the word was out; Taglioni was up to his tricks again. With their economic troubles, if not resolved, at least temporarily put aside thanks to the funds which the government had pumped into the company, including a healthy dollop of development budget, Ducati were able to reveal the prototype. Complete with somewhat odd styling, which fortunately bore no real resemblance to the eventual production model, it appeared at the Milan Show in November 1970.

The technical specification of the new machine made fascinating reading. Though bearing some family resemblance to the single-cylinder range there was little in common between the two apart from the shared system of valve operation; on the prototype this was by single overhead camshaft, with valve springs, driven by a vertical shaft and bevels, of which there were actually no less than nine such gears in the engine. The two cylinders measured 80 × 74.4 mm each, for a capacity of 748 cc, with firing intervals of 270 and 450 degrees

thanks to the 90 degree included angle between the two. Instead of sitting 'upright' in the frame, with the front cylinder horizontal and the rear vertical, the engine was ripped back 15 degrees to move the rear cylinder camshaft drive behind the rider's right knee, and to allow greater ground clearance for the front exhaust pipe. The resultant slight loss in cooling effect was countered by the use of coil valve springs, which in turn kept the rocker boxes narrow and allowed air to pass easily to the rear of the heads. Differential cylinder finning was employed – the source of the 'bitsa' theory when the prototype was first spotted – with the front cylinder having four sets of longitudinal fins and the rear one conventional circular finning. A single plug per cylinder was employed, fitted between the two valves which, however, still sat at an included angle of 80 degrees to each other.

The cylinders were slightly offset in relation to the centre crankshaft axis by just under one inch, the front one to the left, the rear to the right. This also improved rear cylinder cooling and enabled a straighter exhaust run to be employed, again improving ground clearance. The very strong crankshaft assembly consisted of a pair of bobweights forged integrally with their mainshafts

ABOVE *A 750 GT on test for* Motor Cycle *in March 1974. By now, production of the basic model has been finalized with only one front disc (Nutting)*

RIGHT *The 750 engine in its final original production form, with 'round case' styling and points ignition*

and pressed on to a 35 mm diameter single crankpin, the whole assembly supported in a total of four large ball bearings for a very rigid structure. The forged conrods sat side by side on the crankpin, running on caged roller bearings just as on the singles. A 150W alternator was positioned on the right end of the crankshaft, inboard of which was the timing chest containing the set of bottom bevels for the camshaft drive, as well as another shorter bevel-driven shaft driving the contact breakers through a 2 to 1 reduction. A spur gear beneath and behind the crankshaft drove the oil pump, consisting of a simple set of meshing gears for delivery, return to the 4.5-litre sump. The usual Ducati sludge-trap-type oil filter was incorporated in the rear of the crankcases.

In spite of the undue length of the engine unit dictated by the near-horizontal front cylinder, itself a consequence of the 90 degree vee (or L-twin, as it was sometimes rather pedantically called) design, Taglioni had achieved a manageable 60 in. wheelbase thanks to the use of a crossover drive-type five-speed gearbox employing a separate mainshaft and layshaft mounted one above the other to save space; a set of helical gears coupled the mainshaft to the crank, resulting in the engine running backwards. An oil-bath clutch was

employed, as on the singles, with an idiosyncratic withdrawal mechanism which instead of the conventional single long rod extending through the mainshaft comprised, in addition to the adjuster screw mounted in the pressure plate, three rods of varying length, a ball bearing and four rollers. Taglioni's intention was to spread the thrust load over as many different contact areas as possible, as well as to compensate for any slight misalignment of the hole down the centre of the mainshaft.

Unlike the majority of narrower-angle V-twin engines, the Ducati 750's cylinders both had the conventional arrangement of the exhaust ports facing forward for maximum cooling (but offset 30 degrees, with the inlet ports offset 15 degrees), necessitating in turn the use of two separate carburettors but a less than perfect inlet manifold, which was particularly heavily curved on the front cylinder. Unusually perhaps, twin Mark 1 Amal

ABOVE AND BELOW *Two stages in the early evolution of the 750 Sport: above is the original factory styling photo, with graceful exhaust line and black predominating over yellow.*

By the time the bike appeared at the Paris Show in October 1972, the colours had been reversed, the famous Contis had put in an appearance, and a half fairing added

The 750 Sport in final form, with black-painted crankcase and bevel drive covers, and no fairing. A single seat is still fitted, however

Concentrics were fitted to the prototype as well as to the first production bikes until Ducati's regular supplier Dell'Orto came up with a modern generation of concentric carburettors. These were adopted from 1973 onwards.

The much-needed adoption of 12 V electrics was a welcome feature of the new bike, which ran a total ignition advance of 38 degrees, sparking through a pair of coils mounted under the fuel tank. This would be one of the early V-twins' Achilles heels – electricity did not seem to be one of Borgo Panigale's strong-points: Taglioni mistrusted electronic ignition (in spite of having one of Europe's leading manufacturers in the field right next door!) after his experiences with ignition failures on the 500 V-twin racers in 1971. Eventually, though, he gave in and adopted it on the 860 range.

The prototype 750 engine had been fitted with straight-cut bevel and primary gears for development testing, but the production versions adopted helical gears to reduce engine noise and increase strength; even so the V-twin Ducati's mechanical noise was unmistakably that of a gear-driven engine and was to become one of the most distinctive sounds on the road, allied to the booming exhaust note of the Conti 'silencers', which were to become so beloved of the *ducatisti*. Each camshaft ran in three ball bearings, and offered 121 degrees of overlap, allied to an 11 mm valve lift and a considerable degree of dwell. Running on an 8.5:1

compression ratio, with the forged semi-slipper pistons having flat tops with machined-in valve pockets, the 750GT (as the basic model was to be known) produced 50 bhp at the rear wheel at 7700 rpm (60 bhp at the crankshaft).

This most unusual engine, which nowadays seems if not commonplace at least a relatively common sight on the roads of the world yet which in 1970 was the object of much comment and enquiry, was originally housed in a set of cycle parts broadly similar to those the production models eventually adopted, but with a less well-strengthened swingarm pivot area as well as other detail differences of geometry and fitments. By the time the first deliveries began in the middle of 1971, the frame had been modified to what was effectively a scaled-up replica of the Seeley chassis, which had been successfully adopted on the works 500 V-twin racers after being specially commissioned from the British chassis builder at the start of 1971. The tubular-section swinging arm with pull-type axle adjusters was a trademark of Seeley's work, but surprisingly early production models were fitted with a 19 in. front wheel (with 3.25 section tyre), presumably in an effort to achieve what was felt to be necessary increased ground clearance. By 1973 this was found to be no longer necessary and 18 in.

Later, the 750 Sport became slightly more sociable, with the addition in 1975 of a dual seat. The black finish on the engine cases was dropped

rims were eventually standardized front and rear. Marzocchi 38 mm forks with a single 11 in. Lockheed disc brake fitted to the left slider were employed, matched by an sls drum rear; with a dry weight of 430 lb this was deemed adequate to stop the bike from the 122 mph top speed of which it was capable, and indeed the use of the disc brake was the first time this feature had been employed on a Ducati road bike.

The first series of customer bikes offered a lean and hungry look which was undeniably appealing, the styling having undergone drastic revision before a final version was settled on, and the 19 in. front wheel contributed to an attractive 'kicked-out' look. These machines were also fitted with a fibreglass tank of somewhat uncertain quality, blending smoothly in with the line of the dual seat, and the whole ensemble was a favourable comment on the work of Leopoldo Tartarini, whose Italjet studio had been responsible for the final styling touches. A steel tank was required for the model to be sold in the UK, but a standard colour scheme of black and metalflake cherry red (Ducati had discovered the Candy-Coloured, Tangerine-Flake Streamline syndrome in 1972, the 500 and F750 road racers and desmo single being similarly afflicated) was adopted on all machines.

Riding the new Ducati twin brought a new experience into the life of road-testers the world over, once they'd learnt how to kickstart it properly,

for there was no electric starter available as befitted a sports-orientated machine. Vincents and Harleys were rare in Europe and the Guzzi V7 range had electric starting, so until riders of the new Ducati learnt to turn the engine over gently on the kickstart to the compression point on the front cylinder, there was a great deal of unnecessary huffing and puffing. That apart, once started and under way, the 90 degree V-twin's lazy, offbeat lilt proved deceptively easy-going. The new bike was a mile-eater, at home equally on twisting mountain roads as on flat straights, with large reserves of torque that made riding it a delight.

It was only a matter of time before a tuned version was introduced by the factory, and in 1972 the valve-spring 750 Sport arrived on the scene. Employing the same cycle parts as the GT but with clip-ons and rearsets and a single seat (though a later 1975 option was a dual seat), the yellow and black machine ran on a slightly higher compression of 9:1 and used the new generation 32 mm Dell'Ortos with accelerator pumps and no air cleaners, only a wire-mesh stoneguard on each carburettor intake. The superior breathing this afforded raised peak revs to 8200 rpm, at which point the output was 56 bhp at the rear wheel, good for a top speed of 127 mph. Later that year a

ALL *The best-looking Ducati ever built? Many would agree with this claim on behalf of the 750 Super Sport, in its day perhaps the fastest road-legal motorcycle in the world. Above and middle shows the first prototype shortly before its launch in March 1973, with round cases and very close to the Imola-winning works racer. Below, in its final form in 1976, with square cases and 900 SS styling, aimed mainly at the Italian market in which 750 cc production racing was still important (Top two – Zagari)*

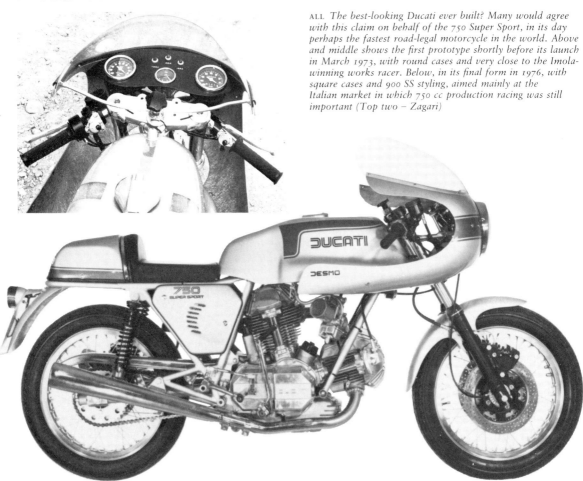

The Giugiaro 860 GTI prototype, at the Milan Show in November 1973. In spite of the headlamp fairing, which disappointingly was not fitted in production, the effect is already soft (Woollett)

European version was introduced, with 40 mm Dell'Ortos as fitted to the works racers and running on 10:1 compression with the engine outer covers and bevel drive housings painted matt black for identification. Top speed in this form was now up to more than 130 mph in standard form, and an electric starter was now available as an optional extra on just the cooking GT version only.

Paul Smart's Imola 200 victory in April of that year had done wonders for the new V-twin's future, and Ducati now seemed to be back on the road to prosperity, with a total production run of 20,000 units planned for that year, and plans to construct a new, modern factory on the site of the old one while still maintaining production. To celebrate their success, the company decided to have the racing department construct a small batch of Imola Replicas (as they were originally to be called), which would be street-legal versions of Smart's winning bike and thus ideal mounts for production and/or café racing. The scrapping of the 500 V-twin racing effort and the 350/3 prototype created capacity for this project in the competition department, but while it was originally intended to build only 25 machines in a single batch, demand was such that

further batches were commissioned and around 200 750 Super Sports, as the model was eventually officially titled (750 SS for short), were eventually made to satisfy world demand. The first run appeared in late 1973, while further batches were produced in 1974, before the arrival on the scene of the 900 SS. Even after that, the 750 SS continued to be produced but using the square crankcase bottom half, to satisfy the requirements of the Italian market, with particular emphasis on production racing, in which the 750 class was paramount.

Indeed, many of the 750 SS machines found their way on to race tracks all over the world, reaping Ducati as well as their fortunate owners a rich harvest of success and publicity benefit. Little wonder, for the bike was in every way the finest production racer in the true spirit of F750 racing yet to emanate from any factory. The sohc desmo heads featured racing camshafts offering increased lift (12 mm) and overlap (125 degrees), as well as the higher revs and increased reliability offered by positive valve control; hairpin feeler springs were, however,

ABOVE *An early 860 GT on test for* Motor Cycle *in the spring of 1974 (Nutting)*

BELOW *The 860 GT in final production form, again on a* Motor Cycle *test run, this time in 1975. A triumph of styling over design (Nutting)*

fitted to close the valves the last couple of thou for ease of kickstarting, as on the desmo singles, though a faulty batch of these on the second run of bikes made had some owners forced to resort to run and bump tactics till their first engine strip-down. 65 bhp in standard form was available at the rear wheel at 8500 rpm, though the engine was safe to 9200 revs, at which point a piston speed of 4000 ft. min. dictated an easing of the throttle: piston rings would also break if the engine was over-revved. Compression ratio was now 9.8:1.

But the 750 SS was more than an uprated Sport model with desmo heads: it was literally the product of the race shop and built to withstand the rigours of competition with little regard for the costs of doing so. Thus the rockers were carefully hand finished after manufacture in a stronger (but more expensive) metal than the desmo singles employed; the I-section conrod polished to perfection; the two-day process of shimming all the gears and valve gear to a state of breathtakingly fine tolerances undertaken; the inlet and exhaust ports carefully flowed to match their manifolds, with the inlets tapered at the head flange to increase gas velocity; and the primary gears now straight-cut, though the bevels remained helical. Dell'Orto's 40 mm

ABOVE *MCW tester John Nutting aboard the 860 GT in 1975*

LEFT *An 860 GTS poses beside a Cornish harbour in the summer of '76. The impractical Giugiaro seat has been replaced and a second front disc added*

carburettors were employed as on the Super Sport, again with accelerator pumps, matching the 40 mm inlet and 36 mm exhaust valves. The whole engine displayed the mark of a thoroughbred racehorse, while at the same time one which could be used for hacking down to the local pub, to be tethered outside the door ready for a lightning canter over hill and dale.

The 750 SS employed the same chassis as the Sport, but was now fitted with 18 in. wheels front and rear, and two cast-iron Brembo 280 mm disc brakes at the front and a single 225 mm rear disc. With a genuine top speed of over 135 mph available in standard form – easily the fastest in the 750 class at the time – the 750 SS could nevertheless be hauled down from a high terminal velocity with complete sureness and safety even in the wet, thanks to these magnificent stoppers which were almost certainly the finest brakes ever fitted to a production motorcycle. Even the slightly spongy feeling of the plastic-reservoir Scarab master cylinder fitted to some machines did not impair this braking power, and indeed at one time it seemed that no two 750 Super Sports boasted the same combination of discs and master cylinders, with components from Scarab, Lockheed and Brembo being fitted quite haphazardly – another indication of the hand-built

aspect of the bikes. Whatever the fitter's hand came upon in the parts box was what ended up on the bike.

While some allegations of poor finish could be levelled at the 750 SS, the purpose of the handsome bike, with its pale green frame and silver cycle parts edged with the same colour, was not to compare it to the plastic perfection of the Japanese products. The 750 SS was a raw-edged street racer which defined the outer limits of road-legal motorcycling, and as such, the ultimate product of the last era before the onset of noise and construction regulations blunted the edge of performance roadsters, was in more ways than one a truly historic machine.

However, in spite of the new V-twin range's success, Taglioni was far from complacent, and was already hard at work on an updated version to keep Ducati in line with the general trend of the times towards larger-capacity machines. The fruit of his efforts duly appeared at the Barcelona 24-hour race in 1973, and as recorded in the next chapter the new 860 cc Ducati engine achieved a victorious debut in this most arduous of races. Four months later, as was now Ducati tradition, the production road version made its first appearance at the Milan Show in the form of the 860 GTI, but also in best Ducati

ABOVE *The heavy-looking 900 GTS whose styling perhaps did much to turn some traditional Ducati customers away from the Bologna firm*

style there was another long wait before deliveries of the new larger-capacity bike began.

This eventually appeared in 1975, in the form of the 860 GT, the first of the so-called square-crankcase models (in fact only the outer covers were styled in this way) which utilized the same chassis components as the 750 series, but now clad in bodywork designed by the noted car stylist Giorgio Giugiaro of the Ital Design studio. The result was an unhappy illustration of the futility of commissioning designers from the four-wheeled world to work

on motorcycles, since for the most part they had no idea of the practicalities involved in day-to-day riding. Thus the stylish, kicked-up seat, for example, fitted at first to the 860 GT was uncomfortable in extended use and would soon collapse, and moreover the somewhat heavy tank and sidepanel lines proved a disappointment after the light and cobby appearance of the early 750 range.

Ducati were desperately trying to keep up with what they saw as overall styling fashion trends, and

BELOW *Along came Tartarini's restyling project, which produced the Darmah — one of the best-looking motorcycles of the modern era. This is the black and gold version*

when the 750 range was phased out almost at once except on the home market, the customer who had been seduced by the near-mystical experience of riding a 750 V-twin Ducati had little option but to plump for the new range if he wished to continue the experience. Fitted at last with transistorized electronic ignition to replace the unreliable points, the new 86 × 74.4 mm engine delivered even more bottom end torque than the 750, as well as improved top speed and still excellent fuel economy, especially when compared with the large-capacity Japanese models that were now pouring out of the big four's factories. Lanfranconi silencers had however replaced the raucous Contis, and weight had increased by 10 kg, taking the edge off acceleration in comparison to the earlier models, but still nevertheless respectable all the same. But there was no getting away from the fact that the 860 GT represented a softening of what had in the space of a little over three years become the muscular image of the V-twin Ducati. Few customers can have been deterred from buying the 750s by this raw-boned character – quite the reverse, for in Britain for example 1974 was Ducati's best-ever sales year – so while less dramatic an example than the disastrous parallel twins whose saga was being enacted at this very period, the change in emphasis of the Ducati image, as typified by the appearance of the 860 GT, was yet another example of the people who controlled the company's fortunes not understanding fully why people bought their products. If the customer wanted a European sports

tourer he almost certainly bought a BMW or, for rather less money, a Guzzi; if he wanted a performance bike he opted for a Laverda or Ducati. There's more than a case for the theory that the Ducati directors of the time were blinded by numbers: having done so well with the initial V-twins, they wanted to turn it into a bike for all seasons and all uses, instead of concentrating on its high-performance, sporty character. Inevitably, they ended up falling between two stools.

This whole attitude was typified by the dropping of the single-cylinder range at the end of 1974 (though unsold stocks continued to be catalogued for the next year or so) and the launch of just about the most uncharacteristic Ducati ever made: the 125 cc two-stroke Regolarita enduro/trial bike. This first appeared at the Milan Show at the end of 1975, and was evidently part of a misguided attempt to cash in on the growing popularity of dual-purpose lightweight two-strokes amongst the sport-mad Italian youth. With no less than 14 other manufacturers all offering similar machines to the home market, not to mention the various other European companies such as KTM and Montesa, who also catalogued similar machines (the Japanese were effectively excluded from the Italian market by a well-erected set of tariff barriers), the effort to persuade youngsters to start out with a Ducati, presumably before progressing on upwards to the big twins, was fated from the beginning. Taglioni was contemptuous of the whole idea and refused once again to have anything to do with it: 'I know

The early Darmah was one of those machines which seemed to change its appearance and lines depending on the colour it was painted: this one is red and white. This has the Campagnolo wheels also

900 Darmah

enough about two-strokes to know that I hate them', was his only comment, and in the wake of Spairani's departure (see the next chapter) the great man found himself increasingly forced to take a back seat in the technical committees which decided future new model plans.

Sadly, Dr. T was proved only too right when the Regolarita spectacularly failed to even cover its development costs, let alone sell well enough to make a profit. The abortive stroker comprised a conventional 54 × 54 mm piston-port cylinder running on 12.4:1 compression and producing 12.8 bhp at the rear wheel at 9000 rpm. The heavily finned alloy barrel with chrome bore was surmounted by a radially-finned head, the whole fed by a 34 mm Dell'Orto carburettor and transmitting the drive through a wet clutch and six-speed gearbox. This conventional engine, which might have been the product of any one of a couple of dozen manufacturers anywhere in the world, was mounted in an equally derivative set of cycle parts, consisting of a twin loop frame with rather flimsy-looking box-section swinging arm controlled by

Sadly, this final version of the Darmah had already lost much of the grace of its predecessors. Demands for a more comfortable, thicker seat led to the compromise seen in this brochure shot

two Marzocchi gas rear units with external reservoirs, mounted in a semi-laydown position. A small headlamp was protected by a wire mesh grille, and the plastic mudguards fitted over a 3.00 × 21 front wheel, with a 3.75 × 18 rear. Fashionable MX bars gave a suitably high-barred riding position, then *de rigueur* for boulevard cruising Italian-style. Dry weight was 237 lb – very heavy compared to most of the competition; the reason was that it was intended that the 125 should be the precursor of a whole range of two-stroke enduro and motorcross machines ranging in capacity from 125 to 400 cc, all using the same cycle parts, which thus had to be beefed up from the beginning to accommodate the larger engine capacities.

Fortunately or unfortunately, depending on one's viewpoint, this was not to be, for the sales performance of the 125 version was so disastrous that all ideas of enlarging it was swiftly dropped. In an effort to stimulate sales one of the leading Italian enduro riders, Italo Forni, was provided with a bike for use in the burgeoning local enduro scene, and at the beginning of 1977 the bike was completely redesigned as a more serious competition mount, and renamed the Ducati Six Days 125 (though it had not in fact been accorded the honour of representing Italy in the ISDT!). The cylinder was re-ported (still with the same 4 transfer/1 exhaust configuration) and compression increased to 14.6:1, with power now steeply raised to 25 bhp at 10,250 rpm at the crankshaft, translating to 19.5 bhp at the rear wheel. This was entirely adequate to make the Ducati stroker competitive in the 125 enduro class (though the high compression ratio made it very awkward to start on occasion) especially since the weight had now been trimmed to 218 lb dry. This enabled the little bike to register the second fastest 400-metre standing-start time in its class, with a top speed of just on 115 km/h; only the successful Aprilia was quicker. Problems with the gearbox now arose, though, for this had not been uprated to cope with the extra power. The chassis *had* been redesigned for a far more workmanlike result, now with the rear units almost upright and mounted upside down, and with a solid skid plate protecting the bottom of the engine.

In its final form the Six Days Ducati was a very attractive little dirt bike, and in some ways it's a pity that it didn't catch on. Customers just didn't associate Ducati any more with lightweight machines, and expecially not two-strokes, when the

BELOW *The 900 SSD was a tuned version of the Darmah which somehow managed to combine the flair of the 900 SS with the line of the Darmah*

rest of the company's range was so far up the capacity and performance scale; the bike suffered from an identity crisis. The introduction of the parallel twins, also announced in 1975, was intended to partially redress this situation, but they too bombed, and the company was left to concentrate on its now-traditional V-twin line.

The 860 GT and its new, re-styled and slightly more sporting counterpart the GTS had not been well received by the marketplace either, accustomed as it had become to the lean and hungry look of the earlier 750s. It had been intended to continue production of an uprated version of the 750 desmo,

ABOVE *A 900 SS in its natural habitat. This is Dave Cartwright's production racer*

By 1982 the 900 SS had evolved into this much less raw-edged but nevertheless purposeful machine: the origins of the later S2 styling can be clearly seen

termed the 900 SS, on the same basis as before, with the racing and development department assembling the model in batches when time permitted. But the reaction of the traditional Ducati rider to the Giugiaro-designed GT had been so unfavourable that instead plans were hurriedly pushed through, after the first small run of 900 desmos had been completed, to transfer the model to the production line where it would be built in series with a steel tank and slight modifications in the interests of more civilized road as opposed to race riding. Thus it was that, as the result of expediency born of desperation, the present situation arose whereby for the first time ever all production Ducatis are equipped with desmodromic valve gear.

The 900SS was the first bike to carry this numerical model designation, though in fact the engine was still the same 86 bore unit as fitted to the 860 GTS but with desmo heads. Based closely on the 750 Super Sport, it now revved to 7000 rpm, at which point an output of 79 bhp at the crank was delivered, translating to 68 bhp at the rear wheel: the desmo valve gear made the unit safe to 8000 rpm, though power tailed off over 7200 revs. Of more importance was the incredibly flat torque curve, practically the same at 4800 rpm as at 6900 rpm, even more remarkable than the 750's already very exceptional performance. Top speed was now a genuine 140 mph, achieved in road tests with a production model, making the Ducati once again

then the fastest road motorcycle in the world, some 7 mph faster than the Z-1 Kawasaki (with an extra 40 cc and twice as many cylinders) and the 1000 cc Laverda triple. Part of the reason for this was the Ducati's incredibly slim profile, only 27 in. wide at the handlebars, themselves the widest point on the machine. The light weight of only 427 lb for the production version with the steel tank also contributed to the bike's performance, and resulted too in impressive fuel consumption figures of better than 40 mpg. The latter was an important point in endurance racing, for which the factory now produced an optional racing kit, including a full fairing, high-level megaphone exhaust system, 13 mm lift camshafts (termed 'Imola' cams), an oil cooler and lightweight long-distance tank; some of these parts had already been available for the 750 SS, and were a requirement for competition riding, especially the exhausts, since the standard pipes, while providing minimal strangulation to the engine were too low-mounted for track use and would ground unless much longer rear units were fitted, which in turn altered the frame geometry. Having fitted the high pipes, the facing owner than discovered that the next thing to ground was the kickstart boss. . . .

Various efforts were made by the factory to

ABOVE *A real street racer – the Mike Hailwood Replica, which was Ducati's best-selling model in the early 1980s. Though the red and green machine was anything but a true replica of the TT-winning bike (whereas the 750 SS was certainly a close relative of the Imola victor), there was sufficient family resemblance to enable its rider to identify with Mike the Bike. This one has the one-piece fairing and steel fuel tank. Other variations were built*

LEFT *Bella Donna – or boy meets girl. A 900 S2, with Pantah-style fairing poses beneath an example of neo-Grecian sculpture somewhere in Britain in 1983. The S2, the first SS with an electric starter, was considered to be detuned from earlier examples but in fact was still an excellent sports motorcycle even if the raw edges had been filed flat (Parker)*

promote sales of the 'square' 860 GT and 'round' 860 GTS ranges; the British importer even took to calling the 860 GTS the 860 Mark 3, for the simple reason that they remembered the Mark 3 single had sold well enough to build up a following, so hoping that some of the respect that the little bikes had earned would be transferred to their bigger brother. When that didn't work the factory started calling it the 900 GTS because that sounded more impressive, even though it was exactly the same identical 864 cc machine as before! Such was the disdain with which the marketing 'experts' and salesmen who were now responsible for the distribution of the company's products treated the enthusiast. 1976 was the nadir of the company's fortunes in terms of their understanding of the market.

Meantime the Borgo Panigale factory had been completely rebuilt, incredibly enough on the same site as before without halting production, and now boasted one of the best-equipped manufacturing facilities in the European motorcycle industry. Some detail changes had been carried out to the GTS, largely at the insistence of the various importers, with at last a more modern version of that traditional Ducati failing – Italian-made switchgear – appearing on the 1977 models. But still the 900 SS desmo was the bike the customers wanted to buy, even taking into account the considerable price differential between it and its more humble valve-spring relation, so it was really remarkable that it took so long for the penny to drop at the factory as to the obvious move.

That move was to install the desmo engine, in a less uncomfortable set of cycle parts which might broadly be termed 'touring', but fortunately it sunk in in time. The result was the 900 SD Darmah (part of a curious obsession with this phonetic word ending that saw other models appear around the same time named Pantah, Utah and the unforgettable Rollah . . . as in Royce, no doubt) which was the consequence of considerable pressure on the part of Coburn & Hughes in particular to persuade the factory to provide a 'softer' version of the 900 SS which they felt, correctly as it turned out, would be a bestseller. Though still something of a compromise – Lanfranconi exhausts were fitted instead of the Contis that customers wanted but which were now marginal for the increasingly stiff noise regulations in various countries, for example – the bike looked stunning, having been styled by Leo Tartarini in the same manner as the 500 Sport parallel twin which debuted at about the same time. The desmo engine with softer cams and 32 mm Dell'Ortos was

A 900 crankcase pictured during assembly in 1979 (Zagari)

A 900 engine undergoing brake tests in the autumn of 1979 at the factory

Few special builders have felt it possible to improve on the factory V-twin chassis. However, Swiss Fritz Egli constructed this machine in 1974 (Minton)

detuned to produce a claimed 68.5 bhp at 7200 rpm at the crankshaft, though strangely this became only 55.5 bhp at 6500 rpm at the rear wheel in independent tests; maximum torque was reached at 4000 rpm according to the factory, but again tests on the *Motociclismo* testbed showed the figure to be nearer 5000 rpm in reality: the discrepancy was never adequately explained.

With a top speed of just on 120 mph – 10 mph faster than the GT – the Darmah provided the sort of performance that a Ducati rider was looking for, if not quite living up to the image conveyed by its name. The original Darmah was a fabled man-eating tiger from Sandokan, near India's northwest frontier! For it was indeed a much more civilized machine in every way than any previous Ducati twin; Japanese instruments and switchgear at last replaced the outmoded and unreliable British and Italian components which had been used before, while gold Campagnolo wheels fitted with the braking system off the 900 SS looked sharp and worked well. A really excellent instruction manual – only available in English, much to the annoyance of the consequently rather miffed Italian press! – replaced the previous half-hearted efforts; electric starting was standardized, though unlike on

Laverdas there was at first a supplementary though very awkwardly placed kickstart for emergencies. The riding position was more upright than on the SS, with one-piece touring bars and no more rearsets, and even at top speed was comfortable compared to the GT.

Numerous other detail improvements combined to make an enormous improvement over previous touring models, and of course the adoption of the desmo engine offered a direct link to the sporting and competition success of the racing V-twins. The frame had been lowered slightly in comparison to previous machines, and the fork angle steepened, presumably to produce quicker steering. Unfortunately, these modifications to a well-proven design resulted in the only real drawback to the new machine, which was a curious imbalance at low speeds in corners: the bike seemed to fall into a turn rather than steer its way round, and the image of the taut, good-handling Bologna twin was unfortunately lost. This same critique applied to the later Darmah SS, a slightly sportier version of the same model, whose clip-on bars exacerbated the defect.

ABOVE *An attempt to cash in on the growing market for small-capacity two-stroke trail bikes: the 125 Regolarita as it first appeared in 1975 – too heavy and too slow*

RIGHT *The 125 two-stroke Ducati engine was a piston-port unit measuring 54 × 54 mm; carburettor was a 34 mm Dell'Orto*

The introduction of the Darmah at the Bologna Motor Show in December 1976, with deliveries commencing later the following year, went a long way towards restoring the company's reputation amongst its faithful clientele. In spite of the extra weight – the bike weighed 475 lb dry – it had a useful performance and was beautifully finished. But in an inexplicable move, the Ducati management decided to narrow the gap between the Darmah and the 900 SS sports bike by detuning the latter for 1977 with the fitting of 32 mm carburettors and Silentium silencers in an apparent attempt to kow-tow to various construction-and-use regulations which were being introduced by certain more bureaucratically minded countries. Thus if you lived in Britain and wanted an SS, you had to accept one fitted with the silencers to meet the Dutch noise regulations, for example. The resultant outcry from not only the UK but other countries which had now become vital export markets for Ducati, such as Japan and Australia, resulted in a hurried about-face by the factory barely a year later, and the 40 mm pumper carbs and slightly modified Contis made a welcome reappearance.

A much more intelligent move was to cash in on the somewhat unexpected success by Mike Hailwood in the Isle of Man in 1978 by producing a Hailwood Replica version of the SS. This was effectively a stylized version of the 900 SS, whose

The 1977 Sei Giorni was a much more serious enduro mount, and could have proved a real sales success had it not been already tarnished

mechanical specification it adopted almost completely, but fitted with a very attractive full fairing, and fuel tank based on the NCR seat/tank unit used by Hailwood in the Island. The ensemble was finished in the green and red livery of Sports Motor Cycles, with white trimming to complete the Italian national colours, and was unquestionably a masterpiece of both styling and marketing. The company enjoyed deserved success with this machine on a world-wide basis (though it was not homologated officially for the USA, some bikes did manage to creep in through a somewhat devious route), and it was Ducati's best-selling model in the 1980–81 model year. Strangely, though, in spite of the full fairing it was actually a mile or two slower at top speed than the standard 900 SS with only a half fairing. The styling added an extra 600,000 lire to the cost of the machine on the home market, and its success was a dramatic vindication of the value of racing success in marketing terms. Indeed, it may be claimed with some justification that when Ducati has tried over the past 20 years at least to build a touring or runabout model it's been doomed to failure, but when they've opted instead for a sports bike, they've been rewarded invariably by success.

At the start of the 1980s it appears that the lesson has sunk in.

Indeed, the last new Ducati design to appear before this book was written typifies in every way the sort of machine that the Bologna factory has excelled at making down the years; the Pantah. Elected 'Bike of the Year' by an international panel in 1980, the Pantah first appeared at the Milan Show in 1977, and represented Ing. Taglioni's riposte to the, as he saw it, gratuitous insult to both his engineering intelligence and the Ducati reputation which the 500 parallel twins had delivered. Ducati needed a middleweight model, which in time would begin to rival the performance of the big V-twins, but he had contended all along that a scaled-down version of the 750/900 range could be made and sold at a profit, rather than the derivative vertical twins which had proved troublesome and disappointing in the extreme.

A true scaled-down replica of the big V-twin was out of the question, for the bevel-driven engine was expensive to manufacture thanks to the multiplicity

The 350 Rollah on its solitary appearance at the Milan Show in November 1977. The belt-driven ohc single-cylinder engine was Pantah derived

the bike in order to test the idea further, but he resolved to adopt it on the prototype of his new machine, which like the bigger bikes would be another sohc 90 degree V-twin, with two-valve heads, but this time with desmodromic valve gear as a standard feature.

The Pantah engine was originally designed in 500 cc form, measuring 74 × 58 mm and thus even more heavily oversquare than had been the case with any production Ducati to date. The vertically split crankcases–another Ducati hallmark over the years– were gravity diecast and incorporated two large ball bearings in which ran the one-piece cast-iron crankshaft. As on the big V-twins, the two forged conrods sat side by side on a common crankpin, but in a new departure for Taglioni, if not Ducati, this was not of the caged roller bearing type but instead employed a plain bearing, with separate conrod caps and Vandervell shells. The purpose of this was to counter some big end problems which had been experienced on the 900 twins in view of the sustained high revs which the desmodromic valve gear permitted the engines to attain. However, a drastic increase in oil pressure was now required, to 70 psi compared to 15–20 psi hot on the bevel-driven, roller crankpin twins, and this was provided by a single gear-type oil pump running off the

of its fine-tolerance gears and careful assembly required. To resolve this problem, Taglioni instead opted for a solution that had already had much currency in the four-wheel world, from the Cosworth-BDA racing engine at one end and the Fiat 128 at the other; camshaft drive by toothed rubber belt. Indeed, he had been the first engineer in the motorcycle sphere to publicly experiment with this concept, when the 500 cc V-twin racer had appeared in Spaggiari's hands in the 1973 season with dohc heads driven by external belts. Factory politics had prevented him from contining to run

The prototype Pantah, showing the final chassis used, but with pre-production finned cambelt covers that were strangely not employed on the final version

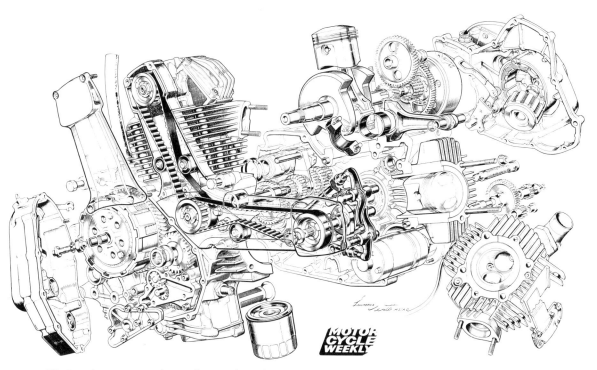

ABOVE *The Pantah engine in production form, as drawn by MCW artist Lawrie Watts*

BELOW *The 500 Pantah's styling in final production form – here seen in late 1979 – was not to everyone's taste, with an awkward combination of lines and planes that made for a rather heavy effect. But the superb mechanical package more than compensated for this (Zagari)*

LEFT *A 500 Pantah engine in the factory racing department in December 1979 being 'studied' for possible (?) competition use (Zagari)*

BELOW *Ingredients of a Pantah cylinder head*

helical primary drive, itself in turn keyed to the right-hand crankshaft taper. Return feed was once again by gravity to a wet sump containing 3 litres of oil, and a new feature was the adoption of a car-type screw-in oil filter in the front right corner of the crankcase bottom.

Another departure from tradition, but this time of even greater moment, was the to some minds long overdue adoption of a 60 degree valve angle on the Pantah, the first time this had been featured on a production Ducati. Sixty degree heads had long been a prerequisite of significant Ducati power on the V-twins since they first appeared on the Imola bikes in 1973; now the customer could have them too. The valves themselves were very large for a 500, a 37.5 mm inlet matching a 33.5 mm exhaust, operated by single camshafts with the conventional opening cams located as on the desmo singles and big V-twins between the two closing cams on each shaft, which in turn ran on three ball bearings as before. This time, however, the camshafts were driven by two Uniroyal PowerGrip toothed belts which had to be adjusted to give 5 mm free play in the middle of their run with a cold engine to allow for thermal expansion. That done, Ducati claimed test runs of over 30,000 km without any problems with the belts being encountered.

The belts were driven by two pulleys sited on the right extreme of a cross-shaft located behind the crankshaft and driven directly off it by a helical pinion keyed to the shaft, inboard of the small flywheel and 200W 12V alternator. Taglioni had insisted on being allowed to adopt what he considered to be the best transistorized ignition system available, rather than be forced out of a mixture of convenience and old loyalties to use the less reliable products of the separate Ducati factory next door, now renamed Ducati Elettrotecnica. Thus the Pantah was fitted with Bosch ignition, actuated by a flywheel trigger and sparking the single plug per head using the dead spark system. Electric starting was standard, without the option of the kickstart being available, and light return springs were fitted to the valves as on the big desmos for ease of starting.

Yet another novel departure, especially for a four-stroke, was the use of Gilnisil (Italian Nikasil) bores in the light alloy cylinders to replace conventional liners. Both cylinder and head finning had synthetic rubber plugs jammed between the fins to reduce resonance, an important source of engine noise which had to be reduced in light of the ever more stringent noise regulations imposed all over the world. This was another reason for the adoption of belt-driven camshafts; indeed the Pantah at first seemed almost unnaturally silent for a Ducati when it first appeared – in spite of the efforts of the manufacturer of the exhaust system, whose name was Conti. . . .

Semi-slipper pistons were employed once again with valve inserts, though these were not as pronounced as on the 900s. A shallow dome had a flat machined on the top, and compression ratio was not high at 8.7:1, dictated by the ever-reducing lead content and octane level of contemporary pump fuel; it started out at 9.5:1 when the first production machines were delivered. Maximum ignition advance of 33 degrees was employed. Twin 36 mm Dell'Orto carburettors with accelerator pumps were fitted, with the same degree of port offset on both inlet and exhaust as on the big twins, for the same reasons.

Another departure from Ducati norm was to be the use of hydraulic action for the clutch adopted from 1981 onwards, in spite of which it was a very stiff pull. Again of the oil-bath variety, the clutch's drum and hub were both made of alloy, and would be a limiting factor in increasing the engine size much beyond 600 cc in the future. A five-speed gearbox was fitted.

But for the time being it was the 500 Pantah that first appeared, the slim, compact and quite light (60 kg) engine being housed in an equally unique frame also designed by Taglioni, and bolted to it at only three points, thus facilitating easy engine removal. The chassis was of a trellis type, consisting of two pairs of parallel tubes running from the well-boxed steering head on either side of the rear cylinder to meet another pair of tubes running up from the rear of the crankcase; two intermediate pairs of bracing tubes provided the necessary structural rigidity. There was no swinging arm pivot as such, since the rear fork actually pivoted in two hefty lugs incorporated into the rear of the crankcase castings, very close to and just behind the engine sprocket and thus providing near constant chain tension for the final transmission. The whole structure was both light, rigid and practical, contributing to a dry weight of 396 lb. Marzocchi 38 mm front forks were fitted, though due to supply problems some bikes were fitted with Paioli units; all carried twin 260 mm

diameter Brembo discs, with a single such brake on the rear. These were cast-iron as usual, drilled for drainage, and actuated by Brembo calipers. The wheelbase was a compact 57 in., in spite of the 90 degree V engine.

The Pantah's styling was as distinctive as the engine characteristics, and not everyone felt the shape of the fuel tank or line of the standard half fairing seemed to achieve the perfection of the Super Sport or the near-ideal of the Darmah. A pair of chrome covers fitted over the belt drive to the camshafts, replacing the prototype's layout that had seen the belts enclosed within the barrel castings which were ribbed on the outside in the same direction as the cylinders to give a much more pleasing effect. Unfortunately it was found necessary to increase the cooling fin area slightly, and so this more attractive layout was replaced by the polished covers.

It was the Pantah's performance that its customers cared most about, and Ing. Taglioni had not disappointed them, for in designing the bike he had produced the fastest 500 cc road machine of its age. Producing 49 bhp at the rear wheel (54.75 bhp at the crank) at 9000 rpm, it also had an incredibly flat torque curve, yielding practically the same figure at 3000 rpm as at 10,500 revs, with maximum pull at 6750 rpm. Top speed of 124 mph with the

Amazing what a good paint job can do: compare this 1981 version of the 600 Pantah shot in California with that on page 163 (Parker)

rider under the screen was however achieved at only 8300 rpm; in other words the bike would not pull its standard gearing (the engine was in fact safe to 10,500 rpm, and thanks to the plain big-end bearing could take this sort of abuse, but the power dropped off smartly after 9000 rpm), and this perhaps accounted for some initial comment that 'more power was needed' from early road-testers. The Pantah possessed such exceptional performance for a mere 500 – and a twin at that – that riders often fell into the trap of comparing it with much larger-capacity machines.

In due course two capacities were introduced, with a variety of states of tune and equipment offered varying from a police version which the local *carabinieri* of Bologna enthusiastically adopted, though an economy model without the fairing, to a touring machine with panniers and one-piece bars. Of the other engines, the 600 appeared first in 1981, with bore size increased to 80 mm for a total capacity of 583 cc (though the racing versions used an 81 mm bore for 598 cc; why Taglioni did not employ this configuration on the standard 600 is something he's not so far decided to explain). This now required hydraulic clutch actuation in view of the heavier springs required to transmit the additional power, which had been increased to 58

The Bologna carabinieri assemble in the city's main square in 1982 to take delivery of the fleet of specially-designed 600 Pantahs

bhp at 8500 rpm at the crankshaft, yielding a shade over 52 bhp at the rear wheel. Top speed was now up to 128 mph, but of more import was the bottom-end torque, which had been increased with the extra capacity and gave improved accleration from a standstill. All other aspects of the bike were the same as for the 500 which continued in production, except for the fairing, which now featured front canard-type projections, to be joined in April 1982 by a 350 version, again a desmo like its two bigger brothers and measuring 66 × 51 mm for a total capacity of 349 cc. This model, dubbed the 350 XL, had been introduced to beat the Italian regulations, which saw a considerable additional sales tax levied on bikes of over 350 cc, and thus appeal to the younger market for which until then Ducati did not have a current model after the demise of the 350 parallel twin and the 125 Six Days. The 350 Pantah

OPPOSITE (BOTH) *In April 1982, two further variations on the Pantah theme were announced. Above is the 600 TL touring model, while below is the 350 XL, another (more successful) attempt to cash in on the Italian tax law which penalises machines over 350 cc*

had a relatively mild state of tune for this reason, since Ducati did not wish to suffer the same sort of accusations as had been levelled at some of the Japanese manufacturers for producing motorcycles aimed at the youth market which were too fast by half: 40 bhp at the crank (35 bhp at the wheel) at 9600 rpm, running on a 10.3:1 compression ratio and twin 30 mm carburettors gave a top speed of 105 mph, with sporting rather than mind-boggling acceleration.

The XL, which was supplied with a handlebar fairing only, was in fact the replacement for a Pantah-inspired machine which, though shown in prototype form at the 1977 Milan Show, did not in fact go into production, for reasons which have never become completely clear. This was the 350 cc single-cylinder Rollah, also displayed in trail bike form with 21 in. front wheel and small-diameter triple disc brakes and called the Utah. The engine was simplistically described as one half of a Pantah, but in reality it was more than that and in retrospect it may well have been that the Ducati management did not feel there to be a sufficient market to justify the development of what was essentially a completely different model line.

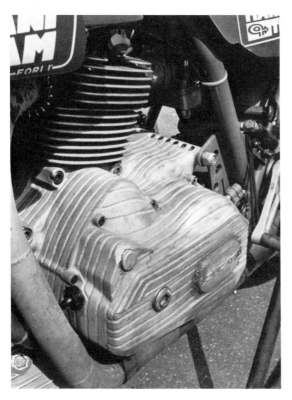

Weight-saving carried to the ultimate degree: this 900 SS was entered for the Imola 200 in 1982

In 1979 Meccanica Ducati was reorganized by the government department headed by the so-called Ministero delle Partecipazioni Statali into a newly created group of state-owned companies whose principal area of manufacture was in the diesel engine sector. Ducati had been steadily building up its stationary engine side, until it now dwarfed the motorcycle sector by a factor of 70/30 in overall turnover and even more in terms of profit contribution, so that the diesel engine business was effectively subsidizing the continued manufacture of motorcycles. The VM Group, as the new conglomerate was now known, also included another famous name from Italian automotive history, for Isotta-Fraschini had built some of the moxt luxurious and powerful cars in the world in the pre-World War II period before shelving automotive production in favour or marine and other diesel units. In 1982, though, VM would make a return to the car world when the company designed and produced a four-cylinder turbo diesel for sale to British Leyland for installation in the Rover SD1 saloon and to Alfa Romeo in their 2400 Turbo Diesel Alfetta. This engine was designed and built in the Ducati factory.

In reviewing current projects at the start of 1979 the new directors of the Group, led by a man sympathetic to Ducati's struggle for survival, Ing. Mario Brighigna, almost certainly decided not to proceed with the Rollah/Utah design. This was a pity, though doubtless dictated by resources, for the engine had all the makings of an outstanding 1980s version of the classic single-cylinder design. The vertical cylinder (in fact inclined forward by 10 degrees in another throwback to Ducati's past) bore a visual resemblance to the rear pot of the 500 Pantah, and like it featured sohc desmodromic valve gear driven by a toothed belt. The compact crankcase was entirely different, housing a five-speed gearbox with gear primary and an electric starter on the Rollah, with kickstart only on the Utah. The one-piece forged crank featured a plain big end as on the Pantah, and the Gilnisil-coated cylinder measured 83 × 64 mm for a total capacity of 346 cc. Running on 9.5:1 compression and a single 30 mm carburettor the engine's output was 27 bhp at the crank and 24 bhp at the rear wheel; with a dry weight of 340 lb for the prototype roadster performance would not immediately have been exceptional, but there was certainly room for development, especially at a price of only 1,700,000 lire in 1978. Sadly, though, the project was not persevered with, and by the turn of the decade the only Ducatis were all desmodromic V-twins.

14

V-twin racers –
two cylinders can be better than four

When word of the imminent arrival of the 750 V-twin Ducati on the large-capacity road bike market first began to surface during 1970, most observers felt it was but a matter of time before a racing version would be announced, to continue the factory's established (and successful) policy of testing new street models in the heat of competition before releasing them in developed state to the waiting market. If along the way they were able to pick up some honourable places and even the occasional win against the pure-bred racing machines they were obliged to compete against, so well and good. It all served to further the sporting image which the company had so successfully built up over the previous 20 years.

The burgeoning interest on both sides of the Atlantic in what was soon to become Formula 750, but which in the two years before the FIM could be persuaded as belatedly as usual to recognize the new category, was simply termed the 'Daytona Formula', lent support to these feelings of inevitability surrounding Ducati's plans for an official return to racing on a grander scale than their support of Spaggiari's efforts in Italian events with the desmo singles in the 1960s. The production-based F750 category was tailor-made for a factory like Ducati, whose emphasis had always been on developing racing versions of their road bikes, rather than designing out-and-out racing machinery with little relevance to the need of the road-riding customer.

Thus it was a major surprise that when the Bologna factory did indeed announce at the end of 1970 that they would be returning to racing officially the following season for the first time since 1960, their chosen field was not to be the fledgling 750 one, but the blue riband of motorcycle road racing, the 500 cc Grand Prix class. However, the machine they were to use in order to challenge Agostini and the MV Agusta team, which had dominated the category for the last three years since

Honda's withdrawal, was closely related to its bigger production-orientated brother; it was, in fact, a 500 cc V-twin.

The reasons for the company's return in this way and at this time were not hard to fathom. The wide-angle 90 degree V-twin layout was a novel one, especially for a sporting motorcycle, and some resistance to the configuration, later to be immortalized by *Cycle* magazine editor and Daytona Superbike winner Cook Neilson as having a 'weird-Harold appearance', could be anticipated. Proving its viability in the international road racing world not only rebut such reservations, but any success earned would rebound to the benefit of the new 750 line. Then too, there were technical arguments in favour of a return to racing; both two- and four-valve heads had yet to be tested under the stringent conditions imposed by competition and the same applied to the frame design, which had yet to be finalized. A return to racing could yield valuable information not otherwise obtainable.

The decision to return to racing was taken at a board meeting in October 1970, at which new company President Arnaldo Milvio and his deputy, now general manager Fredmano Spairani successfully championed the racing cause. From there to the 500's first appearance at the Modena meeting on 21 March, 1971, was but a short six months, but once again Taglioni's tremendous capacity for hard work, plus the fact that as usual he'd done much of the preliminary design some time beforehand and had filed it away ready for later use, enabled the deadline to be met. Spairani took an enthusiastic control of the team. In a style more usually associated with the Japanese teams, the bike proceeded from drawing board to its racing debut in just over five months. And when Bruno Spaggiari became embroiled in a dice for third place in that inaugural Modena outing with Roberto Gallina's speedy 8-valve Paton twin, behind the MVs of Agostini and Bergamonti, it seemed almost too good to be true. It almost was, for gearbox problems dropped the bike back to finish sixth, but the point had been made. For the first time Ducati had a serious 500 class contender.

Even more remarkably, in view of the short time available, two versions of the same 90-degree V-twin sohc valve-spring engine had been made, with two and four valves per cylinder respectively. Taglioni was intent on using the racing experience as a mobile testbed, so to this end two separate frame designs were also employed. The two-valve engine was fitted into a chassis of Ducati's own design, made for them by Verlicchi in Bologna, and it was this machine which Spaggiari rode in the Modena debut. The 8-valve unit, on the other hand, was sent in 'empty' form to Colin Seeley in Britain for a special frame to be designed for it, based on his highly successful Mark 3 chassis which had successfully given a new lease of life to the ageing G50 Matchless engine in Grand Prix and short-circuit racing alike. Seeley had been recommended by Vic Camp as a master in the art of tube bending.

Both engines employed the same cylinder dimensions, once again the hallowed 74 × 57.8 mm oversquare layout, with camshaft drive by the traditional vertical shaft and bevel gears up the right

Pictured in Colin Seeley's workshop in Erith in February 1971, a bare 500 V-twin racing engine receives its British chassis

side of each barrel. These were finned differentially in a way later to become a hallmark of the 750 and 900 V-twin roadsters, but used in public for the first time here, with the forward cylinder finned longitudinally and the rear one horizontally in relation to the cylinder head joint. The protruding wet sump was also finned for cooling purposes, with a gear-driven oil pump fitted on the right of the engine just below another, fairly short bevel shaft which drove the twin contact breakers for the coil ignition. A six-speed gearbox with straight-cut primary gears was fitted, with a multi-place dry clutch tucked well out in the airstream on the left. Though not revealed at the time, included valve angle was 60 degrees on both engines, with squish bands on both the combustion chamber and flat-top slipper piston, which had pronounced valve inserts. Twin 40 mm Dell'Orto carburettors with separate round float chambers were employed, bolted directly onto the heads and fitted with short spun alloy velocity stacks, whose use was good for a couple of extra brake horsepower.

Two riders were signed at the start of the season to ride the machines; the faithful Spaggiari and up-and-coming newcomer Ermanno Giuliano. Spaggiari was deputed to ride the two-valve machine, which produced 61.2 bhp at the rear wheel at 11,000 rpm, with an exceptionally smooth powerband from 6000 rpm upwards. Fitted in the Ducati-designed frame, featuring a single cast-iron front

disc with Lockheed caliper and 200 mm Fontana 2ls rear drum, it resulted in a dry weight of only 297 lb – apparently disappointing nonetheless for Taglioni, who'd been aiming for the 275 lb mark!

Giuliano's Seeley-framed bike housed the four-valve engine, whose cylinder heads were both taller and more heavily finned than the other version. Producing 65 bhp at 11,500 rpm, it however offered a less flexible powerband, with real power only arriving from 8000 rpm onwards. Taglioni admitted later that this experience was the main reason he did not adopt four-valve heads on the Pantah and indeed he was able by careful attention to the combusion process to arrive at a best figure by the end of 1972 of 71 bhp at the wheel for the 2-valver, as opposed to 69 bhp for the less flexible 4-valve.

The frame, made as usual with Seeley products in Reynolds 531 tubing, weighed a mere 21 lb, and consisted of twin top tubes extending back at a narrow angle from the steering head, with a similar, braced pair running down from the steering head to the swing-arm pivot point, enclosing the rear cylinder. A pair of small-diameter tubes originally joined the two runs beneath the seat, passing close on either side of the rear carburettor, but these were later dispensed with. A final pair of tubes ran down from the rear of the steering head to bolt to the front of the sump, leaving the lower part of the frame open and thus employing the engine as a semi-stressed member. A tubular swinging arm with pull-type axle adjusters completed this light and very rigid design.

A Seeley drum front brake and Manx Norton-type rear were originally fitted to the chassis, but were substituted for the same brakes as those on the Ducati-framed bike by the time of Giuliano's scheduled debut at Modena. Unfortunately, the engine had been fitted with electronic ignition (made by the neighbouring Ducati Elettronica firm), which played up on the day, causing him to non-start. The new machine had, however, lived up to expectations in Spaggiari's hands, so after sitting out the following week's Rimini event in order to make modifications to both bikes, the team was next seen in action at Imola in April, after having travelled abortively to Riccione earlier in the month only to see the 500 race cancelled after Bergamonti was tragically killed in a crash on the 350 MV. This would mean the end of the Italian street circuits.

The Imola race brought even more happiness to the Ducati camp, for though Spaggiari once again suffered gearbox trouble, which forced him to retire while holding a comfortable second place, Giuliano's machine ran perfectly on its debut to allow the youngster to take over the runner-up spot and hold it to the end, behind Ago's MV and well ahead of the horde of Kawasakis and Yamahas, as

The 500 V-twin when first revealed to the press in early 1971, here fitted with the Ducati-designed chassis which proved so unsatisfactory (Perelli)

well as the Linto and Paton twins. The following week at Cesenatico he repeated the result, after Spaggiari had given the team even more encouragement by dicing with the MV-mounted world champion for the lead for the best part of the race before his engine seized. The Bologna factory were back in business, and nobody realized it better than then four-times world champion Phil Read, who after winning the 250 race on his private Yamaha had been forced to watch the 500 race from the sidelines after his works Benelli had failed to materialize. Eager for a competitive 500 ride, Read approached Spairani to see if he could get aboard one of the V-twins, and after a short discussion one was promised to him for the Silverstone international meeting in August – not sooner, for the factory had much catching up to do with development in light of the lessons learnt during the hectic round of Italian meetings. Talk was of a magnesium engine scalling close to the magic 275 lb limit, as well as of a dohc version of the four-valve engine producing over 80 bhp, offering a power to weight ratio that would be slightly superior to that of the three-cylinder 500 MV Agusta.

An intensive couple of months' work now followed, with the modifications to the machine tested at a convenient international meeting in June at Skophia Locka in Yugoslavia: Gilberto Parlotti, then making a name for himself on the 125 Morbidelli, scored the 500 V twin's first but sadly only victory quite comfortably on the four-valve-headed version, thanks principally to the superior handling abilities and lighter weight of the Seeley frame; Spaggiari was third. The result was that Seeley was commissioned to make five more frames, and mechanic Giancarlo Librenti journeyed to Britain with the two-valve engine now slotted in the original Seeley frame for tests and modifications. While there, Alan Dunscombe – Vic Camp's sponsored rider then cleaning up in British club racing on single-cylinder Ducati machines – tested the bike at Snetterton and reported that the rev limit had been raised to 11,800 rpm, but the powerband narrowed so that usable power came in only at 9000. Marzocchi forks had replaced the Seeley units once fitted, while both Ceriani and Girling rear suspension was being tested. The following week Read rode the bike at Brands Hatch for the first time, and reported himself well pleased with its performance and handling.

A change of policy now came about at Ducati, who had intended to enter some of the GPs but now found themselves running behind with final development of the 750 road model. The next

The 1972 version of the 500 GP bike (Zagari)

outing would be at the non-Championship but nevertheless important Silverstone meeting, but just before it Read crashed his Yamaha in practice for the Czech GP and damaged a shoulder. The possibility existed that he might not be fit in time for the race, so another rider was invited to test the 500, as well as the inevitable racing version of the new 750 that had now been constructed. His name? Mike Hailwood.

Mike the Bike had been dividing his time between car and bike racing since Honda's withdrawal four years previously, and indeed in 1972 would eventually win the prestigious European Formula 2 four-wheel championship in one of John Surtees's cars. But for now he was still interested in racing motorcycles, and in a hurriedly arranged test session rode a V-twin Ducati for the first time. However, his international race debut on such a bike would have to wait until the 1978 TT, for Read reported fit to ride the new 500, while with the 750 Ducati, now fitted with desmodromic heads, Hailwood reported that the handling was 'not to my liking' and instead confined his outings to a Yamsel 350 twin.

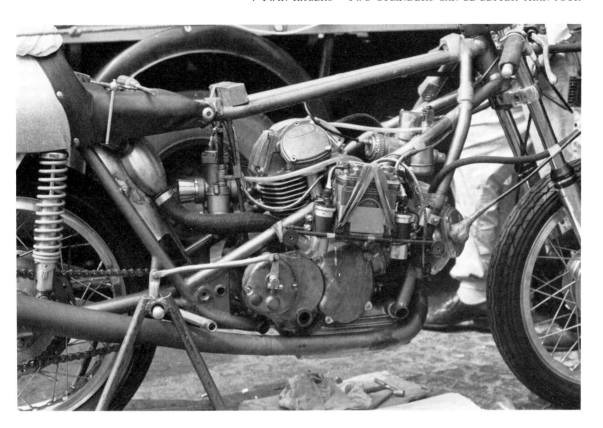

Both Read and Spaggiari appeared on the V-twin 500s, both two-valves engines fitted in Seeley frames, in the 500 race at Silverstone, where each worked up to 3rd place at one stage behind winner Agostini's MV and the Suzuki twin of a rising young star called Barry Sheene. Both Ducatis eventually retired though, Read with a run big end in his first race on the bike, and Spaggiari when the electronic ignition again played up.

Hailwood was mounted on a Benelli four at the Pesaro international the following week but Read sat it out in order to concentrate on becoming the first privateer to win a world title. Aboard his TD2 Yamaha he was neck and neck with Rod Gould's works machine in the points table for the crown he was eventually to win. But Spaggiari and Giuliano lay second and third on 500 Ducatis behind the inevitable MV until the closing stages, when both, like Hailwood on the Benelli retired, the veteran with a broken exhaust and Giuliano with defunct ignition. Two weeks later Read was back on the bike for its classic debut in front of the home crowd at Monza, but could only manage fourth after another slow start and running out of fuel on the last lap to limp home on one cylinder. Spaggiari on the other machine had seemed set for second place

Spaggiari's machine at the Italian GP at Monza in September 1971; he retired after once lying second to Pagani's MV Agusta. The troublesome points ignition can be clearly seen (Heese)

behind Pagani's MV after Agostini's bike had suffered one of its rare retirements, but a broken valve forced him to retire after qualifying third on the grid, once again ahead of all the two-strokes. Both bikes had reverted to points ignition after the troublesome Ducati Elettronica transistorized units had again given trouble at Silverstone.

The final outing of the season was at the San Remo international on 10 October, and it marked a highly satisfying end to this development season. With three Ducatis on the grid for the 500 cc race, they finished in line astern behind Agostini's MV, with Read just beating Parlotti after a race-long duel and Giuliano passing Dave Simmonds's Kawasaki on the penultimate lap to finish fourth. After an inevitably shaky start thanks to the reduced development time available once the decision to construct the machines had been taken, the 500 V-twin had been gradually refined into a well-balanced and mostly reliable machine, especially at home on twisting tracks, where the excellent handling of the Seeley-inspired chassis and light

weight would pay off. It would never be an MV-beater, and while yielding valuable information for their production programme, the twin would have to become a four to get on terms with Agostini.

Some serious thinking went on at Borgo Panigale during the winter break, and at one time plans to build both a four-cylinder 500 and 350 triple were actually considered. True to form, Taglioni had already carried out a preliminary design of the four, and all that was required was the green light from the government controllers to go ahead. After some wrangling, the 500-four project sadly was dropped, but permission was received to proceed with the 350, as well as developing the 500 V-twin for another season.

The principal reason was that a major effort was being planned for the new 750 Formula in an effort to boost sales of the large V-twin road bike, and the factory's racing department would already be at full stretch to cope with this. Money too, was another important reason – or rather the dearth of a sufficiently large budget to develop an exotic four-cylinder GP racer from scratch in the requisite time. And probably most important of all, it was felt that such a machine would not be immediately and recognizably a Ducati, an important factor from the point of view of the publicity department, with both MV and Benelli racing similar machines at the same period. A water-cooled, dohc, 12-valve 350 triple with fuel injection and seven-speed gearbox would be different enough from anything else around to give the marque some useful prestige. Though work proceeded throughout 1972 on this project which was actually bought in from the British engineer Ford-Dunn, and Taglioni's target of 80 bhp at 14,500 rpm was met in brake tests, with the engine safe to 16,000 rpm, it never appeared in public and in all probability was never even fitted to a frame. According to Dr. T the engine hated test-bed running, and did not like the use of fuel injection which he saw as the only way to achieve GP-level power. Intended rider Phil Read instead signed for MV soon after the start of the 1972 season, and Ducati's planned GP comeback was scrapped when a new general manager took over the reins at the

OPPOSITE ABOVE *Phil Read's 500 for the start of the 1971 Italian GP at Monza. Holding the bike is Giancarlo Librenti, while to his right are colleagues Giorgio Nepoti and Rino Caracchi, who that winter were to found Scuderia NCR (Nepoti and Caracchi Racing) (Zagari)*

OPPOSITE BELOW *Franco Farne at Modena in March 1972 with the direct fuel-injected 500 GP machine. Though results were excellent, the fuel injection was dropped because the FIM ruled that the system was a form of supercharging (Zagari)*

Another view of the fuel-injected 500 (Zagari)

start of 1973, when Spairani was ousted from control.

In the meantime though, work continued on the 500 twin, which appeared at the Modena opening meeting in 1972 with a modified four-valve engine giving 69 bhp and safe to 12,500 rpm. Problems with the electronic ignition had been sorted out, and this was now fitted again, and Taglioni had yielded to pressure from the riders to fit a second front disc. Titanium was used for the first time, which helped lower the weight to around 280 lb.

The gearbox problems which had haunted the bike spasmodically the previous year still persisted, and Spaggiari was forced to retire at Modena, when it started jumping out of gear. Giuliano on the other hand only lost third place behind the inevitable two MVs when, after getting the best of Gallina's Paton after a race-long duel, he slid off on the last corner, remounting to finish fourth. There had been no sign of the dozen replicas promised for sale to privateers by this race, and British importer Vic Camp, who had been relying on one for his rider Alan Dunscombe, was understandably disappointed. There seems little doubt that, in spite of the increasing dependability of the two-stroke opposition, Ducati would have had a ready market for these machines had they chosen to construct them.

An all-out effort for success in the vital Imola F750 race – rewarded in full, as we shall see shortly – kept the racing department fully occupied for the next few weeks, and it was not till the Italian GP, run that year at Imola in May rather than on its traditional date at Monza in September, that the 500s appeared again, with Spaggiari this time accompanied by Imola 200 winner Paul Smart, who claimed to find the 500 rather tame after the more powerful 750! After failing to agree terms for the season with Spairani, Read had in fact asked for a ride after the French GP two weeks before, when he found his Suzuki twin to be hopelessly uncompetitive. Ducati were unable to accommodate him, as Smart was flying back from the USA especially for the Italian race, so instead the 1971 250 world champion turned more in desperation than in hope to MV. Much to everyone's surprise he was drafted into the team alongside Agostini, and made his debut for Count Agusta at Imola in the 350 event.

Smart started the 500 Italian GP as he had left off at the same circuit the month before, stunning the huge crowd by moving into the lead on the second lap in front of the two MVs. But it was too much to hope that the V-twin could really be a match for the MV-3s, and first Ago, then Pagani slipped past to go on to win. Smart held third before being forced into

the pits when a carburettor began to fall off (a fault not unknown on V-twin Ducatis down the years!), leaving Spaggiari to take over third spot, which he held to the end. Smart scythed up through the two-stroke ranks to capture fourth position by the end of his only GP of the season.

It was also the 500 Ducati's last appearance that year, for in a remarkable midwinter volte-face the government controllers dictated not only that the 350 project should be scrapped, but also that the 500 twins be no longer ridden as factory entries. Spairani, whose commitment to racing as a valuable publicity and development vehicle was never in doubt, was ousted from control of the company, but Taglioni was permitted to continue at least with work on developing the 500 twin into its final form, and at the same time race-test a new means of driving the overhead camshafts which he intended to employ in the future.

Thus it was that Spaggiari appeared as a semi-private entry at the Imola season-opener in March 1973 aboard the ultimate version of the 500 V-twin, now fitted with dohc four-valve desmodromic heads driven each by a toothed belt instead of the heavier and more costly bevel drive. The change pushed power up to 74 bhp at 12,000 rpm with improved acceleration to boot, but the performance

Giuliano (73) and Spaggiari (9) awaiting the start of practice for an Italian event in 1971 on 500 V-twins (Zagari)

was not sufficient to gain the new model any success. For the modern era of GP racing had well and truly dawned, with the overbored 350 Yamahas and Aermacchis not to mention the 500 Suzuki twins and sleeved-down Konig outboard engine now packing the finishing positions behind Agostini and the hitherto invincible MV. In turn this now faced a works machine from Japan, the four-cylinder 500 Yamaha of Jaarno Saarinen, which had the beating of them all. The age of the four-stroke Grand Prix bike was drawing to an end, and though the 500 V-twins would achieve some satisfactory results in the hands of privateers such as Baronicini and Giuliano, Ducati's long-awaited entrée into the blue riband GP class came too late for worthwhile success. Nevertheless, some useful lessons had been learnt which would bear fruit in the future.

Formula 750 racing was a different story though, for there the factory had been in on the class almost from the beginning, and had produced exactly the right machine at the right time to earn memorable success. After the announcement of the 500 V-twin machine at the start of 1971, some observers unfamiliar with the spirit of enthusiasm at Borgo Panigale had assumed that this would be the sum total of the factory's racing involvement for the immediate future, but nothing could have been further from the truth. Spairani was wedded to publicizing the newly launched 750 range

The final version of the 500 V-twin, which appeared at Imola in March 1973. The 4-valve heads featured belt drive to the twin overhead camshafts, a development soon to be used in the Pantah (Zagari)

through competition, and so when the American production-based 'Daytona Formula' spread to Europe, they resolved to become wholeheartedly involved.

The decision to proceed with a 750 racer was again taken at that significant board meeting in October 1970, but work on the 500 took precedence, so that it was not until the end of July the following year that the prototype 750 was completed. Some hurried testing in Italy knocked off some of the rough edges, and the bike was loaded into the transporter leaving in mid-August to attend the international meeting at Silverstone, where it was planned that it would be ridden by Mike Hailwood on his British short-circuit comeback.

This first F750 Ducati differed considerably both from the later racers and from the road models, being closely related to the 500 GP bike, with which it shared the same set of sand-cast crankcases, with dry clutch and separate casing for the selector

Paul Smart about to take to the track in practice for the 1972 500 cc Italian GP at Imola – just one month after his triumphant works debut on a 750. The ever-present Farne looks on (Heese)

box of the six-speed unit gearbox that was fitted, as opposed to the five-speed road bikes whose delivery was soon to begin. Standard 750 engine dimensions of 80 × 74.4 were however featured, and the roadster's bevel drive to the sohc heads, fitted with desmodromic valve gear that reportedly made the engine safe to 11,500 rpm, was also employed. A power output of around 75 bhp was cited, though bench testing had not been completed before the bike departed for Silverstone. Forty-millimetre Dell'Ortos with separate floats were fitted, straight off the 500s. Hailwood rode the machine in practice for the F750 race, recording the sixth fastest qualifying time behind the works BSA/Triumph triples and Peter Williams's Norton Commando, but on highly competitive terms with the rest of the pack. However, he declined to use the Ducati in the race, preferring the surer handling of his 350 Yamaha, which took him to fourth place in the end. To save time, the factory had placed the 750 engine (with 500 bottom end) in one of the Seeley frames built for the smaller bike. The swinging arm pivot in particular was insufficiently well braced for the extra power, and resulted in some unpleasant squirming when the power was applied hard with the bike cranked over; the single front disc brake fitted to the Marzocchi forks was moreover insufficient to stop a machine weighing around 360 lb, especially combined with the 2ls rear drum. Even on a circuit like Silverstone with only one hard stop a lap, this was a problem.

The abortive Silverstone outing had however yielded much vital information, especially with a rider of Hailwood's talents aboard. A complete redesign took place over the winter, resulting in

machines that more closely resembled the final production model appearing *en masse* at the vital Imola 200-mile event in April. Before then, though, stalwart Ducati enthusiast Vic Camp had produced his own racing version of the 750 roadster, thus becoming almost certainly the first entrant of a big V-twin Ducati on the international scene when Alan Dunscombe took the machine to tenth place in the 1000 cc race at the Good Friday Brands Hatch Transatlantic Trophy meeting. The bike was in fact the first production 750 GT V-twin to enter Britain at the end of 1971, which Camp and mechanic Bert Furness had spent the winter turning into a racer, with the help of some racing cams for the valve-spring engine provided by the factory. After sorting out handling problems with the standard chassis – now basically a beefed-up version of the Seeley frame – Dunscombe went on to achieve worthwhile success in UK short-circuit racing with the bike, which is still to be seen in British classic events.

Meanwhile the parent factory were mounting a massive effort for the Imola race, and Spairani had determined that no expense should be spared to ensure success in this all-important event. The organizers were spending vast sums on publicizing the meeting as 'the Daytona of Europe', and substantial publicity benefits awaited the winner, a fact recognized by no less than nine different factories, all of which entered works or works-supported teams. MV had developed a special version of their shaft-drive 750 for Agostini to ride; the full array of BSA and Triumph works triples

Big brother, little sister: the 750 (right) and 500 V-twins pictured at Borgo Panigale in June 1972. Note the rangy wheelbase of the bigger bike (Zagari)

would be there, as well as a special lightweight Triumph-3 for Walter Villa to ride for the local importer, Beppe Koelliker; the pannier-tanked, low-slung Nortons with their substantial John Player tobacco sponsorship were hoping for a win for their new backers; endurance specialists Laverda and Moto Guzzi entered full teams, the latter with Aussie veteran Jack Findlay on one of the bikes; British Honda specialist Bill Smith had obtained three CR750 works racers for himself to ride with Tommy Robb and John Williams; Cliff Carr had his awesome H2R two-stroke Kawasaki triple from America, while fellow British expatriate Ron Grant was mounted on a US-specification Suzuki; and Helmut Dahne had a nominally private but much-modified BMW that had obviously received some attention from the German factory.

Against this magnificent array of men and machinery, Ducati had opted for a four-man team, including Spaggiari and Giuliano – then the regulars on the 500 GP bikes – and Alan Dunscombe on his first continental outing, in recognition of Vic Camp's enthusiastic support over the years. But Spairani realized that none of these was a potential race-winner, though Spaggiari's intimate knowledge of the Imola circuit would certainly count for much; he therefore determined to secure the services of a real top-liner to lead the squad.

His initial approach was to Jaarno Saarinen, the Finnish ace then considered by many to be the best rider in the world, and an odds-on certainty for the 250 World Championship that year. But the latter was Saarinen's first priority, and so he turned the ride down, reckoning the Ducatis would not stand much of a chance anyway against what was thought to be lighter, more powerful opposition. A similar decision was made by Britain's rising young star Barry Sheene, who though an official Yamaha works rider that year, was free to race another make of machine in F750, provided it was not Japanese. Sheene at one time committed verbally to riding for Ducati, according to Spairani, who also wanted him in his 500 cc team (Yamaha did not at that time have a half-litre GP contender). Lack of confidence in the bike's competitivity, as well as an inability to agree on a substantial fee to ride the bike, resulted in the arrangement with the 21-year-old Londoner falling through; a fall in the French GP in which Sheene injured his back slightly provided a suitable face-saving excuse for all concerned.

With Harley-Davidson not contesting the event – their new XR750 alloy-engined road racer was still to appear in public, having been ineligible for Daytona since less than 200 examples had been constructed – Ducati's next stop was at Harley's Italian subsidiary Aermacchi, whose rider Renzo Pasolini was eager to compete in the Imola event and was certainly capable of winning it. Aermacchi were keen for Paso to concentrate on the GPs as well, and so less than two weeks before the event, Ducati still did not have a winning rider to lead the team. Fortunately, Vic Camp came to the rescue by recommending Spairani to contact one of the leading stars of the F750 class, who had ridden for him on Ducati singles in the late 1960s, but did not have a ride for Imola; Paul Smart. Smart was contracted to the American Kawasaki Team Hansen, and was living in the USA that year with occasional jet-setting flights across the Atlantic to race in Europe as a freelance rider.

ABOVE BOTH *An interesting comparison between the 500 (left) and 750 (right) V-twin racers. Note the way the latter's frame downtubes run inside the upper frame rails, as opposed to the 500's which bend outside. The 750 shown is a twin-plug version – hence the extra set of coils (Zagari)*

With Sheene definitely out of the Ducati team, Spairani took Camp's advice and called Smart's home in California. Ironically, the person he spoke to was none other than Barry's sister Maggie, who was married to Paul Smart. Paul was away racing at Road Atlanta, but his wife accepted Spairani's offer of a works Ducati for Imola on his behalf – then rang her husband to tell him so! Smart's first reaction, as he freely admitted later, was that she should phone Spairani right back and tell him that he refused to ride the bike; he felt, like his brother-in-law, that it would be too slow and unwieldy to be competitive. Maggie Smart had given her word, and thus it was that a couple of days after finishing third at Atlanta on the fire-eating Kawasaki triple, Smart flew to Milan, 8000 miles from his Californian base, to ride what he was convinced would be a no-hoper in the Daytona of Europe.

What he found awaiting him could not have been more unexpected. A total of 10 F750 race machines had been built, two for each rider plus a further two spares for future use. The racing department was humming with organized activity, and in an ingenious publicity gimmick Spairani had ordered a specially built transporter with a glass side to carry the eight team machines to the track, while allowing the enthuasiastic *tifosi* fans to see and admire them.

A last-minute test session at Modena allowed Smart to get the feel of the bike, which seemed rather ponderous and sluggish at first. The lazy off-beat note of the production-based V-twin engine was deceptive, and he ended up lapping faster than Agostini's 500 cc MV lap record, in spite of encountering difficulty rounding the hairpin thanks to the extended 59 in. wheelbase. Spairani was delighted, and the team held high hopes for success in the 200-miler.

Few others expected them to do well against the better-developed racing machines they were ranged against, so it was a major surprise when Smart and Spaggiari qualified first and second fastest in practice. The Ducatis were very closely based on the V-twin road bikes, even to the extent of employing standard frames, based on the Seeley 500 design, with the mounting lugs for the main stand left in place. The Marzocchi forks now featured twin front discs and a single rear, while on the left side a high-level exhaust increased ground clearance, which also required the removal of the kickstart shaft on the right; Smart's then-eccentric 'sitting-off' riding style, nowadays the modern norm but which he was

750 V-twin racer at Silverstone in August 1971. Hailwood practised the bike but did not race it. Note the similarity to the 500 GP bike, rather than to the road prototype (Woollett)

A view inside the famous glass-sided Ducati transporter, taken at Silverstone in August 1972 (Greening)

the first major rider to adopt, was helpful in allowing the machine to remain as upright as possible in corners, and it was noticeable that the 42-year-old Spaggiari had also forsaken his usual 'classical' riding technique in favour of a similar approach, which prevented the machine grounding.

The engine had been completely revised since Hailwood's abortive ride, and now featured standard 750 crankcases as were required by the F750 rules, with desmodromic heads which permitted the engine to be run up to 10,000 rpm in the lower gears, though peak power of 85 bhp at the rear wheel was produced at 8800 rpm. The special camshafts, later to be made available to private owners as the immortal 'Imola' cams with pink and white identification markings, gave a good spread of power from 5000 rpm upwards, offering increased dwell on the valve timing and higher valve lift than the standard ones. Concentric 40 mm Dell'Ortos fed the two-valve cylinders on a 10:1 compression ratio, and the same 80-degree included valve angle was adopted as on the production bikes. A five-speed gearbox replaced the six speeds of the

Hailwood prototype, whose dry clutch was also dropped in favour of the standard oil-bath unit, fitted with beefed-up springs; later, as power outputs increased, the factory would revert to an air-cooled clutch. In spite of the use of so many standard parts, the 750 Ducati racer weighed only 356 lb with oil but no fuel, resulting in a very favourable power to weight ratio compared to the opposition.

When the flag fell at Imola on 23 April, 1972, it was to signal a day that would become as much of a milestone in the history of the Borgo Panigale firm as their first appearance with the 125 desmo in Sweden, or the crushing 1-5 victory in the 1958 Italian GP. Though Agostini roared off into an immediate lead from the clutch start on the 750 MV Agusta, this time the Bologna twins were more than a match for the Gallarate four, and on the fifth lap Smart demonstrated the Ducati's clear speed advantage by passing the red and silver machine on the flat-out straight past the pits, in clear view of a good part of the massive 70,000 crowd. Spaggiari followed through shortly after, and from then on the two silver-faired Ducatis gradually drew away from the rest of the field, hampered only in Smart's case by the fact that he had lost bottom gear early on. However, in those days before the Formula 1 car circus defaced many of the world's leading circuits with the erection of chicanes that were more dangerous than necessary for motorcycle racing, Imola was a very fast circuit, with only one tight corner at the end of the long pit straight. Smart discovered that the enormous reserves of torque of the big V-twin permitted him to take this corner in second without slipping the clutch, or indeed losing much time, if any.

Such was Spairani's confidence before the race, with the two fastest qualifiers in his team, that he had instructed his riders to circulate together until the last five laps, after which it would be every man for himself. Even after the mid-race pitstop Spaggiari shadowed the British rider, the two machines circulating together in an impressive display of reliability and speed. Nine laps from the end the Italian veteran slipped ahead, but Smart responded and the two exchanged the lead several times in the closing stages. On the penultimate lap Spaggiari got in front again, but ran wide on one of the fast corners to allow Smart to resume the lead. By now both bikes were running very low on fuel, and on the last lap both were misfiring because of fuel starvation. The Italian's machine was worst affected, and after swapping places twice on the final lap, it was Smart who crossed the line to win the race in front of an ecstatic crowd, with Spaggiari finishing four seconds behind with the twin now a single and running on fumes from the empty tank. Ironically, the 200-mile race was strictly not that at all, for the 64 laps of the 3.117 mile circuit resulted in a total race distance of 199.515 miles; the outcome of the race might have been very different had an extra lap been run! Villa's standard-framed Triumph-3, which had won the Bol d'Or the year before, was third, 25 seconds behind, and only Read's John Player Norton and Pickrell's works Triumph were also on the same lap as the victorious Ducatis at the finish.

Smart's win netted him around £4500 – a huge amount in prize money now, let alone in those days, and he had shared the honour of fastest lap with Spaggiari and Agostini (whose MV had expired after half distance) at just over 100 mph. His most unexpected prize was yet to come, for in a generous gesture of gratitude Spairani presented him with his winning bike, which he still owns to the present day. Doubtless he remembered to thank his wife for accepting the ride on his behalf!

Once they'd recovered from the euphoria of victory, Ducati were quick to capitalize on their

ABOVE *The 1972 version of the 750 racer, featuring dual ignition and production-derived engine and chassis: note the centre stand is still retained (Zagari)*

success, not only in an advertizing campaign which saw sales of the new 750 road bike boom worldwide, but also by producing a limited edition run of 200 or so replicas of the winning machine for sale to private owners: the 750 Super Sport appeared the following year and offered a desmo-headed twin for the road or production racing for the first time. As already recounted, the majority of these ended up on the track at one stage or another during their lifetime, and earned Ducati another impressive list of successes all over the world.

Having given the best possible boost to their road bike sales, Ducati's principal concern was now to step up manufacture and iron out production snags. With work proceeding on the 350 triple and the 500 twin, the racing department had its hands full too, so there was little further development on the 750 that year. Occasional team rider Gilberto Parlotti was loaned a machine fitted with lights and road equipment with which to carry out his course learning at the Isle of Man TT. He was to ride the works 125 Morbidelli there on which he was leading the World Championship. Tragically he crashed during the 125 race in terrible conditions up on the Mountain and was fatally injured.

The F750 desmo's next outing was at the beginning of July in the Canadian GP at Mosport. It was to be a useful opportunity to promote the road twins, which had just been launched on the North American market, since the demanding road course suited the V-twins better than the speed bowls further south, where flat-out power counted for everything. Three riders were entered; American Ralph White was nominated by Berliner, but retired during the race, as did Spaggiari who fell off while lying fourth, fortunately without injury. The third man saved Bologna's honour by finishing third behind the faster Kawasakis of local ace Duhamel and Cliff Carr; Percy Tait. Even more of a veteran than Spaggiari, Percy had recently been dropped from the Triumph works team, but had turned down the offer of a works Ducati for Imola, preferring to race his own British triple instead. Having doubtless regretted such as hasty decision, he was drafted into the team for Canada and was able to make an interesting comparison between the two machines. Apparently the Ducati was easier to ride, with a much wider powerband and better

OPPOSITE ABOVE *The 750 racer in Imola-winning form; compare it to the photo on page 180 (Zagari)*

OPPOSITE BELOW *Smart's Imola winner, pictured inside the transporter during practice for the race (Heese)*

torque than the pushrod triple, also scoring on acceleration, while the Triumph was faster at the top end. Braking and weight were similar, but Percy offered that the Ducati could easily be lightened.

A similar 'propaganda' race was undertaken by Smart at the end of October, winning the Greek GP on the island of Corfu on a works 750 desmo in spite of a very bumpy track resembling a scrambles course. Before then, he'd ridden the works machine in a series of British events, starting with the Hutchinson 100 run in the reverse direction on the Brands Hatch circuit. Curiously, push-starts were stipulated for all the races, including the F750, and the resultant uphill shove was too much for the short Spaggiari on the second bike, as indeed it was for many others. Smart was able to win the F750 race after a dramatic tussle with Read's Norton, which he passed on the last lap at the uphill Paddock Bend to beat the former Ducati teamster by a wheel, after flinging the big Ducati about in a way that had strong men reaching for support. A second and third place in two other events completed his tally.

Smart was out of luck in the F750 event at Silverstone the following week, retiring with a broken condenser wire (battery and coil ignition was employed that year on all the 750 V-twins) while disputing the lead with, ironically enough, Percy Tait, who was back on his ex-works Triumph. Tait went on to win, but Spaggiari was sixth on the other Ducati, while in the 1000 cc race Smart had some consolation by finishing fourth in a race won by Saarinen's 350 Yamaha. The writing was already on the wall for the big twins.

A fortnight later at Snetterton Smart rode his Imola-winning bike in the Race of Aces, and led Agostini's 500 MV on the first lap, before slipping back as the bike went on to one cylinder forcing him to retire from the meeting. For the rest of the British short circuits that year he reverted to his old but trusty Triumph-3, and indeed the Greek GP marked the Imola winner's last race on a works Ducati, for the following season he was contracted exclusively to Suzuki. He did reappear on a Bologna V-twin, however, in 1975, riding a 900 for the semi-works Spaggiari team at the Imola 200. Sadly his 1972 success was not repeated, for Smart fell in the second heat of the race, breaking his leg.

Spairani had decided after careful reflection that the factory would not be competing in F750 events the following season, having achieved their original purpose in convincing fashion. When after one of the periodic reshuffles inside the company he lost control, Taglioni found himself in charge of the racing effort again and resolved at least to compete

at Imola in 1973. Though the two-strokes were now undoubtedly reliable enough to last 200 miles, as well as blindingly fast, he still had a few tricks up his sleeve which he felt would be sufficient to ensure a repeat victory. He was so nearly proved to be right.

Winter development, and indeed the factory's immediate racing plans, were disrupted by a tragic accident that cast a pall over the team. Taglioni's right-hand man, Franco Farne, and another racing mechanic, Massimo Nepoti (son of one of the men soon to found the semi-works NCR team) collided on the *autostrada* encircling Bologna while out testing two 750 machines. Nepoti was thrown off into a lamp standard and died instantly, while Farne sustained multiple injuries which put him out of action for several weeks.

Nevertheless work continued on a revised version of the 750, which featured a 60 degree valve angle, lumpier camshafts with 14 mm lift instead of the Imola type's 13 mm, and even more oversquare engine dimensions of 86 × 64.5 mm (instead of 80 × 74.4), which permitted maximum revs of 10,000 rpm to be utilized, at which point just on 90 bhp at the rear wheel was on tap. The long-awaited attention to weight-saving, while still employing the standard frame, resulted in the 1973 bikes scaling 343 lb compared to 356 the year before, and both exhausts were of the high-rise type, rather than only the left-hand one as on Smart's winning machine.

A new team of riders matched the new machines: the ever-present Spaggiari was promoted to team leader, but instead of Smart, Giuliano and Dunscombe – the latter two had retired in the 1972 event, the Briton falling off and breaking a collarbone while lying a promising 9th near the end – he was supported by the Swiss Bruno Kneubuhler and Yorkshireman Mick Grant, a former John Player Norton team rider. Grant had spent the winter racing in South Africa, and he had been highly impressed by the speed of one of the 1972 works 750 desmos which the factory had sent out there for local rider Errol Cowan to compete on against Agostini and the other European stars specially imported for a series of races. Cowan finished third and fourth in the 750 races, and wound up fifth in the South African TT on the Roy Hesketh Circuit, a race which Grant had won on his 350 Yamaha.

The Ducati team came very close indeed to repeating their astonishing 1972 Imola victory against a field that was even more star-studded than the year before, and which included for the first time works entries from Harley-Davidson and Yamaha, as well as the race favourites, the

Il film della gara: *the story of the 1972 Imola 200 in pictures. Agostini takes the lead from the start on the shaft-driven 750 MV Agusta, with Smart, fastest in practice, right behind, and Spaggiari on another Ducati just watching (top left). On lap 5 Smart took the lead, and Spaggiari had closed up on the MV (bottom left). Shortly after, Spaggiari too passed and set off after his team-mate (top right). By half-distance the two silver Ducatis had opened up a handsome lead over the field, running nose to tail as they lapped the backmarkers (middle right). During the last five laps the two team-mates scrapped for victory between themselves, but with both running low on fuel it was Smart who took the chequered flag to register Ducati's most important success up till then (bottom right) (Zagari)*

Rider and designer at Imola in 1972: 'Thassa my boy!'

TR750 Suzuki triples of Barry Sheene and Paul Smart. Only the brilliance of Jarno Saarinen prevent Spaggiari from clinching the victory he so badly wanted, but the Italian had to be content with a second and third place respectively in the now two-leg race, giving him his second consecutive Imola runner-up position on the works desmo. Kneubuhler slid off after passing Baumann's Harley for second place behind the flying Finn in the first race, with Spaggiari getting the better of a race-long dice with Cal Rayborn on the other American machine. Mick Grant had burnt his Ducati's clutch out on the line, but finished seventh in the second leg, just behind the 350 Yamaha of a man who would play an important part in Ducati racing history nearly ten years later; Tony Rutter. Kneubuhler had hurt his hand too badly to start the second leg, but a noteworthy performance was that of Italian Claudio Loigo, who wound up 15th overall on his red and silver, semi-official Ducati 750, which marked the entry into international competition of the Scuderia NCR.

The 1973 Imola 200 marked the last official appearance of a works 750 Ducati in a speed event; henceforward it would be left to private owners and local concessionaires to tilt at the two-stroke

windmills. Endurance racing, however, was another matter and Taglioni had correctly identified this as an increasingly important branch of the sport in which Ducati could shine. The Bologna marque's emphasis on building light, slim machines which were not tiring to ride and returned good fuel consumption, thus cutting down on unnecessary pit stops, would stand it in good stead in this type of racing. All of this would yield useful publicity benefits in terms of the Ducati reputation for reliability, especially in important markets such as France and Spain, where such events were more eagerly followed than even Grand Prix racing.

The 750 capacity limit did not apply to endurance racing, and so it would be necessary to increase the size of the engine to compete effectively against the bored-out Honda and Kawasaki fours of more than 900 cc which now threatened to dominate long-distance events. This tied in neatly with Ducati's own plans for a larger-capacity road bike, and so Taglioni quickly developed a bored-out version of the 750 desmo measuring 86 × 74.4 mm, for 864 cc, running on 9.6:1 compression and producing 86 bhp at 8200 rpm with 'endurance' cams.

The resultant bike duly appeared in July for the prestigious Barcelona 24 Horas, doyen of the continental endurance races, to be run at the twisting 2.25 mile Montjuich Park in the centre of Barcelona, which would ideally suit the Ducati's torque and power characteristics. Riders selected were local aces Salvador Canellas and Benjamin Grau, who had won the race the previous year on a works 360 Bultaco single. Team manager was Ducati importer Ricardo Fargas, himself a former winner of the event on a Mototrans single (and Norton twin), and of course the V-twin's appearance marked a return for the factory to an event they had excelled in back in the late 1950s and 1960s, winning outright no less than five times in all. Ing. Taglioni was in attendance to watch over his big bore prototype, while Farne, now recovered thankfully from his injuries, headed the well-drilled team of mechanics.

Apart from an oversize fuel tank, dry clutch and cooling scoops for the rear brake caliper, the 860 was externally similar to one of the 750 SS road bikes, running without a fairing however in view of

OPPOSITE *Ducati were fortunate in having two such strong racers in their team in 1972. Spaggiari (above, in the Imola 200) was the perfect test rider and in fact an extension of Taglioni's own talents. Smart (below, at Silverstone in 1972) was an aggressive and competitive rider then at the height of his career, whose hanging-off style was ideally suited to the long wheelbase V-twin Ducatis with their limited ground clearance (top Zagari, bottom Greening)*

the twisty nature of the circuit and 90 degree Fahrenheit heat; a Manx Norton-like fly-screen was the only streamlining aid. Both exhausts were tucked well up over the top of the crankcases, which were 750 castings with the conventional rounded side covers.

The race represented a triumphant debut for the new 860 model in endurance racing. Canellas took the lead on the third lap from the big Honda four of Jean-Claude Chemarin, and proceeded to pull away into a lead that would only be relinquished once during the entire course of the race, when a rear tyre punctured on a piece of wire and the works Norton monocoque of Williams and Croxford took the lead for just two laps. Then the Ducati got quickly back in front again, and finally won by the massive margin of 16 laps, setting new lap and distance records and covering 1674.58 miles in the 24 hours. The bike ran perfectly from the start to finish, only the need to change the rear chain four times as a precaution representing other than normal maintenance. It was a convincing display of superiority that was naturaly welcomed by the local Mototrans factory, though the latter was manufacturing only

Bruno Spaggiari never won the Imola 200, but he was second twice in successive years. Here he sweeps round Galeazzo Pederneschi in 1973, en route to runner-up behind Saarinen's similar TZ350 Yamaha. Compare the photo with that on the top of page 187 (Zagari)

the 250 and 350 singles, with the V-twins imported separately from Italy.

A subsequent outing with the same machine in the Bol d'Or at Le Mans proved less successful, with Grau/Canellas retiring before half distance. Honour was saved with eight place obtained by a 750 Sport entered by the French importer, but from now on the factory's principal competition activity with the big V-twins would be in the field of endurance racing, though for political reasons the bikes were usually entered by Scuderia NCR (Nepoti and Caracchi Racing), whose workshop was only a mile or so from the factory gate.

In due course a road version of the 860 prototype was announced at the end of 1973, known as the 860 GTI, though not with the square-sided crankcase covers that eventually became standard wear on the entire big twin range. With a modified version of this engine producing nearly 90 bhp, Grau and

Canellas returned to Barcelona for another attempt in 1974. They built up a nine-lap lead before retiring after 16 hours with the gearbox locked in gear; Godier and Genoud's Kawasaki failed to beat the 1973 Ducati record in winning the race.

For 1975 a serious attempt was made on the FIM Coupe Endurance championship, with Grau as the spearhead and NCR the vehicle for thinly veiled factory participation; Canellas had too many commitments as a topline car rally driver to be able to take in all the rounds. He teamed with his fellow-countryman to score another relatively un-challenged victory at Barcelona, beating their previous distance record by 11 laps into the bargain. A win in the next race, the 1000 km event at Mugello, this time accompanied by a new young rider named Virginio Ferrari, seemed to set Grau up for the title. Sadly, things went downhill therafter, with no points in Belgium followed by a first-lap spill in the Bol d'Or at Le Mans, which left the bike well downfield before eventually retiring with another seized gearbox. In spite of this, Grau came to the final round at Thruxton holding a single point lead in the championship, thanks to his two earlier victories. Sadly, new co-rider Carlo Perugini threw the bike away early on and with it Ducati's championship chances. Grau wound up third overall in the series behind Godier/Genoud's Kawasaki and the Japauto-Honda of Ruiz/Huguet.

The 1976 season started off well enough, with

Salvador Canellas earholes through the twists and turns at Montjuich Park in the heart of Barcelona en route to victory in the 1973 24 Horas aboard the 860 Mototrans Ducati, fitted with a TT100 front tyre

Practice for the 1973 Montjuich 24 Horas, with Canellas about to take to the track on the prototype Ducati 860, while Benjamon Grau takes a rest and Ing. Taglioni assumes the role of eminence grise

scratch pair Pentti Korhonen and Christian Estrosi finishing second in the opening round of the championship at Mugello on their NCR-entered bike. Two engines had now been developed for endurance racing, an 808 cc small-bore unit producing 96 bhp at 9400 rpm, and the larger 860 cc one, which had the same power output but achieved at only 8800 revs, with better torque. Rear cylinder cooling had become a problem, with the full fairings now a necessity for straight-line speed on fast circuits such as Spa and to a certain extent Mugello. The new silencing regulations of 115 dBa which had spelt the end of the MV Agusta team's involvement in GP racing also posed an equally frustrating problem to the Ducati factory. It was achieved, but only at the cost of some power and megaphonitis.

The big Ducati's principal weapon was still its slim profile and good power to weight ratio; with a dry weight of only 160 kg complete with lights and a generator it was, together with the less powerful BMW, much the lightest machine in endurance racing. This told particularly at the Barcelona event, where local riders Jose Torres and Alejandro Tejedo on a 90-bore 950 cc machine entered by Ricardo Fargas clinched third place behind the all-conquering RCB works Hondas. 1976 was the end of Ducati success in endurance racing. Indeed, the increasing dominance of the Japanese factory teams and their importers, backed by ever-bigger race budgets that Ducati and NCR could never hope to match, spelt the end of the Bologna marque's success on any scale in the endurance series to become a full World Championship in 1980. There were bright spots, to be sure, not least Benjamin Grau's astonishing record in the Barcelona 24 Horas, an event he seemed almost to make his own. Always mounted on a big Ducati, he not only won in 1973 and 1975 with Canellas but also finished third with him in 1979, sixth with Victor Palomo in 1978, second with Enrique de Juan in 1981, and fourth with the same rider accompanied by Carlos Cardus in 1982. In all an incredible record of consistency in one of the world's most demanding road racing events, in which Ducati were to score one final victory in 1980, when Mallol and Tejedo outlasted the works Hondas and Kawasakis to give the twins a final moment of glory.

As Ducati's star dimmed in the Coupe d'Endurance sky, it was to dawn again in two new road racing classes which could almost have been dreamt up with the products of the Italian factory in mind. One of them was to yield the firm as much beneficial publicity as practically any other form of racing they had ever participated in; the TT Formula World Championships.

The Isle of Man TT races had by 1976 become an anomaly in modern road racing terms. Parlotti's death in 1972 had been the last straw: the 99th man to die on the Mountain Circuit, his demise hastened the end of the TT as a world championship Grand Prix, since the leading contenders, led by Agostini and the MV Agusta team, no longer contested the June races. As well, the prospect of having to spend a full two weeks, involving at least two costly ferry crossings, in order to contest just one World Championship Grand Prix, made increasingly less economic sense to works teams and privateers alike, beset by the ever-mounting costs of going racing. Too late, the ACU and Isle of Man authorities began pouring vast sums of money into the races in order to try to retain the services of the leading riders and thus the TT's status as a major international event; but the die had been cast, and though the mystique of the Mountain races continued to attract a special breed of rider, the

stars of the Continental GP circus, new and old alike, had by the mid-1970s almost entirely deserted the event in droves.

Under these circumstances, it was farcical to continue featuring the TT as a World Championship GP event, since with a very few exceptions (mostly in the sidecar class) none of the riders who scored points at the TT did so at any other other races; indeed, hardly any of them even contested them. The time had come for a rethink of the TT's role in the modern world of motorcycle racing, and in 1976 this took place and resulted in a compromise solution that eventually turned out to be in the interests of all parties. A new British GP was instituted, initially at any rate held on the flat, relatively safe mainland circuit at Silverstone, while in order to ensure that the TT retained its World Championship status, and thus a protected place in the racing calendar, a new title category was created; the TT Formula World Championships.

The brainchild of Neville Goss, a senior British ACU official who had long been concerned with the running of the British round of the FIM Endurance series and the Thruxton long-distance race before that, the TT Formula concept was intended to achieve three objectives. To ensure the continuation of the IoM races as an international event; to answer the complaints of those who attributed the increasing doubts about the circuit's safety to the speed of the new breed of ultra-specialized racing two-strokes, by reverting to a category based on production road-going engines; and to achieve a balance between two- and four-stroke machines by means of an equivalency formula.

The latter resulted in four TT Formula classes being established. TT F1 catered for four-strokes from 601 to 1000 cc, and two-strokes from 351 to 500 cc; TT F2 was for 351–600 cc four-strokes and 251–350 cc two-strokes; TT F3 encompassed 201–400 cc four-strokes and two-strokes from 126–250 cc; while the smallest class, TT F4, was in fact never run on the Isle of Man and ironically only caught on successfully in the one country which had more than any other been responsible for the demise of the TT as a World Championship GP event – Italy. Catering for 51–125 cc two-strokes and 51–200 cc four-strokes, it attracted the horde of small Italian manufacturers contesting the market for 125 cc machines.

Indeed in due course the TT Formula classes, with some local modifications, were to become so well accepted in Italy that the national Junior championships were run to this production-based formula, which was, after all, nothing more than an

ALL *Three views of the winning 860 Ducati at Barcelona in 1973. Apart from the dry clutch, the machine is remarkably similar to a standard 750. Note the rudimentary cooling scoop attached to the rear brake caliper in order to combat the effects of Montjuich's fierce braking in the heat of the Spanish summer (top, above Woollett; right Zagari)*

Grau advising his Canellas that they've just beaten their previous distance record for the Barcelona 24 Horas in 1975. They beat the mark by 11 laps – about 25 miles

updated version of the MSDS and Formula 2/3 classes which Ducati and other manufacturers had excelled at in the 1950s.

Other rules for the World Championship, which for its inaugural season in 1977 consisted of just one event, the IoM TT itself, included a requirement that at least 1000 examples of an engine used must have been manufactured and made available for sale to the public through normal commercial channels. Also that its original equipment should have included both a starting device (whether electric or manual) and a generator, both of which could, however, be removed for racing; and that no alteration to the stroke of production engine could be made, though over boring was permissible. To encourage fuel-efficient designs, a series of maximum fuel tank capacities was established for each class, which were later to provoke contention when riders of certain thirsty Japanese four-cylinder machines were to be observed beating in the side of the tank with their fists after crossing the finishing line at the TT in an apparent effort to reduce its capacity before the technical inspection. On one occasion the race winner's fuel tank was found to be stuffed full of plastic containers, not all of which were necessarily air-tight. Such measures were unnecessary with the less profligate, fuel-efficient twin-cylinder machines such as Ducatis, but two other aspects of the original regulations did cause confusion until they were cleared up. A carburettor rule was featured which aimed at the use of the same size and type – meaning the same identical instrument(s) – of carb(s) as fitted to the original road bike, but after complaints from the Japanese

teams and primarily from Honda, who could not extract the type of performance they deemed necessary from the standard road units, this rule was altered so as to allow racing carburettors, which needed only to be of the same general type and choke diameter as the originals. Additionally, the rules originally stipulated that the crankcases, cylinder heads and barrels had to be of unaltered external appearance, but in due course this was amended so as to require that the crankcases in particular should be those of the original road model. The importance of this change as it affected Ducati will be seen shortly.

The new TT Formula 1 class seemed tailor-made for Ducati, even though it had doubtless been evolved to attract the Japanese factory teams back to the Isle of Man. The 900 SS had already made its mark on the Mountain Circuit in the 10-lap 1976 Production TT, run to a ludicrous handicap system which required the 250 class runners only to complete nine laps while the 501–1000 cc category machines needed to do ten! Not surprisingly, the leader board was swamped with smaller machines, but the race was noteworthy for the magnificent ride by Welshman Roger Nicholls and young Steve Tonkin on a near-standard 900 SS Ducati, who led the race on a scratch basis from laps two to eight before retiring with engine trouble after having got the better of a titanic dice with the works-assisted BMW of Dahne/Butenuth, who went on to win the class. Before retiring, however, Nicholls had set a new lap record which was to stand for ever as the IoM Production mark, of 21 min. 57.0 sec., a speed of 103.13 mph – some going for a very slightly modified road-going machine, complete with lights and silencers, though the fact that the latter were the ubiquitous 105 dBa Contis may have had something to do with the performance!

The big Japanese multi-cylinder production bikes had completely failed to register in the Production TT, which was never won on scratch by an Oriental machine. Their substantial power outputs were not then matched by commensurate cycle parts, a deficiency which the Mountain course exposed mercilessly. The experience of requiring both sides of the road to steer a Z-1 Kawasaki down the Sulby Straight at speed was not one which the leading TT riders were eager to acquire, and the factories were understandably reluctant to have their four-cylinder superbikes humbled by better-handling, though less powerful, European machines.

The TT Formula was a different matter though, and the fact that it was originally conceived as a class catering for standard road engines with a

relatively small degree of tuning, slotted into racing frames, was a direct sop to the Japanese factories. Strangely, though, of these only Honda, who were no longer involved in the Grand Prix scene and were following a strict four-strokes-only policy in their production range, were tempted in. A TT F1 racer was constructed around an overbored 810 cc version of the CB750 sohc engine, and an astonishing publicity coup saw the seven-times World champion Phil Read, who had been one of the most vociferous critics of the TT as a GP event in the early 1970s, recruited to ride the new bike on the Isle of Man. Interestingly, the complexities of frame design suitable for the TT and other road courses continued to elude the Japanese technicians, and it was not until later when a frame was ordered from the leading British TT Formula chassis manufacturers, Peckett & McNab, that the works Honda started to handle properly.

Surprisingly, the possibilities of the TT Formula and the suitability of the 900 SS as the basis for a successful contender, appeared not to be recognized at first at Borgo Panigale. There were two reasons for this: first, the TT had now become a *bête noir* of the Italian press after Parlotti's death and MV's refusal to race there, so any developments regarding it were extremely ill-reported, if at all. This might not have mattered, but for the second reason; Ducati had come more and more to rely on the efforts of their local importers not only to keep the company's flag flying and its sporting image

ABOVE *Benjamin Grau about to push off from a midnight pitstop in the 1976 Bol d'Or 24 hours, while Farne gives a hasty wipe to the screen. The NCR Ducati 900 eventually retired with a seized gearbox, after a first-lap spill*
BELOW *Salvador Canellas again at speed at Montjuich Park in 1975. Due to car rally-driving commitments, he was unable to contest more than this one race that year*

enhanced by entering machines in local competition, often with considerable competition and sales success for all concerned, but also to keep them appraised of developments in their own countries which the factory might respond to. There were many examples of this, not least the success of the Australian distributor in defeating the Japanese marques in the prestigious local production bike races, which eventually resulted in Australia becoming Ducati's second-largest export market in the early 1980s, after Japan and ahead of the USA and Europe.

Unfortunately, a new British concessionaire had been appointed at the end of 1973, replacing the enthusiastic Vic Camp, whose company was claimed too small to handle the substantial sales of the new V-twin range which the factory rightly hoped for. The new distributor was an offshoot of one of the UK's largest retail companies, Coburn & Hughes, and in spite of the fact that such market penetration as Ducati had and would achieve was based on the public's perceived image of the marque as a sporting one, the group of hard-headed businessmen who ran the company paid only token lip-service to the idea of becoming involved in or even supporting a road-racing effort indirectly or directly. Their principal interest was to increase the sale of 'units' by conventional means only and thus maximize profit margins. They were too short-sighted to understand what really makes a potential

Ducati owner tick and hence had no interest in furthering the image of the marque through competition involvement.

Fortunately, there were individual dealers and privateers who thought otherwise. Thanks to their efforts Ducati achieved some considerable success in British events, in spite of rather than thanks to the UK concessionaires. This band of enthusiasts originally had no direct contact with the factory and depended on Coburn & Hughes to keep Bologna appraised of developments. Coburn & Hughes had refrained from involvement in the 1976 Production TT, (beyond entering their workshop manager on his own bike) even though a Ducati had an excellent chance of winning this prestigious event, and thus either didn't understand the portent of the new TT Formula rules or, if they did, failed to realize its potential for the marque which they represented.

It was left to one of their largest dealers, Sports Motor Cycles of Manchester, to step into the vacuum created by the UK distributors. Though one of the biggest multi-make retailers in the country, Sports concentrated on Italian bikes in general and on Ducatis in particular, and under the enthusiastic leadership of the company's managing director, Steve Wynne, who himself was a racer of no little talent, had successfully campaigned a large team in

Franco Uncini rode a Ducati 750 SS in 1974 and 1975 after some success on a private Laverda 750 SFC in 1973. He was destined for greater things

the Avon Production series in the mid-1970s. The Nicholls/Tonkin 1976 TT bike was a Sports Motor Cycles entry, and indeed the firm had in the eyes of the British *ducatisti* already begun to assume the position in the competition world which the British importers had relinquished by default.

Thus when the TT Formula regulations were announced it was left to Steve Wynne to ensure that the Bologna marque put forward a competitive entry for the inaugural event on the Isle of Man in June 1977. An initial direct contact with Italy seemed discouraging: there could be no question of a works bike being entered, for the combined racing and development department at the factory were working full speed ahead on the Pantah prototype in order to have it ready for the Milan Show later that year, at which it would make its public debut. Wynne, on the other hand, realized that even some further tuning on the Production TT lap record machine would not make it competitive with the Hondas and other Japanese multis, now that these were permitted proper racing frames which would cancel out the Ducati's intrinsic handling advan-

Welshman Roger Nicholls was to set the all-time Production TT lap record in 1976 at over 103 mph on this 900 SS machine entered by Sports Motor Cycles. Helmut Dahne isn't closing here at Waterworks (Nicholls)

tage. A more powerful engine was required, and eventually his persistence won through, so that Sports Motor Cycles were able to buy one of the semi-works NCR endurance bikes for use in the TT. There was no question of the factory preparing the machine though, or even providing it on loan. Wynne's company had to purchase the bike, and would be responsible for running it in the Isle of Man, without even a blessing from the UK importers.

When the Ducati eventually arrived in Britain it was found to have led a very hard life, and apparently had not been rebuilt after its last endurance race. But it did have the desirable 60 degree heads (as compared to the 80 degree included valve angle of the 1976 Nicholls bike, which was actually Wynne's own Avon series production bike, that in turn started out life as a 750 SS), and moreover had the factory dry-clutch conversion by means of a specially cast magnesium outer cover.

The 864 cc desmo engine had the same broad specification otherwise as the road bikes, and the frame was similarly close to standard, though fitted with eccentric rear wheel adjusters, and a full fairing and one-piece seat/tank unit.

Roger Nicholls was nominated to ride the newly acquired bike in the TT after Wynne had completely stripped and rebuilt it from top to bottom with many new parts, while Irish road-racing star Tom Herron was entered on the 1976 lap record production racer. Practice proved Wynne's fears to be justified, with Read on the Honda lapping at over 105 mph, but Nicholls qualified fifth fastest at 101 mph, just behind one Tony Rutter on another, privately entered Honda.

Conditions for the five-lap F1TT could hardly have been worse, with torrential rain and strong, bitterly cold winds sweeping the 37.75 mile circuit. They were instrumental in negating the Hondas' power advantage, and though few of the supposedly knowledgeable press appeared to realize it either at the time or in retrospect, the easier power delivery and more controllable handling of the Italian V-twins, with their long wheelbase and great reserves of torque, made them now the pre-race favourites.

One man who *did* realize this was Gerald Davison, team manager of the Honda Britain equipe. To make matters worse, the fuel-tank capacity restriction would require Read to make two pit stops in the five laps, since the Honda could not carry enough fuel to complete three laps non-stop, even at the reduced speeds dictated by the foul weather. The Ducatis on the other hand, would

The author sweeps round Coram Curve at Snetterton on his 750 SS in a 1977 British production race to place second behind an 810 cc Honda

only need to make one stop, since they could easily complete three laps on one 25-litre tankful, and could even do four at a pinch under wet conditions. The inaugural F1 TT started with Davison a worried man, for he had been the person primarily responsible for persuading Honda to return to road racing in the new category, and his Japanese bosses would not take kindly to having their expensively developed machine beaten by a privately entered Italian V-twin.

Such fears appeared to be groundless, as Read swept into an immediate lead from the start of the race; but Nicholls on the Ducati, racing with a broken thumb after a practice fall the night before the race, was belying the practice time form book by placing second, ahead of the other four-cylinder bikes. Herron too was going well, lying fourth on the PR bike and moving up to third on lap 3 as the multis made the first of their pit stops. Sadly, a badly riveted chain broke on the same lap, depriving him of a certain top three finish.

Nicholls experienced no such problems, and when Read made a lengthy first refuelling stop at the end of lap 2, taking 52 seconds to rejoin the race after troubles with a misted-up visor, a Ducati victory seemed on the cards. Both men were scheduled to stop at the end of the third lap, Nicholls for his only refuelling session, Read for a top-up before the final two laps. To make matters worse, Read's engine was consuming vast quantities

A pit stop for the NCR 900 Ducati during an Italian endurance race at Misano in 1976. While Caracchi refuels, Nepoti checks the rear, and rider Virginio Ferrari prepares to dismount to hand over to Carlo Perugini. Note the bike's dry clutch (Zagari)

Roger Nicholls aviates the front wheel of the Sports Motor Cycles Ducati at the bottom of Bray Hill on the first lap of the 1977 Formula 1 TT. After the race was shortened in controversial circumstances, he finished 2nd behind Phil Read's works Honda

of oil, requiring several pints for topping-up at the first pit stop, another reason for the lengthy delay.

What happened next depends on who's telling the story. What is certain is that Davison needed badly to get the race stopped. Although conditions had not appreciably worsened the FIM jury now met at Honda's urging to consider doing so, short of the full five-lap distance. However, instead of announcing their decision over the public address and Manx Radio commentary so that all competitors would learn of it simultaneously, the organizers allowed Davison to receive advance information. Through a journalist to whom the news had been leaked he was told that the flag would be put out at the end of the fourth lap, stopping the race in accordance with Honda's wishes. Prized with this vital knowledge, the Honda team manager raced to his pit, so as to be able to wave Read on when he came into the pits for his second fuel (and oil) stop. Without the slightest hint that the race was going to be stopped after four laps, the Sports Motor Cycles team brought Nicholls in and refuelled the Ducati in the normal way. What made their doing so doubly ironic was that the bike would have been able to complete the truncated race non-stop. Soon after, Read arrived at the pits, slowed down then accelerated away when he saw Davison frantically waving him on, and in doing so retook the lead to win by the slim margin of 28 seconds; the missed pit stop had been crucial.

Though Roger Nicholls's second place was still a fine result, Wynne and his team felt justifiably robbed of victory and a prized World Championship, thanks to the ineptitude of the organizing ACU, coupled with the machinations of the Honda team. From the point of view of the Ducati factory they had only themselves to blame, for had they sent an official works entry to the race the Italian Federation would in all probability have sent an official delegate to safeguard their interests, and the result of the inaugural Formula 1 TT race might well have been very different. The following year would see justice done.

A supporting TT F1 race was held at the British GP meeting at Silverstone in August that year, in which Nicholls at one time lay third on the Sports ex-NCR machine before crashing spectacularly at Becketts after tangling with Richard Peckett's P&M Kawasaki. The meeting, however, was of far more significance from Steve Wynne and Ducati's standpoint since it marked the team's first encounter with Mike Hailwood.

Mike had retired from a four-wheel GP career when his McLaren had crashed at the Nürburgring in 1974, injuring his right foot so badly that he was unable to use it to change gear on a motorcycle. With wife Pauline and their two children he'd emigrated to New Zealand and a quiet life to recover from what he termed the 'bullshit factor' of GP car racing. While there, he began riding bikes again, first an old Manx Norton in Australian classic events, then later renewed his lengthy acquaintance with the Bologna marque on a Ducati 900 SS in endurance racing.

The quiet life might suit many people after a hectic and successful career on two and four wheels, but not Mike Hailwood. Visiting the UK to spectate at the British GP in 1977, he entered into negotiations with the ACU to make a return to the Isle of Man TT as a competitor the following year. Mike loved the Island and enjoyed racing there; with nothing left to prove after winning 12 TTs on the Mountain course, he wanted to renew his acquaintance with the bike-racing world and have an enjoyable race, rather than throw himself back in at the deep end as Phil Read had done that year as a full member of a Japanese works team who expected him to win.

Thus it was that while wandering round the Silverstone paddock, Mike came across Steve Wynne and the Sports Motor Cycles team, fettling Nicholls's Ducati. Commenting that it looked like the kind of bike he used to remember riding – 'a vintage racer', as he put it – he sat on it for a while, fielded a crack by Wynne to the effect that if he fancied a ride on it he could have one, and wandered off again. It was the beginning of a beautiful relationship. . . .

Two weeks later the news broke that Hailwood would be returning to the TT in 1978, 11 years after he last rode there on a works Honda. This time though his name was linked with Yamaha, who were however the one Japanese company who did not have a competitive TT F1 engine. Though he did end up riding for Yamaha in the other classes, Mike wanted badly to compete in the Formula 1 class, on what he saw as 'his' kind of bike. Thus when Steve Wynne received a call some weeks later from Hailwood's agent Ted Macauley, it was to ask if a Ducati could be made available for Mike to ride in the Island, against a riding fee of a scant £500.

It was the offer of a lifetime for a TT entrant, and was to prove equally attractive, and exciting, for the Ducati factory, many of whose key employees, especially Taglioni and Farne, had fond memories of and respect for Mike during the previous connections with him over the past 20 years.

Hailwood's involvement, together with Wynne's successful efforts in 1977, persuaded the factory to become more heavily interested than had been the case before. However, this stopped short of full factory involvement, and Hailwood's arrangement was with Sports Motor Cycles, who funded the entire arrangement out of their sponsorship budget, with no help at all from Coburn & Hughes. Indeed, though the factory built two machines for the race, one for Mike and other for Roger Nicholls, Wynne was required to pay up front in full for one of them (Hailwood's bike), and was given until the end of the year to come up with the cash for the second one. Curiously, the factory would only supply him with the machines through Coburn & Hughes, who apparently had the nerve to level a mark-up before passing the Hailwood bike on to Sports. C & H ended up buying the Nicholls machine off the factory themselves; they refused to sell it to Wynne at year's end as per the arrangement, instead putting it on display in their Luton showroom.

The bikes arrived from the factory just before Christmas 1977, and proved to be not too different from the ex-NCR machine. That bike was refurbished to be ridden in the 1978 TT by Jim Scaysbrook, an Australian mate of Mike's who'd been instrumental in getting him back on a bike in the first place in classic racing down-under. The new machines had again been built largely by NCR and sported a slightly altered chassis. Like the previous year's bike it had been built by Verlicchi on the standard jig, but out of lighter, thin-wall tubing that resulted in a useful loss of weight. The footrest mounts and various other lugs and fittings were modified, but the biggest change for 1978 was the adoption of a standard-type swinging-arm and adjusters, which was however much wider than on the road bikes to accommodate the 6 in. rear slick now fitted. The rear brake caliper was mounted above the swing-arm for speed of wheel removal, while the lower mounting bracket for the rear suspension units was copiously drilled to offer a choice of preload positions. An oil cooler was mounted in the nose, with the fairing drilled for ventilation.

The engine was to the same general specification as the previous year, with 60 degree heads and a dry clutch, but this time a set of specially made sandcast alloy crankcases, one of 20 such pairs made with strengthening webs incorporated as then permitted under the TT Formula rules, was employed on each of the two bikes. This also permitted the use of a screw-in type oil filter such as was used later on the Pantahs.

On receipt of the bikes from the factory, Sports followed what was to become standard practice and

BOTH *Two views of the California Hot Rod during its triumphant defeat of the Japanese four-cylinder opposition in the prestigious Daytona Superbike race in 1977. Above, rider Cook Neilson gloves up for the start while tuner Phil* Schilling (left) juggles with the polishing cloths. Below, Neilson sweeps the Duke through Daytona Speedway's Turn 3, en route to a convincing win (Greening)

dismantled them to the last nut and bolt, incorporating certain modifications to the gearbox that experience had shown to be desirable to prevent the bike jumping out of gear as the dogs wore. Wynne rebuilt them to TT racing specifications, with extensive use of Nyloc nuts and the like to prevent vital parts working loose and falling off under the Mountain course's merciless pounding. Hailwood was taking his IoM comeback seriously enough to fly in to Britain some weeks in advance of the TT (he in fact returned to live permanently in the UK near Birmingham until his tragic death in a car crash in 1981) in order to make himself available for extensive test sessions at Oulton Park, near Wynne's Manchester base. Both he and Nicholls, as well as other leading riders such as Barry Ditchburn and Percy Tait, rode the machines, which were refined to perfection in readiness for the big occasion. Hailwood's bike ended up producing 87 bhp at 9000 rpm.

Though few of even the most ardent of his many supporters could have hoped for it to turn out thus, Mike Hailwood's return to the Isle of Man in 1978 will go down in motorcycle racing history as one of the most incredible feats of all time. Eleven years after he last rode there, seven years after he last raced a bike of any kind in an international event, and with a damaged right foot that made even walking sometimes painful, he demolished the might of the Honda works team in the TT Formula 1 race aboard the red and green Sports Motor Cycles Ducati, in spite of giving away two cylinders, around 20 bhp and several million yen to the Japanese multis. There's no substitute for talent, and thanks to the speed and reliability of the V-twin which Wynne and the Ducati factory had provided for him, Mike was able to record one of the least expected but most popular victories in the long history of the TT races.

Hailwood dominated the F1 class throughout the week, recording the fastest practice time at 111.04 mph, 2 mph faster than Tom Herron's Mocheck Honda and the works Japanese bike of Phil Read; Nicholls was 8th fastest at over 105 mph, a lot faster than the dry times he had put up the year before, reflecting the improvements which had gone into the 1978 machines. In the race Hailwood led almost from the start, catching and passing Read, who had started ahead of him on the road, and whose Honda expired with terminal engine problems in the effort to keep up with the lazy-sounding flying Ducati. Before then, the thousands of spectators thronging the course – Mike's return had ensured the largest TT crowd in a decade – had experienced a feeling of

déjà vu, as they watched two of the greatest and most distinctive stars of the golden age of Grand Prix racing pass by together machines very different from those they had raced each other on then. It was a magical moment that all who were there to experience it will never forget.

Hailwood crossed the line to win by two minutes at 108.51 mph from John Williams on the second works Honda, having set up a new TT F1 lap record at 110.62 mph. He did so not a moment too soon, for just as he finished the bottom bevel gear on the rear cylinder sheared and the engine expired, a fact which Wynne and works mechanics Franco Farne and Giuliano Pedretti, who had come over for the race, only became aware of when they came to prepare the engine for the next meeting. But it had kept going long enough to ensure a famous and popular victory that also recorded Ducati's long-awaited first-ever World Championship.

Nicholls had not enjoyed such good fortune, for he'd been forced to retire when the sight glass on his engine's sump had shattered, spilling oil all over the rear of the bike, not to mention his leg. Scaysbrook too, on the other Sports entry, had suffered misfortune at Governors Bridge when a coil bracket fractured under the tank of his Ducati, jamming the throttle wide open as he approached the tight hairpin and leaving him with no option but to lay the bike down in order to avoid serious injury: he was fortunately relatively unscathed after this horrific experience. It was Mike the Bike's day and 3 June, 1979 will live for ever as one of the great dates in motorcycle history.

A week later an in some ways even more astonishing victory came Hailwood's way at the Post-TT Mallory Park meeting, when in spite of an evident top speed deficiency he soundly defeated both Read's Honda and the P&M Kawasaki of eventual British TT F1 champion John Cowie after a breathtaking dice with the pair of them aboard the TT-winning Ducati. Forced to come from behind after a slow start, Mike showed that he had lost none of his short-circuit magic either as he took on and beat the best of the current British scratchers by exploiting to the full the superior handling characteristics of the Italian V-twin. At the finish, his right boot was worn away to the flesh – just like the old days! It was a superb victory that set the seal in every way on his two-wheeled comeback, but just to show he was human Hailwood fell off the bike at the next meeting, on Donington Park's treacherous surface.

The Ducati's speed disadvantage compared to the Japanese fours was more than even Mike could

BOTH *Two pictures of the Scuderia NCR 900 SS endurance racer from 1976. The detail work on the machine is superb,* *and by any standards this was a most delectable motorcycle. Note the duplex drive chain in the upper photo*

cope with at the final race he contested that year at Silverstone, whose wide open stretches placed practically all the emphasis on power and almost none at all on handling. Even so, Hailwood finished third in the TT F1 race on the Ducati, in spite of a boxful of neutrals, beating many faster machines, but forced to take a grandstand seat for the breathtaking fight to the finish between Cowie and Mocheck Honda rider Tom Herron; the Kawasaki privateer swooped though on the inside after Herron made a mistake at Woodcote on the last lap to register a well-earned win by less than a length.

Hailwood's return to the TT, with a couple of short circuits thrown in for good measure, had originally been intended as a one-off event strictly for his own satisfaction and enjoyment. With typical modesty, he was as amazed as any of his countless fans at his unexpected success, which was matched by the delight experienced by all at the Bologna factory at the prestige his victories had brought the marque. In an inspired piece of marketing, Ducati swiftly brought out the Mike Hailwood Replica version of the 900 SS, already described in the previous chapter.

After a good long think Mike decided to return to the Island for one last fling in 1979, but this time he decided to put almost all his eggs in the Ducati basket: the Yamahas he'd also ridden in 1978 had not been much to his liking and he'd enjoyed little success on them, while feeling much more at home on the Ducati. The ACU were, however, keen for him to ride in the 500 cc Senior race, so he decided to take advantage of an offer to ride an RG500 Suzuki provided by the British importer, while concentrating on the Ducati for the TT F1 and open Classic race.

The Ducati factory were naturally delighted at the news, and this time decided to enter an official factory team, with Steve Wynne as team manager but the bikes owned and prepared by Bologna. Wynne was chary of this arrangement; he'd been striving to get the factory involved in racing again on a direct basis, so welcomed this part of the deal, but felt that they tended to underestimate the rigours of the IoM circuit, hence final preparation needed to be carried out in Britain. A compromise was struck whereby the bikes would be built and fitted by early in the New Year, then shipped to Manchester for race testing, but January came and went, and with it no sign of the promised machines – one for each of the two races.

Eventually by the middle of April the word came from Bologna that both machines were ready to be tested, but instead of this being done in Britain,

Hailwood would have to go to Italy to carry it out. Pat Slinn had by now joined Sports Motor Cycles from Coburn & Hughes to concentrate on running the racing team in conjunction with Steve Wynne, who needed to spend more time on the retail side, and it was he who accompanied Mike to Misano for the first test session. Mike had covered over 100 laps on the two bikes, and was reportedly pleased with their performance on the flat, smooth Adriatic track, but it all ended in disaster. The factory had reversed the gearchange pattern from the one-up, four-down arrangement Mike was really accustomed to on the left to a one-down, four-up pattern on the same side. Since the gearbox was also hitting false neutrals, it was only a matter of time before the inevitable happened. Mike found neutral changing from third to fourth rounding the fast left-hander on to the main straight, and in the flap to find a gear stamped on the gear lever the wrong way, hitting second instead. The bike broadsided and he was thrown off, breaking three ribs and was fortunate not to be more badly hurt. A series of events now occurred which threatened his participation in the TT on a Ducati, and almost certainly was responsible for the disappointing performance of the bikes in the Island.

Hailwood's testing crash had made front page news in Italy, and had been noticed by one of the key executives in EFIM, the government-owned holding company which controlled Ducati. That person professed concern that the firm was not adequately insured against a lawsuit for damages on the part of one of their riders, should he be injured riding a factory-entered bike. It was impossible to arrange adequate coverage through an insurance company. Less than four weeks before the start of TT practice, Ducati cabled Wynne to say that they were withdrawing their entries, and would not be able to provide a bike for Mike to ride!

Fortunately, Wynne acted quickly, contacting Bologna and offering to buy the machines off them so that Hailwood would once again be riding for Sports Motor Cycles instead of Ducati Meccanica. The factory agreed, provided that if Mike won again, they could buy the bike(s) back off him. 'A hiding to nothing' is how Steve Wynne later described the arrangement, but conscious of how many people were about to pack the Island in order to see Hailwood ride again, he agreed to the terms.

The problem was that when the two machines arrived in Britain two weeks before the TT, it was evident that development on them had stopped while the confusion over the insurance policy was being sorted out and they were consequently far

Hailwood makes a point to Steve Wynne during practice for the Silverstone TT F1 race in 1978 (Greening)

A historic moment, as Mike Hailwood prepares to mount a Ducati V-twin for the first time in a race, during the Castrol Six Hour race at Amaroo Park in Australia in November 1977: Jim Scaysbrook is his co-rider

from ready to be raced in the TT. The F1 bike turned out to be a slightly modified wet-clutch production 900 SS which, moreover, lacked the special one-piece seat/tank unit. Fortunately, Wynne was by now selling this component as a bolt-on accessory and was able to fit one of his replica versions. The Classic TT machine was a specially-developed racer, though.

An Oulton Park test session with Mike and George Fogarty, for whom another works bike had originally been promised, aboard revealed that the Ducati's traditional handling advantage had completely disappeared on the Classic machine. Unknown to the team then, the factory had altered the steering head angle and had also raised the engine 2–3 in. in the frame in order to provide additional ground clearance for the new breed of longer-lasting sticky slick tyres to do their stuff. A titanium box-section swinging arm had been fitted

ABOVE *The 1978 TT-winning Ducati 900 (Greening)*

RIGHT *A famous photograph: Mike the Bike sweeps effortlessly round Quarter Bridge on the Sports Motor Cycles Ducati en route to a historic win in the 1978 Formula 1 TT*

to permit use of an even wider section tyre on the Classic TT bike, which also had a wider rear frame loop to allow high-level exhausts to be employed, with the rear pipe exiting from the rear cylinder between the frame members. The engine on this machine (but not the TT F1 bike, which remained an 864 cc unit) had been bored to 947 cc, and measured 90 × 74.4 mm; the factory claimed 115 bhp from the unit, but it's doubtful if the output much exceeded 100 bhp, and in any case the extra power was an embarrassment thanks to the frame modifications which nobody involved with running the bikes had been informed of.

Though Wynne and Slinn together with their helpers and two factory mechanics worked long and hard throughout TT practice week, they failed to find the right formula to make the bikes even as competitive as the 1978 machine. Hailwood did one lap with the 950 Classic bike, clocking 89.97 mph in the dry, and reported it was 'all over the road – absolutely unrideable'. He decided to race his 500 Suzuki in the Classic, and concentrate on trying to get the TT F1 bike in a competitive shape. Everything was tried, even the 1979 engine in the 1978 frame, but the bike simply wasn't as fast as the previous year, and of course the Japanese teams, who had now come into the TT Formula class in a

big way, had carried out a whole year's intensive development since being humbled by the Ducati in 1978. Ideally, the solution would have been to race the 1978 machine, but owing to the change in regulations its crankcases were no longer legal.

Mike's best practice time for the 1979 F1 TT was a mere 105.88 mph, when he'd clocked over 111 mph the year before. Had he been able to repeat that time, he'd have been second fastest in practice to Alex George's works Honda. He did in fact achieve that position in the 500 class on the Suzuki at over 108 mph, and as history records he went on to win the Senior TT, setting a new lap record at 114.03 mph; he was riding better than ever. Sadly the Ducati was this year no match for its rider's talents, and though Mike was able to grit his teeth sufficiently to lie third at half-distance in the F1 race, he lost top gear as he started his last lap. Then coming down the Mountain for the last time the extra vibration caused by over-revving the engine in fourth (the fact that it put up with this abuse was nevertheless an excellent advertisement for desmodromic valve gear) caused the battery bracket to fracture and the battery itself to dangle by its connecting wires, some of which were broken. The engine cut out and Mike, believing that it had blown up at last, toured all the way to Hillberry, where he had to dismount if he wanted to push home. It was then that he saw the loose wires, and though his mechanical knowledge was legendary for its slightness, he claimed later that he managed to pick up enough tips from the marshals and policeman on duty to rewire the battery, which he wedged in place above the rear mudguard. Much to his surprise, he was able to restart the engine, and toured in to finish in fifth place, having averaged 106.06 mph, with a best lap of 109.45 mph. After last year's victory it was a disappointing result for Mike and his thousands of fans, but at least the leader-board finish was some consolation for the days of hard work put in by Steve Wynne and Pat Slinn.

Hailwood had been contracted to do five other meetings on the Ducati, including the Post-TT and Race of the Year Mallory meetings and the British GP TT F1 round at Silverstone. The performance of the bikes had been so disappointing that he dropped the idea, and then when he broke his collar-bone in a practice crash at Donington on the Suzuki, the career of the greatest motorcycle racer of all time was over. Uncharacteristically, Mike was so upset at the performance of the bikes that he actually went so far as to say in a newspaper interview he felt the Ducati factory had let him down: the most charitable observer would have to say he was right.

Though a variety of riders such as Fogarty, Eddie Roberts and others continued to ride the big bevel-drive Ducatis in TT F1 events for Sports Motor Cycles during the next couple of seasons, Hailwood's 1979 TT performance was effectively the model's swansong in that class of racing: the Japanese multis were now so powerful, and their chassis technology beginning to keep up with engine development, that the twin-cylinder Dukes were no longer remotely competitive. The 1980 TT saw two significant appearances in the later context of Ducati World Championship hopes. Tony Rutter rode one of the big V-twins for the first time, when Wynne cobbled a bike together for him at the last moment after he'd been let down with his Honda ride; though it only lasted one lap before a porous rear cylinder began spewing sufficient quantities of

No ground clearance problems here! Richard Schlachter thunders his way round the Loudoun track in New Hampshire ahead of Wes Cooley's Kawasaki in a 1979 Superbike event, aboard the George Vicensi 900 Ducati

oil to make further progress undesirable, the relationship between Rutter, the team and the Ducati marque (he was actually a dealer in Staffordshire) had been struck.

The other significant debut was that of the Ducati Pantah engine, with its belt-driven desmodromic ohc design, in TT Formula 2 racing at the Isle of Man. The Pantah had been announced somewhat prematurely at the end of 1977, but it had not been until 1979 that deliveries effectively began. Even so, it was surprising that it took so long for the usually sharp-minded *ducatisti* to realize the potential that the smaller engine offered for the TT2 class, and it was not until portly, bespectacled German tuner Alfred Baujohr brought an overbored version of the Pantah, which was then only available to the public in 500 cc form, to the Island in 1980 that this suddenly became apparent. Baujohr's modified engine measured 81 × 58 mm, for a total capacity of 597 cc, and though it was housed in a lightly modified standard frame, he caused quite a commotion amongst the riders of the thinly veiled TZ350 Yamaha racers which then dominated the class by qualifying sixth fastest in practice on his first visit to the Island at 94.19 mph. Though the damp conditions on race day resulted in a lowly finishing position for the cautious first-timer, his little Ducati had shown others the way of the future.

At almost the same time it was announced by the Italian Federation that the 1981 national Junior championships would be run according to TT Formula rules, with all four classes catered for. The only amendments in comparison to the World (meaning IoM/ACU) title regulations would be the retention of the original starting device (which neatly disposed of the TZ350s and their ilk), and the abolition of the fatuous carburettor rule, which had resulted in smooth-bore Keihins and flat-slide Lectrons – racing units which had never graced a production motorcylce – becoming standard wear in British TT Formula events.

This move, which had come about after concerted lobbying by several Italian manufacturers, including Ducati, Laverda, Bimota, Villa, Malanca and many others, resulted in a reappraisal of the current policy towards racing participation at Borgo Panigale. It was decided that, instead of entrusting the company's fortunes to even closely connected private teams such as NCR, Ducati Meccanica would build and develop a TT2 racer and would enter a team of riders in the 1981 Italian championship.

The TT F2 World Championship, extended that year to encompass the Ulster GP as well as the TT itself, did not feature in their plans. So it was left once again to Sports Motor Cycles, in the absence of any interest on the part of the British importer in earning the new Pantah road model some of the

charisma which the Imola 100 and IoM TT victories had lent to its bigger brother, to try to achieve a second world title for the Bologna marque. A meeting at the Cologne Show in September 1980 between Pat Slinn and Cosimo Calcagnile saw the factory agree to supply Sports with a Pantah engine and tuning parts free of charge for entry in the TT and Ulster. Sports would have to provide a chassis and build the bike, and due to their Italian title series commitments the factory would not be able to send a mechanic along to help out, as in the past.

In the first couple of months of 1981, one of the first customers that Steve Wynne's retail firm had sold a road Pantah to unfortunately crashed it on the street, and the bike was written off by the insurance company. Wynne bought the bike from

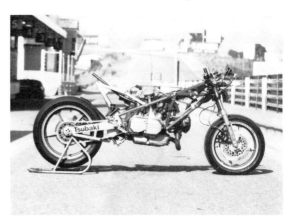

RIGHT *Monoshock Ducati from Tecfar in Spain. So far perhaps the most exotic big V-twin seen (Noyes)*

BELOW *Malcolme Tunstall and his tuner father Syd have been the backbone of Ducati racing for the past 20 years in the USA. His 950 cc Superbike sweeps into the Donington chicane in August 1982 (Francis)*

Herman Jolink's 860 drag racer. So far it's managed 10.689 sec over a standing start 400 m in Holland

them, and set about turning the wreck into a potential TT race-winner. One of the conditions of being given the factory's engine was that Sports should engage a rider for the bike who was also a potential race-winner. Tony Rutter had already won two Junior TTs on Yamahas, and moreover had a very good record on the Dundrod circuit in Northern Ireland, on which the Ulster GP would be held. He agreed to ride the bike in both TT F2 races in 1981.

Unfortunately, when the promised factory engine duly arrived, it turned out to be a development hack that had not been rebuilt after running for several hours on the brake for fuel-testing purposes. It was moreover a 500, and would need to be converted to the 600 cc capacity limit for TT F2 four-strokes. Pat Slinn set to with a will to build a racing engine unit out of this somewhat unpromising material. He began by fitting a pair of 750 liners and boring the engine to 81 mm, as Baujohr had done the year before. A set of specially made 10:1 pistons were ordered from Omega, then

carefully balanced before being fitted to the standard rods. The inlet tract was opened out to 36 mm, the maximum carburettor size permitted for the model, but instead of the standard Dell'Ortos a set of flat-side 36 mm Lectrons were used, with converted Moto Guzzi valves originally fitted to the Le Mans model. The factory had sent a special set of camshafts offering increased lift, and these were fitted with standard rockers which had been carefully shot-peened. A standard wet clutch with longer springs matched a gearbox which also contained standard road ratios. Since the engine was never put on a brake no performance figures were ever determined, but peak revs were 10,500 rpm, with a wide spread of power from 7000 rpm upwards and excellent bottom-end torque. A factory two-into-one exhaust was fitted.

An original test session at Oulton Park was distinctly unpromising, with Rutter reporting poor handling and steering, and the engine well down on power. When it seized after a handful of laps, victory in the TT looked a remote possibility indeed. But Wynne and Slinn set to to sort the bike out, and the frame was entrusted to Maxton chassis builder Ron Williams to modify for racing purposes. When Rutter next tried the bike at Aintree just before the TT it had been transformed. Powerful and easy to ride, it now handled superbly thanks to Williams's alterations, which consisted of positioning the twin Koni rear units vertically for increased suspension travel, bracing the swing-arm, and rearranging the geometry of the bracing struts connecting the parallel tubes of the trellis frame design. An extra bracing tube was added to increase steering head rigidity, and Dymag wheels and a set of adjustable Marzocchi front forks with magnesium sliders completed the bike's transformation from insurance wreck to TT winner.

For that is indeed what it became, with Rutter qualifying fastest in practice after a spot of gearbox trouble at 101.26 mph and leading from start to finish on race day, never lapping below the magic 'ton' and setting new race and lap records at 101.91 and 103.51 mph respectively as he completed the four-lap race non-stop to finish $1\frac{1}{2}$ minutes ahead of Odlin's four-cylinder Honda. Once again Ducati had won on what was effectively the marque's first time out in a new category, though this time the credit was all Steve Wynne's and Pat Slinn's in terms of producing the winning machine, and in Tony Rutter they had selected the near-ideal rider for the TT2 class.

Still to come was the second round of the World Championship in Ulster, and victory was far from certain on the tighter Dundrod circuit, where the top-speed superiority that the Ducati's slim profile had helped to assure would count for less. At this point the factory decided to pitch in, and promised to provide Rutter with a works 600 TT2 bike for the deciding race. In fact, Franco Farne and export director Franco Valentini turned up with two machines, on one of which Rutter broke the F2 lap record in practice by no less than 15 seconds over the 7.4-mile road circuit. A bad start left him well down in the race, but in spite of the miserably wet conditions he scythed through the field to what he thought was the lead. In fact, he'd misread his pit signal thanks to a misted visor, and 'Plus 14 seconds' turned out to be minus that amount, but second place behind eventual winner Phil Mellor's 350 Yamaha was sufficient to earn Tony Rutter his first world title and Ducati their second. George Fogarty finished fourth on Rutter's TT-winning bike, to

Ing. Taglioni holding one of the Verlicchi-made frames for the 600 TT2 Pantah works racer: it weighs a scanty 7 kg

position. Marzocchi 35 mm front forks were used at complete a memorable day for the Italian firm.

The bike which Rutter had ridden to second place in Ireland was one of the five factory TT2 machines which had been constructed for the Italian championship. Though naturally using the Pantah engine as a basis for the design, these otherwise bore no relation to the standard road bikes, having been designed by Taglioni from the frame up as outright racing machines. In many people's opinion, not least the author's, the 600 TT2 Ducati is the ultimate four-stroke racing motorcycle.

The red and yellow machines – whose colours denoted a renaissance of the traditional Squadra Corse livery of the 1960s – encompassed all Taglioni's insistence on light weight, efficient air penetration, wide power band and ease of handling that he had striven to achieve ever since the Marianna first appeared over 25 years before. The standard Pantah frame was replaced by an incredibly light multi-tube triangulated unit, also made by Verlicchi, which weighed only 7 kg and was fitted with monoshock rear suspension employing a Marzocchi unit in the cantilever

the front, of a multi-adjustable type with magnesium sliders, and both 16 and 18 in. lightweight Campagnolo alloy front wheels were tried, though most riders including Rutter preferred the large diameter; an 18 in. rim was standard wear at the rear. A 55 in. wheelbase ensured quick and positive steering, and fully floating discs with Golden Brembo calipers were fitted front and rear. The attention to detail in the design of the frame was remarkable, even to the extent of having a groove moulded into the fuel tank to accommodate the sweep of the throttle cables. Care was needed though in removing the engine, as it was possible to distort the frame in doing so since it was not well supported at the balance point above the rear cylinder. Attention to weight-saving details resulted in a dry weight of 128 kg complete with the heavy self-starting equipment required by Italian TT Formula rules.

A highly competitive power to weight ratio was obtained thanks to effective tuning of the road-based engine, which was bored to 81 × 58 mm, as opposed to the street version of the 600 Pantah which had by then been announced. It measured 80 × 58 mm for 583 cc compared to the racer's 597 cc. Semi-slipper pistons gave 10.5:1 compression compared to the road bike's 9.5:1, and oversize valves (40.4 mm inlet against 37.5 mm on the production model, with a 35 mm exhaust against 33.5 mm) offered improved breathing, especially when mated with the 40 mm Dell'Orto carbs permitted in Italian TT events; Rutter was obliged to make do with 36 mm units for the World Championship races. Specially developed racing desmodromic camshafts of the type fitted to the 1981 TT winner completed the basic engine modifications; careful assembly and tuning were the additional factors responsible for the remarkable performance of an engine not very far removed from the road bike on which it was based. Standard engine cases and gearbox ratios were employed, with a bolt-on magnesium cover for a hydraulically operated dry clutch. The V-shaped cover over the toothed belt drive to the cams was jettisoned to save weight, with a battery positioned somewhat precariously in the tail of the seat representing the only compromise on this beautifully designed machine to enable it to be changed quickly in endurance races. Eventually, the resultant top-heaviness was avoided by placing it in a special box under the engine, just in front of the rear wheel.

Tony Rutter in the dip at Governors Bridge en route to victory in the 1981 Formula 2 TT on the Sports Motor Cycles Pantah, built up from an insurance write-off

Ignition was by Bosch electronic unit, running 32 degrees of advance. Maximum torque was achieved at 7500 rpm, and peak power of 78 bhp at the rear wheel at 10,500 rpm, but with the engine really coming on song from as low as 6000 rpm it was an extremely easy bike to ride, especially on the demanding road courses which the TT Formula was originally designed to encompass.

The inaugural Italian TT2 championship saw a season-long duel between the works Ducatis and a factory-entered team of Kawasaki-powered Bimota KB2s, whose four-cylinder engines had been bored out to the maximum 600 cc limit and were more powerful than the Bologna V-twins; the occasional overbored Laverda Montjuic also featured at the front of the field, but after Ducati signed up the leading Laverda rider, Walter Cussigh, in mid-season, the threat from Breganze was minimal.

Bimota meant business, and their very strong team of riders included Giancarlo Lazzarini, younger brother of the 50 and 125 cc world champion, and Massimo Giumbini, one of the most promising new Italian riders. But Ducati too had their own star of tomorrow in Massimo Broccoli, and though Giumbini won the third round at Vallelunga and was able to beat Broccoli on at least one other occasion in a straight fight, Ducati's

The works Ducati Pantah, here seen in 500 cc form: this is the bike that Massimo Broccoli rode to 7th place against the Suzuki and Yamaha 2-strokes in the 500 cc race at Mugello in October 1981

astute recruitment of Cussigh meant that the Bimota threat could be negated, especially on handling circuits like Mugello. Broccoli took the title by finishing second to Cussigh in the final round at Monza, in which Ducatis occupied the first four places. Just to top off a highly satisfactory return to racing for the factory, Carlo Perugini and Mauro Ricci won the Italian Endurance Championship on an NCR-tuned 900 SS, handsomely defeating a horde of Japanese four-cylinder specials.

The performance of the 600 TT2 Ducati was such that Taglioni could not resist sleeving one of the bikes down to the 499 cc Pantah dimensions of 74 × 58 mm and entering it in the last round of the Italian 500 cc title series at Mugello in October. In his first race against the likes of Lucchinelli and Uncini, Broccoli rode the booming Ducati to an incredible seventh place against a field of TZ500 Yamahas and RG500 Suzuki Grand Prix two-strokes, which he actually accelerated away from out of the tight corners of the Tuscan track. The Ducati's surefooted handling and smooth power delivery on a greasy track, where an overabundance of sudden

The works Pantah: note the bolt-on magnesium cover for the dry clutch conversion. The camshaft drive belt covers have been jettisoned to save weight

power embarrassed many of the GP bikes, was the principal reason for success, but more than one rider of an exotic Japanese production racers suffered the ignominy of being passed down the main straight by the four-stroke twin. It was a truly remarkable result that perhaps even more than its TT F2 victories at home and abroad served to place the 600 TT2 Pantah in its proper perspective as one of the great racing motorcycles of all time.

1982 saw a repeat version of the factory's victory in the Italian TT2 series, but this time with Walter Cussigh as the eventual champion; he won every round against opposition that now mostly consisted of other Ducatis, for Bimota had pulled out after having their very expensive machines humbled by a less powerful but more efficient twin. During the winter the factory had constructed a short line of 20 600 TT2 replicas which differed only from the works bikes in having wet clutches and minor detail modifications. It was, however, a brace of dry-clutch specials which the factory provided Tony Rutter with in order to defend his World TT2 title in 1982, now extended to three rounds with the inclusion of an event on the round-the-houses street circuit at Vila Real in northern Portugal. Though two factory mechanics travelled to each round to look after the bikes, Sports Motor Cycles continued

to pay all the expenses of running the team, and entered Rutter in each of the races.

Once again Ducati ended the season as World TT F2 champions – the factory's third world title – after a series of races in which Rutter literally pulverized the opposition. At the Isle of Man in June, after lapping at a remarkable 108.22 mph in practice, he wound up winning at an average speed of no less than 108.50 mph by almost four minutes from the TZ/LC Yamaha in second place, with Fogarty on a 600 TT2 replica in fifth position after surviving a collision with TT veteran Bill Smith on the approach to Ballaugh Bridge, which left the latter seriously injured. Fogarty himself was lucky to be alive, having earlier crashed the ex-Hailwood TT winning bike which he was riding in the F1 event on the approach to Quarter Bridge; the historic machine caught fire and was tragically burnt out. Rutter's TT F2-winning speed would have been enough to earn him third place in the F1 event against the 1000 cc fours, and his new TT2 lap record of a staggering 109.27 mph, almost 6 mph better than his own previous mark, confirmed his comment that the little Ducati was 'the perfect Isle of Man motorcycle'.

A month later in Portugal, Rutter won again just as convincingly, leading home a Ducati 1-4 sweep followed by German Rainer Nagel and Scotsman Alex George on 600 TT2 replicas, and Welshman John Caffrey on a home-brewed Pantah special with his own design of monoshock frame. Just for good measure, Rutter turned out in the F1 race on one of Steve Wynne's replicas, nominally overbored to make it eligible for the larger-capacity class, and finished seventh with his eye on the more vital TT2 crown.

The 40-year-old Midlands veteran clinched his second title at the Ulster GP in August, averaging over 100 mph to win the race and thus score maximum points in the championship. By finishing third and seventh respectively, Fogarty and Nagel scored sufficient points to wind up second equal in the points table, and Rutter's fastest lap of 104.40 mph was a convincing new lap record for the class on the 7.40-mile Dundrod circuit. To complete the story of the factory 600 TT2's international appearances in 1982, the factory loaned the author Rutter's title-winning bike, fitted with a right-foot gearchange, to ride in the Macau GP in November, run on the 3.8-mile Guia circuit around the streets and along the waterfront of the Portuguese colony on the shores of the Chinese People's Republic. It was the first time for over 10 years that a European bike had appeared in the race, and though the little machine's top speed of 145 mph placed it at a severe disadvantage against the 500 and 750 two-strokes and 1000 cc fours along the fast straights beside the South China Sea, its incredible torque and precise handling made it one of the quickest bikes of all through the short, sharp squirts of the city street section. In spite of being torpedoed at the hairpin by one of the local riders, resulting in my having to finish the first part of the two-leg event with no front brakes, I was able to gain a midfield position in the final results thanks to the effectiveness of the little V-twin Ducati on this type of circuit.

Meanwhile Taglioni had not been idle in considering the possibilities of enlarging the Pantah's capacity, especially with the lowering of the 1000 cc four-stroke upper limit for the TT Formula 1 coming into effect for the 1984 season; since not only were the TT Formula championships but also one of Ducati's traditional areas of expertise, the Endurance World Championship, to be run to these rules, there was even more reason to explore the potential of the smaller V-twin engine.

Accordingly a heavily oversquare prototype version of the 600 TT2, measuring 88 × 61.5 mm for a total capacity of 748 cc, appeared in the hands of American Jimmy Adamo at the 1982 Imola 200, in which it finished a remarkable 13th overall, once again embarrassing the riders of several supposedly more powerful 500 GP bikes and TT F1 machines. Producing 94.8 bhp at the rear wheel, at 10,250 rpm, the bored and stroked version of the 600 TT2 engine nonetheless retained the flexibility of the smaller bike, with maximum torque again developed at 7500 rpm. Top speed was up to just under 155 mph, but the most remarkable improvement was in acceleration out of corners – already a Pantah forté – and in mid-range performance. Externally, the bike was identical to the smaller-engined machines, with the substitution of 41 mm carburettors for the 40 mm units on the 500 and 600 cc versions.

Adamo had been invited to ride the machine at Imola at the last minute when original jockey Carlo Perugini crashed in practice and hurt himself, thanks to his success the previous year in winning for Ducati the inaugural US championship for a fast-developing new class, the Battle of the Twins, which catered for twin-cylinder four-strokes over 500 cc. The origins of the category lay in the street bike-orientated Superbike class which had sprung up in North America in the mid-1970s, and was originally the field for a fascinating technical and racing duel between the powerful but ill-handling Japanese fours, principally the Z-1 Kawasaki, and the better-handling but less powerful European twins, led by BMW, Moto Guzzi and Ducati.

Ducati's involvement in a class of racing which seemed to be tailor-made for the products of the Bologna firm, in what was their most important export market in those days, began in a surprisingly low-key fashion. In spite of the V-twin model's success at Imola in 1972–73, the US importers Berliner had by now adopted an even more obdurate 'no-racing' policy than their British counterparts, and Ducati participation in the National Production class, which eventually evolved into the Superbike Production category for the 1976 season, was minimal.

Fortunately, however, a pair of committed Californian *Ducatisti* stepped in to fill the vacuum which Berliner had left: *Cycle* magazine editor Cook Neilson and his colleague Phil Schilling. Having become deeply appreciative of the engineering behind the 750 Desmo Super Sport in particular (the pair owned a trio of the rare models between them), they resolved to race one of Neilson's bikes in local West Coast events. Success came readily, thanks to a combination of Schilling's meticulous preparation and Neilson's underrated skills as a rider, and in spite of giving away up to 150 cc to the

Kawasaki fours, the Ducati was often able to lead them home in Production races and invariably to win the 750 class. When a separate such category was created for the 1975 season at the prestigious Daytona event in March, Neilson won it easily, finishing fifth overall after being trapped at 138.25 mph on the banking – over 12 mph faster than the next 750 cc machine.

Though up until now the Ducati had been running in more or less standard form, a change of rules and the creation of the Superbike category for 1976 prompted the duo to go for broke, boring the engine to 885 cc (87 × 74.4 mm, compared to the standard 80 mm bore of the 750 or 86 mm of the 860 road bikes). Using the vast resources of motorcycle technology and artisan ingenuity of the Los Angeles area of Southern California, the pair built what they came to refer to as the 'California Hot Rod', a compendium of special parts and trick stuff that resulted in one of the most individual racing Ducatis ever built.

Tony Rutter splashes his way to a world championship for himself and Ducati at the Ulster GP in 1981: he finished second behind a Yamaha, after misreading a pit signal

Faced with a refusal by Berliner's to obtain factory tuning parts for a serious effort to win at Daytona and elsewhere against the works-supported BMWs and Kawasakis, and unable to communicate directly with Bologna, Neilson and Schilling instead were forced to roll their own. Having bored out the 750 crankcases to accept 450 Ducati liners, they commissioned special pistons from first Venolia, then later ForgedTrue, fitted with gudgeon pins from a Toyota car and piston rings from an XT500 Yamaha. The standard crankshaft was rebuilt locally, and a mixture of Polish, German and American bearings fitted in the reworked cases. Cylinder heads were re-ported by ace flow expert Jerry Branch, and fitted with oversize inlet valves off a Harley-Davidson (44 mm against the originals' 40 mm) and exhaust ones from a BMW (38 mm against 36 mm). Standard 40 mm

Steve Wynne, the man behind Hailwood's and Rutter's TT Formula successes, is no mean racer. Here he sweeps one of the factory 600 TT2 replicas through Donington Park on to the 600 cc class win in the BoT race in August 1982 (Francis)

Dell'Orto carburettors were retained, but mounted on modified inlet stubs and with the accelerator pumps backed off. The flywheel was removed, and all internal engine parts regularly Magnafluxed for signs of incipient disaster. This was particularly vital in the case of the gearbox, for though in late 1976 the American pair had been able to acquire a genuine factory close-ratio cluster, this was reduced to scrap at the first meeting they used it at when a piston circlip broke up. In any case, local experts reckoned that the gears were made of the wrong material, and would not last long anyway. The result was a US-built Webster cluster, a copy of the factory gearbox but in graded materials.

The same philosophy was carried over to the chassis and external mechanical parts. The standard battery ignition was retained, but the coils junked in favour of a pair from the local K-Mart supermarket which gave a massive spark, coupled with a set of Accel condensers from a similar source. The oil system was rerouted so as to be partially external, with a Volkswagen oil filter incorporated into it. The chassis was reinforced round the steering head to ensure that it could cope with the grip of modern slick tyres just then becoming required wear in racing, though the Italian bike's handling was throughout the period of development practically above reproach, thanks partly to a set of longer 13.2 in. S&W rear units, which also gave added ground clearance especially when combined with the set of specially made high-rise exhaust pipes designed after extensive testbed research. To reduce weight from the standard 750 SS's 460 lb several steel parts such as the front wheel spacers were remade in alloy, and some aluminium components like the rear brake caliper mounting plate reworked in magnesium. Plasma-sprayed alloy front discs replaced the original cast-iron Brembo ones, like the alloy calipers a product of Harry Hunt's Northern Californian company, while a Hunt disc at the rear was gripped by a magnesium Fontana caliper – practically the only non-American part to be fitted to the machine as a modification. The result of this and other work was a reduction in the weight to 398 lb with oil and half a tank of fuel, and still fitted with lights and other required paraphernalia.

The effect of this Californian development was to produce an externally near-standard street racer whose performance was on a par with the racing machinery contesting the upper-midfield positions of the Daytona 200 and other such events. Trapped at 149.50 mph at Daytona in 1977, the California Hot Rod produced 90.4 bhp at 8300 rpm, and was almost certainly a 150-plus bike, but one which at the same time offered a flat torque curve (with maximum torque achieved at 6500 rpm) and made power from as low down as 3000 rpm. Though somewhat self-deprecating in true Malibu style, Neilson was also no mean rider, and his second place at Daytona in the inaugural Superbike event in 1976 was followed up a year later by well-deserved victory in the race he and Schilling had striven so hard to win. The Ducati led almost from start to finish, drawing away from the twin- and four-cylinder oppostion, all of which with the exception of Cooley's Yoshimura Kawasaki were remarkably enough slower than the Ducati through the speed traps. It was a win which delighted a large section of the road racing fraternity all over the world, not all of them Ducati enthusiasts, who had followed the sometimes painful efforts of the pair to develop the lone Ducati into a race-winner using only their own resources and ingenuity, coupled with a wide range of local contacts and the burning of much midnight oil.

One person who rode the Neilson/Schilling Ducati at a Laguna Seca test session in 1976 was none other than future World 500 cc champion Kenny Roberts, who, not normally known for his ability to do other than call a spade a spade, reported himself impressed and surprised by its performance. Neilson's successes at Daytona on a model which had not up until then been highly regarded by the leading US entrants and their riders, opened the doors for other well-known stars of the present and future to opt for the Bologna V-twin in US Superbike competition. Amongst these were future Honda GP star Freddie Spencer and leading American road racer Richard Schlachter, who both rode Ducatis in the Superbike race at Daytona in 1979. Spencer, then only 17 years old, seemed set for a certain second place on what was by then considered an obsolete machine against the speed and might of the works-supported Yoshimura Suzuki team, until sadly his rear wheel sprocket stripped its teeth not long before the finish. It was Spencer's first indication in an international event of the promise that he would fulfil so dramatically in the future.

Schlachter finished a sound twelfth in that race, but in 1981 he returned to race a Ducati at Daytona again in the new Battle of the Twins class's inaugural championship event. The category had come about the previous year in an effort to provide a means by which the large number of twin-cylinder Superbikes, by now largely obsolete in the face of the 140 bhp fours which at last handled reasonably well, could continue to be raced at major US events. The new class caught on rapidly with both participants and spectators alike, and provided another theatre for continued competition success on the part of the big Ducati V-twin.

Schlachter finished second in that initial Daytona Cycle Week race, riding a Modified Production 900 SS Ducati. But the winner of the race, and the man who would dominate North American BoT racing for the first two seasons of its evolution, was New Yorker Jimmy Adamo on a 989 cc Ducati prepared and entered by expatriate Italian and former factory employee Reno Leoni. Producing just under 100 bhp at 9000 rpm, the 92 mm bore Leoni Ducati ran on a 10.8:1 compression with standard 80 degree heads fitted with oversize 44 mm inlet and 39 mm exhaust valves, the former breathing through 41 mm Malossi carburettors that were in effect reworked Dell'Ortos. Though outwardly remarkably standard-looking, even to the extent of boasting standard 860 cases with a wet clutch, the bike was nevertheless almost certainly the fastest V-twin Ducati ever built, being trapped at 161 mph at the Daytona meeting in 1982, where it once again won the Battle of the Twins race comfortably.

Against Adamo's machine were ranged a large number of other well-modified twin-cylinder racers, though the grids were traditionally dominated by Ducatis, almost all of which were, at least until the end of 1982, the bevel-driven ohc desmos rather than the smaller Pantah version. The main reason for this was the emphasis on straight-line speed placed by the running of several of the rounds on combined banking and infield circuits such as those at Talladega and Pocono, as well as the better-known Daytona. Many of these privateer Ducatis displayed at least as much ingenuity as the California Hot Rod had done, exemplified by the machine on which British-born Florida resident Malcolme Tunstall finished as runner-up to the Leoni bike in the US BoT series in 1981 and 1982.

Tunstall's father Syd had worked for Berliner in the early 1960s, before exchanging the New Jersey snows for the Florida sunshine, eventually settling in St. Petersburg, where he opened a business which became the Stateside equivalent of Sports Motor Cycles, specializing in tuning parts and equipment for Ducatis, which he and his son both raced with great success in local and national events. Syd's Cycles were one of the principal early supporters of both Superbike racing and the Battle of the Twins, and for the latter class Tunstall senior prepared a very special Ducati incorporating many of his own home-made modifications. Bored to 947 cc using a 90 mm piston and standard stroke, it employed a left-hand rounded 750 crankcase for increased ground clearance and all-external oilways. Oversize valves and a modified inlet tract assisted breathing, with all-external braided line oilways and a modified gearbox to prevent the by now common Ducati problem of jumping out of third and fourth gears under racing conditions once the dogs had worn on the pinions. Tunstall's own design of electronic ingition with fixed advanced was fitted, running off a battery mounted just in front of the rear wheel beneath the engine. The Marzocchi forks were converted to compressed air damping, and many other Tunstall-designed goodies such as multi-adjustable clip-ons, specially tuned 2-into-1 exhaust and so forth were evident in the machine. At the end of 1982 it was equipped with a new short-wheelbase Tunstall frame which offered quicker steering, traditionally one of the few bugbears of the big Ducati standard frame's handling, allied to reduced weight which enabled the bike to scale in at 360 lb dry without the use of such exotic components as magnesium outer cases and titanium fittings. Running on the proverbial shoestring, the Tunstall family had no possibility of affording such parts.

At the end of 1982 Ducati's continued competition success with their V-twin model range seemed certain to be carried on in both the TT Formula and Battle of the Twins categories, albeit with threats on the horizon in the latter category from Harley-Davidson and the 8-valve Krauser BMW specials. But the continued and dedicated efforts of enthusiasts such as Steve Wynne, Syd Tunstall and Reno Leoni, as well as many others like them in almost every country in the world where motorcycles are raced, is bound to withstand the strongest test.

Often the most daunting obstacles to further Ducati successes achieved by these determined men, united as they are by a common commitment to racing the products of the Bologna factory, have been the actions of that very factory itself. But at the same time it must be remembered that Ducati Meccanica SpA is a government-owned company, subject to quite different checks and pressures than a privately owned firm, even a public one. While there's no doubting the enthusiasm for racing and eagerness to see Ducati's name on the winner's rostrum that runs through the blood of those in charge of the day-to-day running of the factory, from Ing. Taglioni and his men in the development department to the commercial and sales managers, they've always lacked the freedom from government supervision that would permit them to offer greater assistance to the many people all over the world who have helped to make the Ducati name synonymous with performance and competition success. It is largely thanks to these enthusiasts, and to the man whose designs have consistently over the past 30 years offered a unique combination of engineering excellence and riding pleasure, Ing. Fabio Taglioni, that today one name is synonymous above all others with the image of a sporting motorcyclist's motorcycle: Ducati.

Epilogue

On 1 June, 1983 it was formally announced in Milan that an agreement had been concluded between Meccanica Ducati and the Cagiva motorcycle company whereby Ducati would gradually phase out the manufacture of complete motorcycles in favour of producing engine/gearbox units only, which would be sold exclusively to Cagiva for them to install in machines of their own design.

The announcement was greeted with dismay throughout the world, for enthusiasm for the Ducati marque was such that even many non-owners were saddened that such a famous and historic name should apparently be set to disappear from the ranks of motorcycle manufacturers. Ducati tried to defuse the situation somewhat by sending out a press release stating that they intended to continue with motorcycle manufacture up till the end of 1984 at least, and indeed at around the same time did indeed introduce an updated version of the Mike Hailwood Replica, with electric starting as standard and numerous other detail changes of both a styling and technical nature.

But the terms of the agreement in black and white were clear enough. Lasting initially for seven years and thereafter renewable automatically, it called for Ducati 'from now on to produce only motorcycle engines which will be sold to Cagiva exclusively', with cubic capacities ranging from 350 to 1000 cc. The engines would continue to bear the Ducati name on the cases, and minimum quantities were stipulated for the first three years of the agreement: Ducati undertook to supply, and Cagiva to purchase, at least 6000 such engines in 1984, 10,000 during 1985 and 14,000 in 1986 and thereafter. It was agreed that Cagiva would handle the marketing and sales of the complete bikes, even those made by Ducati in the 1984 model year, leaving the Bologna firm to concentrate on the development of new engines.

The announcement had Ducati enthusiasts the world over thumbing through their catalogues to find out just who were Cagiva. The two firms could not have been more different. While motorcycle production at the State-owned Ducati plant had gradually declined over the previous decade, to the point that only 7800 complete bikes were made in 1982 against a production capacity of 9000 machines, with an even lower target of 6000 planned for 1983, Cagiva had been steadily increasing their output from 7800 machines in 1980 up to the 1983 figure of nearly 50,000. The flourishing, privately-owned company had actually emerged out of the ashes of the former Aermacchi Harley-Davidson concern on the site of the old seaplane sheds beside Lake Varese north of Milan, who had ironically been one of Ducati's principal competitors in the lightweight field in both the USA and Italy before the Bologna firm moved up the capacity scale in the 1970s, while the American-owned company in turn languished in the wake of the Japanese takeover of the small-capacity North American market. By 1977 Harley-Davidson had had enough and closed the company down. The following year it was rescued by a pair of local motorcycle enthusiasts, the Castiglione brothers, who acquired the assets from H-D and restarted production on a much smaller scale, concentrating on the home 125 cc market in which they were soon to excell. The name of the new company was derived from that of their father, CAstiglione GIovanni of VArese: Ca-Gi-Va.

An active programme of expansion and new model development, coupled with an aggressive sales policy and prestigious involvement in both road racing and off-road sport, made Cagiva the only company in Italy to be actually increasing its volume sales at the start of the 1980s. By 1981 they commanded the largest share of the vital 125 cc Italian market, and were already moving up-market with 250 cc machines as well as a 350 sohc 4-stroke

Taken in Mid June 1983 was this 'sneak' photograph of a Cagiva Pantah. There isn't much to say except that it must have been conceived somewhat in advance of the official press announcement of co-operation plan. Interesting shape, though

trail bike. But except for the latter, the company's entire model range was exclusively two-stroke orientated, and so the road towards the range of middleweight and large-capacity four-strokes that the Castigliones saw as imperative for them to tread in order to stimulate the continued growth of their company would be a long and expensive one. The development of a range of big four-stroke engines could prove financially crippling for the concern, whose entire future would be mortgaged to their success.

At the same time Ducati had increasingly become a manufacturer of engines rather than of motorcycles. The company's first diesel engine had appeared in 1969, and this side of the business had by the early 1980s become the life-blood of the Borgo Panigale factory, subsidising the continued manufacture of the unprofitable motorcycle range. Dropping the production of complete bikes, or at least running it down gradually in favour of making only engine units appeared an attractive option to the VM Group's controllers who ran the company. When the possibility of the deal with Cagiva materialised, it seemed too good to be true. Contrary to the scare-mongering conclusions blazed in two-inch headlines by magazines who should have been less irresponsible, the agreement was far from being 'The End for Ducati', but rather a way for the future of the desmodromic 4-stroke engine line to be assured. To real Ducati enthusiasts the world over it matters little what name or emblem is on the side of the tank: Ducatis are made to be ridden and enjoyed, and so long as the basic concept of the machine housing the Bologna-built engine was not altered, there seemed little ground for concern. Both Cagiva and Ducati executives were eager to stress that the arrangement was a true

partnership, and indeed it seemed probable in the early days of the liason that each had something to offer the other. A trail bike version of the soon to be announced 650 Pantah engine was one of Cagiva's main priorities, to attack the market sector that the more ungainly R80GS BMW had proved to exist. A street version of the same machine, whose engine dimensions were rumoured to be 81 × 61.4 mm (i.e. the same bore as the 600 TT2 Pantah and the same stroke as the 750 racer) for 635 cc, with lighter, less all-enveloping Cagiva styling than the standard Ducati range, was also due to be released at the 1983 Milan Show, together with a 350 cc version aimed at the home market.

Cagiva's strong belief in the value of sporting involvement seemed likely to see an intensification of the V-twin Ducati engine's competition career, with TT Formula 1 and 2, and endurance racing the principal targets: TT F1 was due to be run to a 750 cc capacity top limit in 1984, making the bored and stroked version of the Pantah engine a top contender. As well, an official entry in the Paris-Dakar marathon and other long distance off-road events with the new V-twin trail bike was a likely result of the agreement.

At the same Milan Show in 1983 the debut was scheduled of a 90-bore version of the venerable bevel-drive V-twin, to be known as the Mille or 1000 Ducati. Available in both Hailwood Replica and S2 versions, the latter with bikini fairing only, the new engine incorporated many of the improvements to be found on the updated version of the 860 cc engine which had been introduced earlier that year. These included the use of Nikasil liners as on the Pantah, electric start as standard employing the small Nippondenso unit, a hydraulic dry clutch, crankcase oil window, a screw-in oil filter again as on the Pantah but still retaining the models original roller-bearing bottom end, adjustable Marzocchi rear units with remote gas reservoirs fitted as standard, and restyled crankcases and fibreglass to give a more airy feel to the bike as a whole. The large-capacity engine produced considerably increased torque and acceleration, and in all the Mille was to be in every way the culmination of the process of continuous development which Ing. Taglioni and his team had wrought in the 15 years since work on the original 750 V-twin was first commenced.

But for Taglioni the agreement with Cagiva brought with it hopes that an even more significant step could result: the continued development of his cherished V4 project, which in the summer of 1983 was sadly to be found lurking beneath a dust cover in the racing and development department, untouched for several months while its future was decided by the money men and commercial interests. Fortunately, Cagiva regarded the V4 as the jewel in the Ducati firmament, and at the time of writing it seemed probable that an agreement would be reached between the two companies for development work to be recommenced, with a view to a four-cylinder bike being launched towards the end of 1984.

Ducatisti everywhere will be hoping fervently that such an arrangement is made, for the V4 project represents the fulfilment of Taglioni's lifetime in engine design. A 90 degree V4, it has the two inside cylinders pointing upwards, while the outside pair point forwards, the whole engine designed to be tipped back slightly from vertical as on the V-twins. The most radically oversquare Ducati engine yet, the four cylinders measure 78×52 mm for a total capacity of 994 cc, yet the whole engine is only 100 mm wider than the Pantah V-twin from which it is vaguely descended, and whose profile it exactly matches when viewed from the side. The single sohc desmodromic valve gear employs two valves per cylinder, with a single camshaft per pair of separate cylinders, running through tubes connecting each pair of cylinder heads, and driven by a pair of toothed rubber belts running off pulleys on the left of the engine. A one-piece forged, Nitrided crankshaft is employed with plain big ends as on the Pantah, each pair of rods sharing the same crankpin. A mixture of air and supplementary oil

cooling to the cylinders, with the oilways grooved along the external circumference of the Nikasil liners, is employed, with the cylinders cunningly cast to maximise airflow especially around the exhaust ports. Two separate oil pumps are fitted, one for lubrication, the other for cooling, but the two systems share the same 5-litre wet-sump oil supply.

The V4 Ducati unit is remarkably compact – one of the principal reasons why Taglioni opted for such a heavily oversquare unit was to reduce the engine height accordingly. THe complete unit, with 5-speed gearbox driven by helical gear primary, weighs 98 kg – light by current Japanese 1000 cc standards but too heavy for Taglioni to consider producing a 750 version: instead, his process of developing the Pantah V-twin into a full 750 cc machine was completed and track-tested to his satisfaction by the magnificent victory in the 1983 Barcelona 24 Hours of a 750 Pantah ridden by Benjamin Grau and Enrique de Juan. A production version would follow soon after.

Instead, the V4 was intended as a large-capacity but nevertheless economical top of the line machine, with the capability of being bored out to 1050 or even 1100 cc if necessary. Producing 105 bhp at the rear wheel at 9500 rpm with touring cams and silencing equipment meeting all present noise regulations, the engine was capable with the minimum of tuning, but running on open exhausts, of generating no less than 132 bhp, again at the wheel, at 11,000 rpm, running on four 40 mm Dell'Orto carburettors. Fuel injection, using a SPICA fuel pump specially-designed for Ducati by the same firm who supplied their fellow State-owned company Alfa Romeo's F1 car team with similar equipment, was expected to produce an even more dramatic increase in performance, as well as superior throttle response. Power was produced from as low down as 3000 rpm, and a flat 50 degree included valve angle provided the best cylinder filling yet on a Taglioni Ducati, with electronic ignition firing a single 12 mm plug per cylinder.

By the time work on the project was suspended at the end of 1982, Taglioni had completed bench testing of the engine unit and was in the process of constructing a low, multi-tube chassis around it similar to the one adopted for the TT Formula Pantahs, when the word came down from on high to stop work on the project. If the agreement with Cagiva does nothing else but to assure that this superb power unit is actually put into production, as the ultimate testament to the genius of Ing. Fabio Taglioni, it will all have been worthwhile.

Acknowledgements

Having read this sort of 'thank-you' section in other books, I always regarded it as pretty meaningless: after all, the facts and photos are all just lying around waiting to be picked up, aren't they? How wrong I was. After being talked into writing the Ducati story in the first place by my editor Tim Parker, backed up by those leading lights of the British Ducati Owners Club, Jilly and Mike Penegar, to all of whom I am deeply grateful for tipping me over the edge into the abyss of writing my first book. Without the people who contributed information and photographs which enabled me to piece the fragmented history of Ducati Meccanica together into a single work, this book could literally not have been written.

Pride of place amongst the many people who helped me thus must go to the man whose own personal story this book really is too: Ing. Fabio Taglioni. His assistance and positive encouragement, pushed me beyond words to see a project which I was rapidly beginning to perceive as impossible through. Franco Valentini, Dr. Cosimo Calcagnile, and the gorgeous Nadia Pavignani, all key executives with Ducati Meccanica, also provided much factual help and great encouragement. Luigi Giacometti of Cagiva was also of much help in writing the epilogue.

Armando Boscolo, Carlo Perelli and especially Silvano Piacentini of *Motociclismo* magazine in Italy kindly allowed me to live in their office for a week, and to have free run of their files and bound volumes without which I could not possibly have pieced together the early history of the company. Similarly Brecon Quaddy of *Bike* and Graham Sanderson of *Motor Cycle Weekly* in Britain permitted me unlimited access to their photographic files: thanks to them and to another racing journalist, Dennis Noyes of *Motociclismo* in Spain, as well as to *Cycle World*'s Allan Girdler for the loan of other photographic material. And to that ultimate of journalistic *Ducatisti*, *Cycle*'s Phil Schilling – the co-creator of the Californian Hot Rod.

Mick Walker placed his unrivalled knowledge of the technical aspects of the road singles and V-twins at my disposal for which I am deeply grateful.

A long-time admirer of Ing. Taglioni's prowess, Vic Willoughby, also offered encouragement and help especially with the loan of material for which I am sincerely grateful to this doyen of racing journalists. Others who helped to fill in the various gaps in my researches include John Surtees, Syd Lawton, Sammy Miller, Giuseppe Pattoni and Franco Farne in Europe, and Syd Tunstall and Reno Leoni in the USA. My thanks go to all of them for their time and assistance in this project. Especial thanks go to Steve Wynne and Pat Slinn, and to Tore Bertilsson of Sweden, whose constructive criticism worries me not half as much as he seems to imagine.

My 'Austrian uncle' Dr. Helmut Krackowizer, was a tower of strength throughout the writing of the book, and not only placed his extensive archives at my disposal but also offered help and encouragement of a practical nature.

I hope that one of the most attractive aspects of this book to the reader will be the selection of photographs, the vast majority of which have never been published before. In addition to the people mentioned above, I must express my unreserved debt of gratitude to my old friend Franco Zagari. Franco obviously took full advantage of living so close to the Bologna factory for the past 20 years or so, and it is most generous of him to have laid the fruits of this contact at my disposal for this book.

Finally, I should like to dedicate this book to four people without whom it's most improbable I should ever have taken on the task of writing it – or even been in the position to do so. My American friend and motorcycling mentor Jeff Craig was responsible entirely for my starting to race in the first place. I'll always be grateful to Jeff for bullying me into making the right decision, as well as to the late Vic Camp and his colleague Bert Furness whose support in the early stages of my racing career and enthusiasm for the products of the Ducati factory did much to further my regard for the Bologna marque.

And lastly, my particular thanks to two special people: first, if everyone had a mother-in-law like mine the seaside comics would be out of business, and by permitting me to strew assorted piles of Ducati material all over her house in Perth, Western Australia, Betty Todd allowed me to shut myself off from other interruptions earlier this year to get stuck in finally to the task of writing the book. I honestly doubt if I'd ever have got down to it if not for that. And thank you most of all to my wife Stella, whose constant support for my motorcycling activities goes far beyond most bike widows' resigned tolerance to a degree of positive enthusiasm.

Index